The Early Years

The Early Years
Child Well-Being and the Role of Public Policy

Edited by

Samuel Berlinski and Norbert Schady

Inter-American Development Bank

palgrave
macmillan

First published 2015 by
PALGRAVE MACMILLAN

Palgrave Macmillan in the UK is an imprint of Macmillan Publishers Limited, registered in England, company number 785998, of Houndmills, Basingstoke, Hampshire, RG21 6XS.

Palgrave Macmillan in the US is a division of Nature America, Inc., One New York Plaza, Suite 4500, New York, NY 10004-1562.

Palgrave Macmillan is the global academic imprint of the above companies and has companies and representatives throughout the world.

Hardback ISBN: 978–1–137–53647–1
Paperback ISBN: 978–1–137–53648–8
E-PUB ISBN: 978–1–137–53650–1
E-PDF ISBN: 978–1–137–53649–5
DOI: 10.1057/9781137536495

Distribution in the UK, Europe and the rest of the world is by Palgrave Macmillan®, a division of Macmillan Publishers Limited, registered in England, company number 785998, of Houndmills, Basingstoke, Hampshire RG21 6XS.

Library of Congress Cataloging-in-Publication Data is available from the Library of Congress.

A catalogue record of the book is available from the British Library.

Contents

Boxes

Figures

Tables

Preface

As the nations of Latin America and the Caribbean face an increasingly challenging economic environment, governments have a singular opportunity to help one of our most precious resources—our youngest children. There are about 50 million children in the region under the age of 5, who will eventually be the core of our workforce and our social and political leadership. It is in our best collective interest to make sure their foundations are solid as we will all be standing on those foundations in the future.

This book looks at what governments can do to more effectively help our youngest flourish in the early years. It is based on the broad consensus that quality interventions during the first 8 years of life will help our children become not only more productive but also more fulfilled citizens of the future.

In many ways, we have made great strides. Boys and girls in our region are less likely to die at childbirth or when they are very young than they were just a few decades ago. They enjoy better health and nutrition. Almost all attend school. In the year 2000, two out of every five of the region's children lived in poverty. Today, just over one out of every five is poor. Over the past 20 years, the IDB has helped countries bring about these important improvements through more than 150 grants and loans involving early childhood development, for a total in excess of US$1.7 billion.

But, as this book explains, Latin American and Caribbean children continue to lag behind in the critical areas of language and cognition. The problem begins in the first five years of life, when many children are not receiving the stimulation required to ensure proper cognitive development. Tests show that poor children know fewer words than their richer peers, and that children in our region know fewer words than those of more developed nations. This also means that too many of our boys and girls are just not ready when they begin school.

This book forcefully argues that this deficit is not just the responsibility of parents. Governments can—and should—make a major positive difference. According to a landmark study, simple parenting interventions by social workers decades ago in Jamaica produced adults who not only did better in school and earned higher wages, but were also less likely to resort to a life of crime.

An investment in a well-crafted government program, using the tools that we know today to be highly effective, can have a huge development impact. Early childhood development programs are the foundations for successful social investments over the lifetime of an individual, especially for the poor. Investing more in this area is one of the most effective ways governments can improve economic mobility.

Many governments are taking this lesson to heart and have increased investments in the early years. However, the evidence indicates the region is still spending too little. On a per capita basis, for example, governments are spending three times more on children aged 6–11 than on those aged 0–5. Moreover, early childhood investments tend to disproportionately favor physical infrastructure such as daycare facilities, while neglecting vital training and human capital. Recent research shows that some of the biggest returns on investment can come from modest programs that focus on improving the critical early interactions between young children and adults, be they parents, teachers, or caregivers.

Finally, in most of the region's countries, no one actor clearly "owns" the issue of early childhood development. The absence of coordination between multiple actors and levels of government creates a daunting obstacle to improving the quality of services.

Today, the challenge is to ensure that we have smarter institutions capable of directing investment toward programs that have a measurable impact on early childhood development. It is not an easy path, but it is the right one if our countries are to harness the full potential of their citizens.

LUIS ALBERTO MORENO
President
Inter-American Development Bank

Acknowledgments

Development in the Americas (DIA) is the flagship publication of the Inter-American Development Bank. This issue was produced under the direction of Samuel Berlinski, principal research economist of the Research Department, and Norbert Schady, sector economic adviser for the Social Department. The general editor of the volume was Rita Funaro, publications coordinator of the Research Department, who was assisted by Maria Fernanda Barragan-Santana, Cathleen Conkling-Shaker, Nancy Morrison, and John Dunn Smith. José Juan Ruiz, the chief economist and general manager of the Research Department, and Héctor Salazar, manager of the Social Sector, provided extremely valuable guidance and advice throughout the life of this project, and Santiago Levy, the vice president for Sectors, provided overall support for it.

The principal authors of each individual chapter are as follows:

Chapter 1: Samuel Berlinski, Luca Flabbi, and Florencia López Boo

Chapter 2: Norbert Schady

Chapter 3: Samuel Berlinski, Florencia López Boo, Ana Pérez Expósito, and Norbert Schady

Chapter 4: M. Caridad Araujo and Norbert Schady

Chapter 5: Yyannu Cruz-Aguayo and Norbert Schady

Chapter 6: Edna Armendáriz, Martín Ardanaz, Jere R. Behrman, Julian Cristia, and Diana Hincapie

Chapter 7: M. Caridad Araujo, Yyannu Cruz-Aguayo, Analia Jaimovich, and Sharon Lynn Kagan

Chapter 8: Samuel Berlinski and Norbert Schady

A scientific committee participated in meetings to discuss the scope of this publication: Orazio Attanasio, Steve Barnett, Sharon

Lynn Kagan, Michael Kramer, Jennifer LoCasale-Crouch, Andrew Prentice, Robert Slavin, and Hiro Yoshikawa. Others also reviewed specific chapters: Helen Baker-Henningham, Raquel Bernal, Maureen Black, Sally Grantham-McGregor, Christine Powel, Miguel Szekely, and Hiro Yoshikawa. Jere R. Behrman and Ariel Fiszbein read the whole report on more than one occasion. Their advice has been invaluable.

Many researchers were involved in the preparation of background papers employed as the basis for this report: Lorena Alcázar, Steve Barnett, Raquel Bernal, Daniela del Boca, Matias Busso, A. de Cavalcanti de Almeida, Maria Marta Ferreyra, Tomás Guanziroli, Bridget Hamre, Sadie Hasbrouck, Marcia E. Kraft-Sayre, Jane Leer, Jennifer LoCasale-Crouch, Carolina Melo, Milagros Nores, Robert Pianta, Alan Sánchez, and Sara C. Schodt.

The following research assistants contributed to the preparation of the project: Juliana Chen, Jenny Encina, Tomás Guanziroli, Alejandra Ramos, Dario Romero, and Romina Tomé. Special thanks go to Mayra Sáenz Amaguaya for her dedication to this project.

Several individuals provided useful inputs at different stages in the production of this volume. In particular, Monserrat Bustelo, Gustavo Garcia, Julia Johannsen, Matthew Kearney, Fabiana Machado, Sebastián Martínez, Juan Carlos Navarro, Claudia Piras, Andrew Powell, Ferdinando Regalia, Marcos Robles, Marta Rubio-Codina, Carlos Scartascini, and Emiliana Vegas.

This book could not have been produced without the immense effort and dedication of the administrative team of the Research Department and, in particular, Monica Bazan, Myriam Escobar-Genes, Ana Lucia Saettone, Mariela Semidey, and Federico Volpino.

Contributors

M. Caridad Araujo, a citizen of Ecuador, received a PhD in Agricultural and Resource Economics from the University of California at Berkeley. She is a lead economist in the Division of Social Protection and Health of the Inter-American Development Bank.

Martín Ardanaz, a citizen of Argentina, received a PhD in Political Science from Columbia University. He is a specialist in the Fiscal and Municipal Management Division of the Inter-American Development Bank.

Edna Armendáriz, a citizen of Mexico, received a PhD in International Economics from the University of Cambridge, UK. She is a lead fiscal economist in the Fiscal and Municipal Management Division of the Inter-American Development Bank.

Jere R. Behrman, a citizen of the United States, received a PhD in Economics from the Massachusetts Institute of Technology. He is the William R. Kenan, Jr. Professor of Economics and Sociology at the University of Pennsylvania.

Samuel Berlinski, a citizen of Argentina, received a PhD in Economics from the University of Oxford, Nuffield College. He is a principal research economist in the Research Department of the Inter-American Development Bank.

Julian Cristia, a citizen of Argentina, received a PhD in Economics from the University of Maryland at College Park. He is a lead research economist in the Research Department of the Inter-American Development Bank.

Yyanu Cruz-Aguayo, a citizen of Mexico, received a PhD in Economics from the University of Maryland at College Park. She is an economic specialist in the Social Department of the Inter-American Development Bank.

Luca Flabbi, a citizen of the United States and Italy, received a PhD in Economics from New York University. He is a senior research economist in the Research Department of the Inter-American Development Bank.

Diana Hincapie, a citizen of Colombia, received a PhD in Public Policy from George Washington University. She is an education senior associate in the Education Division of the Inter-American Development Bank.

Analia Jaimovich, a citizen of Argentina, received master's degrees in Politics and Education from the Universities of Harvard and Cambridge. She is an education specialist in the Education Division of the Inter-American Development Bank.

Sharon Lynn Kagan, a citizen of the United States, received DEd from Teachers College, Columbia University. She is the Virginia and Leonard Marx Professor of Early Childhood and Family Policy at the Teachers College of Columbia University.

Florencia López Boo, a citizen of Argentina, received a PhD in Economics from the University of Oxford. She is a senior economist in the Social Protection and Health Division of the Inter-American Development Bank.

Ana Pérez Expósito, a citizen of Mexico, received a PhD in Nutrition from the University of California, Davis. She is a specialist in the Social Protection and Health Division of the Inter-American Development Bank.

Norbert Schady, a German citizen, received a PhD in Public Policy from Princeton University. He is the sector economic adviser for the Social Department of the Inter-American Development Bank.

I

Raising Children: The Case for Government Intervention

Well-being is "the state of being happy, healthy, or prosperous," according to the Merriam-Webster Dictionary. *The Early Years: Child Well-Being and the Role of Public Policy* focuses on the well-being of children in the early years of their lives, from conception to approximately 9 years of age. Scientists in the fields of biology, psychology, and economics have a clear view of what outcomes (and trajectories) define a happy, healthy, and potentially prosperous child; they are discussed in this chapter. What is less clear is how to raise children in order to achieve these outcomes and who should be involved in that process. Why should the government be directly involved in the welfare of children?

The first reason is that children have a legal identity and a set of interests that are separate from their parents' and worth protecting. This notion of children's rights is relatively new but widely accepted. The United Nations Convention on the Rights of the Child is the most widely ratified human rights treaty, signed by 194 nations. However, historically, social programs have taken the needs approach, with children as beneficiaries of policies, and governments acting out of patronage and charity (see Box 1.1). Instead, the rights approach recognizes them as individuals with legal rights who are equal before any law and policy.

The second rationale for government involvement is that children that flourish in the early years are more likely to become productive citizens. An investment in a child's well-being is an investment that generates returns over the long term, and affects the prosperity and viability of society well into the future. Nevertheless, families are

Box 1.1   A History Lesson: Childhood and the Emergence of Children's Rights

The concept of *childhood* has varied greatly through time and across cultures. The first modern study of childhood history was Philippe Ariès's *Centuries of Childhood*, published in 1962. In this influential book, Ariès argues that the term "child" started to develop its current meaning sometime between the seventeenth and twentieth centuries.

In modern society, it is generally accepted that "childhood" is a stage of life with certain traits that differentiates it from infancy and adulthood. In medieval society, children at the age of 7 acted—and were treated—as smaller versions of the adults around them; they were introduced to an adult world at a very early age through both labor and sexual exploitation.

The modern status of the child is concomitant with decreases in infant mortality, changes in the educational system, and the appearance of a separate isolated family unit. For most of human history, a significant proportion of infants did not survive to adulthood. Ariès (1962) argues that high mortality rates influenced parents' feelings of emotional indifference. These attitudes changed as survival became more likely.

The emphasis on the importance of education became widespread in the eighteenth century, thanks to the Enlightenment view that children needed to be educated to become good citizens. The development of schooling and its gradual extension and intensification were essential for defining a new idea of childhood, because schooling provided a transition phase between infancy and adult life (Clarke 2004).

An important precedent of child protection was the Poor Relief Act (1601) in Elizabethan England, which, for the first time, made poor children the responsibility of the parish. Among other things, the law established that pauper children would become apprentices. For the next three centuries in England, the parochial overseers of the poor took responsibility for the welfare of children whenever parenting failed or was absent.

While a new notion of childhood was emerging during the eighteenth century, the process of industrialization intensified the exploitation of many children. Although children always worked in preindustrial society, the emergence of the factory system made things worse for working children: many of the tasks they did were dangerous, and work conditions were unhealthy. This situation led to a relatively new notion during the nineteenth century: the child as the object of pity or philanthropy.

A growing number of reformers, alarmed at the conditions in which children were toiling in factories, worked to enact legislation that would control these practices. Even in the laissez faire atmosphere of Victorian Britain, it was accepted that childhood was a period of life in need of protection and that it was appropriate for the state to intervene on behalf of children (Lowe 2004). This was probably the first time the state accepted ultimate responsibility for protecting the well-being of children.

By the end of the nineteenth century, while poverty and illness was still frequent among children, the idea of children as the focus for policymaking had firmly taken root, paving the way for the twentieth century to become—as Ellen Key noted in her 1909 book—"the century of the child." In her book, Key imagines the century as a period of intense focus around the rights, education, and well-being of children.

During the twentieth century a clear view emerged that children's welfare is not merely a family responsibility: children are increasingly viewed as the responsibility of the state, which intervenes in their education, health, and upbringing in ways designed to improve national well-being by developing its future citizens.

This paradigm shift is reflected in some landmarks in children rights. In 1924, the League of Nations adopted the Geneva Declaration on the Rights of the Child. This was the first (nonbinding) historical text that recognized specific rights for children. The United Nations Fund for Children (UNICEF) was created in 1946. Following the Declaration of the Rights of the Child in 1959, childhood became a central issue in international cooperation programs and children began to be seen as having rights. In 1989, 140 states signed the Convention on the Rights of the Child.[1]

understandably more concerned with their needs today than with those of society tomorrow. The danger that the focus of child rearing will be biased much more toward the needs of the present than the future is another reason why public policy may have an important role to play in children's welfare.

Child Development: A Long and Winding Road

The foundations of child well-being start well before birth. During pregnancy, the fetus develops through a number of processes. In the first trimester, the formation and differentiation of organs takes place. In the second trimester, the fetus undergoes major cellular adaptation and increases in body size. Finally, during the third trimester, the organ systems mature and ready themselves for life outside the mother (Mullis and Tonella 2008).

The process of child development starts once the baby is born; it can be described as "the psychological and biological changes that occur as a child transitions from a dependent infant to an autonomous teenager" (Fernald and others 2009). These changes include physical development (changes in the size, shape, and physical maturity of the body, including physical abilities and coordination) and the development of language/communication skills (learning and using language), cognitive skills (the ability to reason, solve problems, and organize ideas), and socioemotional skills (gaining a sense of self, the ability to empathize and express feelings, and how to interact with others).

Child development is hardly a linear process in which outcomes change or progress smoothly from one stage to another. Rather, development accelerates and decelerates at different ages and stages. However, the development process is cumulative and events occur during predictable time periods. As a result, lack of development in certain areas or at certain points in time may have permanent consequences and may affect the well-being of an individual over her entire life cycle. The discussion that follows provides examples of how this cumulative, nonlinear process unfolds for many of the outcomes related to children's well-being and development.

Physical development: The rapid physical growth experienced during early childhood is captured by several anthropometric measures including length/height-for-age, weight-for-age, and head circumference. These measures represent important markers of physiological growth and are typically used as proxies for well-being. The World Health Organization (WHO) has created international standards that assess the growth and development of children from birth to age 5.[2] In general, children grow very rapidly in the first 6 months of life. At birth, the median child[3] is 49.5 centimeters long, weighs 3.25 kilograms, and has a head circumference of 34.2 centimeters.[4] Growth accelerates during the first 2 months of life and continues at a declining rate thereafter.

Studies have shown that weight, height, head circumference, and growth pattern, particularly during the period of intrauterine growth and the first two years of life, are good predictors of outcomes later in life. Low gestational growth and low early childhood height-for-age predict short adult stature (Victora and others 2008).[5] Longitudinal studies for developing countries show that growth failure in the first two years of life is associated with poor cognitive and other educational outcomes (Hoddinott and others 2013).

The process of physical development also includes motor skills (the ability to control the use of muscles). First, children learn to sit without support. This is typically followed by crawling on hands and knees, standing without assistance, walking with assistance, standing alone, and finally walking alone (WHO Multicentre Growth Reference Study Group 2006). Children acquire these developmental milestones during predictable time periods.[6] For example, most children learn to sit without support between 4 and 9 months and are walking alone by 17 months.

Language/communication: Children's language development begins long before they utter their first word (Bloom 1998) and develops differently from one year to the next. Children babble at 2–4 months and make noises and try new and different sounds at 4–6 months. They point and gesture at around 12 months and say their first words and sentences in the first two years. They finally experience an explosion of words between ages 2 and 3 years (Woodward and Markman 1998). At 3–4 years, children speak well in sentences and are able to chant rhymes and enunciate clearly enough to be understood. As children move into the preschool years, indicators of language development include children's production and understanding of words, their ability to tell stories and identify letters, and their familiarity with books.

Reading is a complex developmental challenge that is related to other developmental processes, including attention, memory, language, and motivation (Snow, Burns, and Griffin 1998). Standardized tests of children's vocabularies and their knowledge of letters and print at the start of school are good predictors of their reading scores throughout childhood (Powell and Diamond 2012; Wasik and Newman 2009). Table 1.1 describes an example of the cumulative

Table 1.1 Development of Literacy Skills

Recognizes specific books by cover	Knows that alphabet letters are a special category of visual graphics that can be individually named	Knows parts of a book and their functions	Begins to read aloud with accuracy	Uses knowledge of print-sound mapping to sound out unknown words	Reads aloud with fluency and comprehension of any text designed for this grade
Pretends to read books	Recognizes local environmental print	Begins to track print when listening to a familiar text being read	Uses letter-sound correspondence knowledge to sound out unknown words	Reads and comprehends fiction and nonfiction designed for this grade level	Reads longer chapter books independently
Listens to stories	Uses new vocabulary in own speech	Recognizes and can name upper and lower case letters	Can accurately spell short words	Shows evidence of expanding language repertory, including increasing use of more formal language registers	Summarizes major points from fiction and nonfiction texts
Comments on characters in books	Understands and follows multistep oral directions	Learns most letter sound correspondence	Uses basic punctuation and capitalization	Connects and compares information across texts	Correctly spells previously studies words
Begins to purposefully scribble	Shows an interest in reading	Correctly answers questions about stories read aloud	Creates own written text for others to read	With organizational help, writes informed, well-structured reports	With assistance, suggests and implements editing and revision to clarify and refine own writing
	Writes messages as part of a playful activity using letter-like forms	Writes messages with invented spelling			

Source: Authors' compilation.

process that leads to the development of literacy skills from birth to third grade.

Cognitive skills: Cognitive skills include analytical skills, problem solving, memory, and early mathematical abilities (Johnson 1998). When children respond to their own name at about 12 months and learn to stack or nest objects at 15–18 months, they are developing their cognitive abilities on schedule. By age 3, most children are capable of solving simple puzzles, matching colors and shapes, and also show awareness of concepts such as "more" and "less" (Kuhn and Siegler 1998). Cognitive development at school age is associated with the knowledge of letters and numbers, the ability to retain information, and the knowledge of basic information like one's name and address. Standardized tests of reasoning, problem solving, memory, and mathematical abilities at the start of school are reliable indicators of children's cognitive development and are strong predictors of scores throughout primary and secondary school (Duncan and others 2007; Duncan 2011).

How do humans control and coordinate their cognitive operations? A relatively new concept in neuropsychology named "executive function" (the ability to control impulses, initiate action, sustain attention, and persist in actions or attainment of goals) tries to address this issue. Executive function is an important determinant of how well young children adapt to and learn in school. The concept and its measurement are described in Box 1.2.

Box 1.2   In a Child's Mind: Executive Function

Executive function includes a set of basic self-regulatory skills that involve various parts of the brain, particularly the prefrontal cortex. The concept comes from neuropsychological research in the 1980s and 1990s that studied the consequences of damages to the frontal lobes. Executive function starts to develop in infancy but changes dramatically in early childhood, as the frontal lobe develops (Anderson 1998).

These abilities are distinct from cognition or knowledge of information such as vocabulary (Jurado and Rosselli 2007).[7] Although there have been competing definitions of executive function and how to measure it, there is a growing consensus that executive function includes three broad domains: inhibitory control, working memory, and cognitive flexibility. Sometimes, attention is added as a separate domain.

Inhibitory control refers to the ability to suppress impulsive behaviors and resist temptations. Working memory refers to the ability to hold, update, and manipulate verbal or nonverbal information in the mind for short periods of time. Cognitive flexibility refers to the ability to shift attention between competing tasks or rules. Attention is the ability to focus and disregard external stimuli, which is why it is often grouped with working memory.

In toddlers older than 2 years, the processes most commonly cited as measurable are: working memory (e.g., holding information in mind for a short time, such as a series of numbers); inhibition of behavior or responses as demanded by the situation or task (such as not opening a box until a bell rings); and paying attention as required or being able to switch attention as necessary (such as shifting focus from the color of a stimulus to the shape of the stimulus) (Carlson 2005).

Different components of executive function can be measured separately and at different ages, but it is the ability to coordinate them to solve a problem or reach a goal that is most important to assess (Welsh, Friedman, and Spieker 2006). Executive function is an important predictor of children's learning trajectories and long-term outcomes, including in the labor market (Moffitt and others 2011; Séguin and Zelazo 2005).

Socioemotional skills: During the first two years of life, children learn whether their caregivers will respond to them and how much they can trust them. Sensitive and responsive relationships with caregivers are essential for teaching children to trust others and to deal effectively with frustration, fear, aggression, and other negative emotions (Thompson and Raikes 2007). Healthy infants and toddlers show preferential attachments to caregivers: they recognize their parents' faces at 1–4 weeks of life, smile at 4–5 weeks, respond to parents' voices at around 7 months, and indicate their wants at 7–15 months. They are also eager to explore novel objects and spaces, and are able to reach for a toy at 4 months, play ball with a caregiver at around 10 months, feed a doll at 12 months, and play board games at 32 months. Finally, they enjoy initiating and responding to social interactions, such as waving bye-bye, at 7 months; imitating activities and drinking from a cup starting at 9 months; helping in the house, using a fork/spoon, and removing clothes between the first and second year of life; and brushing their teeth and washing and drying their hands between 18 and 24 months.

In the preschool years, social and emotional development expands to include children's social competence (how well children get along with other children, teachers, and adults), behavior management (ability to follow directions and cooperate with requests), social perception (how well children can identify thoughts and feelings in themselves and in others), and self-regulatory abilities (emotional and behavioral control, especially in stressful situations). All these skills are critical for children's success in school (Thompson and Raikes 2007) and throughout their lives.[8]

The brain plays a key role in the process of language, cognition, motor, and emotional development. Neuroscience has discovered much about the development of the brain during the past 50 years, but much has yet to be discovered. Although the connection between neuroscience and child policy is still tenuous, Box 1.3 describes some basic facts about brain development and the critical role of good early experiences in the development of the brain.

Box 1.3   Early Experiences and Development of the Brain

At the time of delivery, the baby's brain has not completed its development, although the brain's structure (which is genetically determined) is already formed. At birth, the human brain has a minimal set of connections and neural pathways. In the first three years of life, brain development is at the core of the development of a child. From birth until about age 3, synapses in the brain develop very rapidly and efficiently. At the age of 2 years, the number of synapses in the brain of a child has reached the typical amount in an adult; at age 3, synapses in the brain of a child (about 1,000 trillion) are double those of an adult brain. This number is maintained until about 10 years of age, at which time the synaptic density of the brain begins to decline. By the end of adolescence, only 500 trillion synapses will remain.

Brain development can be considered a process of production and disposal of synapses. In the first three years of life, production is greater than disposal; for the rest of the first decade of life, production and disposal reach a certain balance; and upon entering adolescence, elimination is the dominant process (Bedregal and Pardo 2004).

In the brain's process of producing and disposing synapses, the individual's interaction with the environment (reaction to stimuli; collection, processing, and storage of information) plays a major role (Fox, Levitt, and Nelson 2010). Apparently, brain activity is directed by genetically configured neural patterns, while the details of such patterns (the amount and type of synaptic connections) are largely determined by the interaction with the environment (Greenough, Black, and Wallace 1987). The brain is able to modify its organization and functions according to experience—an ability known as brain plasticity (Greenough, Black, and Wallace 1987; Masten and Coatsworth 1998). When a stimulus activates a neural pathway, all the synapses that comprise that pathway will receive and store a chemical signal and will be strengthened by the repetition of that incoming signal. When the signal exceeds a certain threshold (which varies depending on the area of the brain), that synapse is exempt from elimination. Similarly, synapses that are not sufficiently reinforced by the stimulus are candidates for removal. Different regions of the brain's cortex increase their size (via the increasing number of dendrites in each neuron) when exposed to stimulating conditions; the longer the stimulation, the larger the growth of dendrites in each neuron and the larger the dendrite trees. Brain plasticity is particularly high during the first decade of life; after that, synaptic density decreases.

Recent neurological research (Weaver and others 2004; Rommeck and others 2009, 2011; Nelson, Fox, and Zeanah 2014) suggests that warm, stimulating childcare has a profound impact on brain development via the development of neural connections and patterns. For example, research on institutionalized Romanian orphans has shown that profound and prolonged neglect in early childhood is associated with lower IQ and a variety of psychiatric illnesses (including ADHD and conduct disorders). Among these children, those who were placed in early foster care showed substantial improvements relative to those left in institutionalized care, although they generally did not catch up with other children who had never been institutionalized (Nelson, Fox, and Zeanah 2014; Rutter and the ERA Study Team 1998).

Measuring child development outcomes: Table 1.2 shows some measurable outcomes of child development, including examples of the most widely used instruments. Child development assessments are usually based on four domains—physical development, language/communication, cognitive skills, and socioemotional skills. However, there is no consensus on a single measure for assessing the development of a child (such as height-for-age standard scores for physical development); therefore, the table presents the most used instruments in the literature (in parenthesis). For example, the Peabody Picture Vocabulary Test (PPVT) is a validated and widely used test to measure language in children, while the Bayley Scales of Infant Development (BSID) measures cognition, language, motor, and socioemotional outcomes. Further details on each instrument are provided in Box 1.4.

Table 1.2   Outcomes by Developmental Stage and Examples of Associated Measures

Antenatal/natal/neonatal	Early childhood
• Fetal development (weeks of gestation, birth weight, birth length, and head circumference) • Morbidity and mortality of newborns	• Morbidity and mortality of infants and children • Physical development (length/height-for-age, weight-for-age, and head circumference) • Cognitive development (e.g., Bayley Scales of Infant Development [BSID], Wechsler Inventories, the Denver Developmental Screening Test) • Language development (e.g., Peabody Picture Vocabulary Test, BSID) • Executive function (e.g., tests of inhibition, working memory, attention) • Fine and gross motor (e.g., Ages and Stages Questionnaires, BSID, Denver Developmental Screening Test) • Socioemotional development (e.g., Denver Developmental Screening Test, BSID) • School performance and learning (e.g., math and literacy standardized achievement tests scores)

Source: Authors' compilation.

Box 1.4 Measuring Child Development

Many instruments have been designed to measure child development.
Child development tests can be divided into two broad categories:

a. Diagnostic tests are designed to provide a detailed assessment
   of the developmental level of a child. They are characterized by
   psychometric properties of sensitivity (and specificity), meaning
   that they accurately identify (and rule out) children at risk (not
   at risk) of a developmental delay. They are also characterized
   by properties of validity (face validity, concurrent and predictive validity) and reliability (internal consistency, test-retest).
   Diagnostic tests are administered by specialized psychologists
   with training in the use of these instruments. Their administration is usually lengthy, and it combines the direct observation of
   children and parental reporting. The Bayley Scales of Infant and
   Toddler Development or the Complete Battelle Developmental
   Inventory are examples of diagnostic tests that have been
   administered to large evaluation samples in countries like Chile,
   Colombia, Mexico, and Peru.
b. Screener tests are designed to identify at-risk children, and therefore, their properties focus more on their sensitivity than on their
   specificity. Clinically, they are most often used as a first stage in
   a process of a developmental diagnostic. Screeners are simpler to
   administer. They contain fewer items than diagnostic tests. They
   tend to rely more on parental reporting than on direct observation of the child. The Ages and Stages Questionnaire (ASQ),
   the Screening Test of the Battelle Developmental Inventory, the
   Denver Developmental Screening Test, the Nelson Ortiz Scale,
   and the *Prueba Nacional de Pesquisa PRUNAPE* are examples of
   screeners that have been administered to large evaluation samples in Argentina, Brazil, Colombia, Ecuador, Honduras, Mexico,
   Nicaragua, and Peru.

Developmental tests often assess multiple dimensions of child
development, such as cognition, receptive and expressive language,
fine and gross motor development, socioemotional development, and
adaptive behavior. This is the case of tests like the Bayley, the Battelle,
the Denver, or the ASQ. There are also tests designed to focus on one
particular developmental area. For example, the MacArthur Bates

Communicative Development Inventories are designed to assess receptive and expressive language in children younger than 3 years of age; the Strengths and Difficulties questionnaire is a screener test for behavioral problems—emotional, attention, conduct, relationships, and prosocial behaviors—for children as young as 3 years of age.

There is no consensus on which is the best child development test. The choice of a test depends on many elements, among others, the purpose and scale of the measurement, the age of the child, and the resources available (time, money, and personnel) to carry it out. Diagnostic tests have been administered in large samples as part of evaluations aimed at measuring the impact of programs. Screener tests have also been added to household surveys to measure the impact of policy interventions. Aggregated at the classroom level, screener test scores have also been used to monitor provider quality. Not all developmental tests are designed to cover the same age ranges. The Bayley can be used from birth to 42 months of age, while the Battelle covers children up to age 7, the ASQ up to age 5, and the Denver up to age 6.

Child Experiences: The Stories That Make the Person

When human beings become embryos, their complete genetic makeup is determined. The individuals they turn out to be is the consequence of the interaction between this genetic makeup and their life experiences. In a few cases, life experiences have no bearing on some important features, such as sex. In most cases though, the path is highly uncertain and strongly dependent on life experiences.

Mounting causal evidence indicates that early experiences often have persistent, long-lasting, and significant effects on a wide array of important youth and adult outcomes. First, since developing countries have few mechanisms to cope with risk, environmental and economic shocks—such as severe weather, epidemiological events, or armed conflict—can generate long-lasting negative effects, usually by way of their impact on nutrition.[9] For example, Maccini and Yang (2009) look at the effect of rainfall in the Philippines; Almond (2006) studies the persistent impact of the Spanish influenza of 1918 in the United States; and Akresh and others (2012) analyze the effect of growing up during the Nigerian civil war.

Second, the behavior of parents, the daycare center their children attend, and early schooling experiences (all of them central issues of this book) also have long-lasting impacts. For example, a 20-year follow-up (Gertler and others 2014) of a randomized experiment in Jamaica, where the mothers of malnourished children were encouraged to play with their 9- to 24-month-old children, found that those who received the stimulation intervention eventually had earnings around 25 percent higher than those in the control group.[10] Children from low-income families randomly assigned in the 1970s to high-quality childcare in Chapel Hill, North Carolina, in the United States (Campbell and others 2001, 2014) were less likely to drop out from high school and more likely to attend a 4-year college at age 21. Berlinski, Galiani, and Manacorda (2008) used the dramatic expansion of pre primary education in Uruguay during the 1990s to look at how participation in preprimary education affected the completion of school grades. At age 15, those who attended preprimary education had completed 0.8 years of education more than those who did not attend.

Finally, the education received in the very first years of schooling also has long-term effects. Chetty and others (2011) look at the long-term impact of Project STAR (Schanzenbach 2007), an experiment conducted in the US state of Tennessee in the mid-1980s, to evaluate the effect of smaller class sizes. Students assigned to smaller classes were significantly more likely to attend college and exhibit improvement in an index that combines information on savings behavior, home ownership, marriage rates, mobility rates, and residential neighborhood quality.[11] Also, conditional on classroom assignments, students who had a more experienced teacher in kindergarten had higher earnings.

Experiences in the early years are shaped by the interactions between the child and various caregivers. These interactions occur simultaneously in four different environments: the home, the daycare center, the school, and the community.[12] Home and community are always central to an individual's experiences. This is particularly salient during the early months of life. As children grow, some of the care they receive may begin to occur outside their homes, in institutions such as daycare centers. Most children move into primary schools when they reach school age.

In these environments, children interact directly with many caregivers (parents/guardians, family members, family friends, and teachers) who have different resources available to them. Examining the key aspects that determine these interactions reveals the potential role for public policy.

It All Starts at Home

Parents and guardians make an infinite number of choices (consciously or unconsciously) that determine children's experiences in the early years of life. They start by choosing when and how to bring them into this world. Then, they decide what and when to feed them, where they will live, and what clothes they should wear. They also make choices about when to take them to the doctor and whether to follow their advice. They make nonmaterial decisions, such as whether to raise them in a nuclear family, how and when to talk to them, and how to encourage acceptable behavior and discourage unacceptable reactions. Of course, they may also decide to delegate some of the caring time to daycare centers, schools, or directly to other people, such as relatives or nannies.

This is a complicated set of choices for parents to make, and it is complicated for those interested in child development to understand. Ultimately, however, if the objective of public policy is to affect choices and child development outcomes, it is useful to provide a framework to interpret the determinants of these choices. Economists, for example, characterize this problem as one in which parents are trying to fulfill their needs and the needs of those they care about subject to two constraints (Becker 1981, 1993). First, parents are constrained by how the resources they spend (time and money) translate into what they want for their children. Second, the cost of fulfilling these needs cannot exceed the resources available to cover these costs. These concepts are discussed in more detail in the paragraphs that follow.

Start with preferences. Human decisions are driven by the desire to fulfill one's own needs and those of others one cares about. Various dimensions of needs are important to consider when looking at the decisions parents make. The first dimension is a temporal one.

How much are parents willing to trade off the satisfaction of current versus future needs; that is, how impatient are parents? This factor is important, as many of the decisions parents make on behalf of their children involve current sacrifices in exchange for future rewards. Crucially, parents make the sacrifices, and many of the benefits are likely to be reaped by the children as adults, which prompts the second dimension. How much do parents care about the needs of others and, in particular, of their children; that is, how altruistic are parents? This consideration leads to the first rationale for policy intervention: parents may not value future outcomes as much as society as a whole (they may be too impatient) or they may not be willing to make the sacrifices that will result in the optimal allocation of resources for society (they may not be altruistic enough).

Within a given set of preferences, the choices that parents make are subject to two main constraints. The first one is technology; for purposes of this analysis, technology can be considered the process that governs the transformation of experiences and genetic make-up into child development outcomes. Experiences depend on resources (such as time and money) allocated by individuals. For example, if the outcome is language acquisition, the inputs are "conversations/talk time," books, and the time devoted to reading.

Experiences also depend on many factors outside parents' control such as the disease environment or the decisions of others (e.g., governments). Experts in child development usually call experiences that may have a negative impact on development "risk factors" and those with a potentially positive impact "protective factors." The impact of experiences on development may be complex; for example, a child may have to suffer many developmental insults for them to have a negative impact.

With child experiences, as with so many things, timing is everything. At the core of the definition of "developmental milestones" is the idea that stages of development occur during predictable time periods. Child development specialists have long studied whether there are sensitive periods for physical and skills development and, therefore, whether technology is age-dependent.[13] Nobel Prize–winning economist James Heckman, among others, has argued that there might be a sensitive age range in which acquiring a given skill requires fewer resources or the absence of some experience may have permanent developmental consequences.

A classic example of a sensitive age range refers to the acquisition of vision. Nobel Prize winners David Hubel and Torsten Wiesel (Wurtz 2009) conducted experiments with cats and showed that if the animal is deprived of a normal visual experience during a critical period at the start of its life, the circuitry of the neurons in its visual cortex is irreversibly altered. Conversely, if the eye of an adult cat is deprived of vision, the responses of the cells in its visual cortex remain identical to those of a normal cat. This is why it is so important to detect vision problems early in life; otherwise, the ability to see and learn visually can be impaired permanently.

How resources translate into outcomes depends on innate and accumulated traits of children. If the child has hearing problems, her ability to acquire language through speech is impaired. Interestingly, children who are known to be deaf and learn through sign language exhibit no problems acquiring language or learning to communicate. Moreover, the more children are spoken to, the more language they know; therefore, talking more to them may allow them to acquire language in subsequent periods at even faster rates. This relation between early accumulation and later outcomes is described in economics by the concept of dynamic complementarities (Cunha and Heckman 2007; Heckman 2008). Dynamic complementarities and sensitive age periods imply that the timing of interventions, by parents, caregivers, or public policy operators, may also be important.

This complex dynamic relation is one of the main reasons behind the second rationale for policy intervention: parents may not make the best decisions on behalf of their children because they are ill informed about the relationship between experience and outcomes; that is, they have imperfect information. For example, they may think toddlers' tantrums (something biologically natural at this age) are an expression of bad behavior and try to elicit appropriate behavior by hitting them. Of course, systematic failures in parental behavior are not linked only to lack of knowledge; there may be other contributing factors such as parental stress, depression, and lack of self-control.

The second constraint relates to the cost and availability of resources. Producing experiences and generating outcomes is costly. Costs include the time and resources allocated by individuals over time, including all the early years of a child's life and beyond. Costs, therefore, can be current, occurring in the present: for example, a sick day that a mother takes to care for her sick child, or the current expense of a book or toy she buys for them. Other costs are experienced only in the future. For example, a child with cataracts who is not treated early on is likely to develop serious eyesight problems. This will create health care problems in the future, reducing her well-being and her productivity as an adult.

Of course, parents can only spend the money they currently have or that they can borrow. Frequently, the lack of money and resources create a binding constraint to increasing the investment in children to the desired level. The problem could be solved if capital markets were able to provide parents with resources today in exchange for some of the returns in children's investment that will be realized in the future. If capital markets can provide this only imperfectly (only partially or to a subset of families), then constraints in the access to credit generate a third rationale for policy intervention.

In many circumstances, the costs of resources are not borne exclusively by parents, and the benefits are not enjoyed solely by them and their children. This leads to what economists call "externalities" (negative or positive). Suppose, for example, that a parent fails to vaccinate her child against a preventable disease—an action that can be completed at a relatively low cost for the individual. If the child becomes sick because she was not vaccinated, and the associated health care costs and negative long-term consequences are completely borne by the individual, then there are no negative externalities. However, if society shares some of the short- and long-term costs of the disease, either in terms of medical outlays or by increasing the chance of illness for those that cannot be vaccinated, then the parent is imposing a negative externality on society. The presence of negative or positive externalities generates the fourth rationale for policy intervention.

Finally, the process that leads to parental choice is neither deterministic nor static. In particular, parents must contend with uncertainty about three fundamental aspects: their child's initial endowment, how their actions translate into outcomes, and the long-term benefits of investing in their child's development. They hold beliefs about all three aspects. Because parents update their beliefs with the arrival of new information, the process of child rearing is naturally a dynamic one. For example, in Puebla, Mexico, parents of 10-year-old children had incorrect perceptions about how overweight or obese their children were (Prina and Royer 2014). Distributing report cards featuring their child's body weight increased parental knowledge and shifted parental attitudes about children's weight.[14]

Daycare Centers: The Second Line of Care

When the main care providers for a child decide to work, they must pursue alternative modes of childcare for their children. In urban and semi-urban areas of Latin America and the Caribbean, parents increasingly rely on daycare centers. Government support for the expansion of daycare centers has been historically associated with offering public incentives for women to look for work (Araujo and López Boo 2015). In Latin America and the Caribbean, daycare services are delivered through different institutional arrangements: private providers, private/community providers with partial subsidies from the state, and public providers.

In choosing a childcare provider parents must balance convenience, price, and quality of care (Blau and Currie 2006, 2008). Convenience is reflected in the distance to their house or their job and the hours of operation of the center. There is evidence from developed countries that prices (e.g., Baker, Gruber, and Milligan 2008; Havnes and Mogstad 2011) and convenience (e.g., Neidell and Waldfogel 2009) are important determinants of daycare choice. However, how the well-being of children is affected by attending a daycare center instead of being cared for by their parents or other childcare providers at home hinges crucially on the quality of care. This is true even when taking into account the additional resources that are available to the households if parents are working (Bernal and Keane 2011).

How is quality determined? The institutional arrangement for the provision of services influences the quality of services that are offered. Childcare services are what economists call an experience good[15] (a good whose quality consumers are likely to ascertain only after consuming it). The main issue in this environment is information: How do parents determine the quality of a childcare provider when it may take a long time to determine quality or negative experiences may have long-term consequences? What incentives do the providers have to offer high-quality services?

In private markets, prices may provide some signals about quality. Economic research (Tirole 1988) has shown that where direct information can be obtained (even at a cost), informed consumers can improve the quality of the products offered. Moreover, as the fraction of well-informed parents increases, the likelihood that valuable information will be revealed increases as well. As a result, the public benefit of an informed parent is greater than the private cost the parent is willing to pay. This positive externality provides a rationale for public policy intervention in the childcare market. Standards and licensing systems guaranteeing minimum levels of quality could be seen as an answer to this need. Parents know that a licensed childcare center provides at least that minimum level of quality.

However, imposing a minimum level of quality has its limitations. Enforcing regulation is very difficult and costly because this is a market with many small providers. Even assuming perfect enforcement, regulating the minimum quality may not generate the variety of quality demanded by parents. If the standard is too low, the market may offer too many providers close to the minimum quality, leaving the demand of parents willing to pay for a higher standard unsatisfied. If the standard is too high, the total supply of childcare services may be too low to satisfy demand, particularly for low-income parents, which may drive them to a completely unregulated sector (Hotz and Xiao 2011).

Subsidized childcare provision or voucher programs cannot solve the information gap issue. However, voucher programs may be effective in changing the average quality at which demand and supply meet because they allow parents to buy more expensive care. Importantly, a combination of vouchers and regulation of private providers may prevent some parents from moving to the unregulated sector after regulation is introduced.[16]

Schools: A Common Denominator

In Latin America and the Caribbean, primary school education from around age 5 is compulsory, publicly provided, and mainly free. Enrollment in primary school from age 6 onward has been virtually universal across most countries since the 1990s. The emphasis on parental choice is therefore very different in the case of primary school compared to daycare. Parents have fewer choices in this case because they must send their children to school and frequently cannot choose which public school their children will attend.[17]

The core objective of the primary school system is to help children achieve appropriate levels of literacy, numeracy, and socioemotional competencies. Going back to the relationship between experience and technology, the evidence shows that the process of acquiring academic skills is only loosely age dependent. Although starting too early or too late may be costly, reaching a satisfactory level of literacy and numeracy is feasible at almost any age, and the age interval during which the cost of acquisition is very similar and relatively low is quite large. For example, Finland, a country routinely ranked at the top of children's achievement indicators, starts compulsory teaching of literacy and numeracy at age 7, two years later than the average in the Latin American and Caribbean region.

From an organizational point of view, it is crucially important for a given country or very large community to determine a common school age. This coordination is necessary because it is far less expensive to teach a relatively large number of children who are similar in terms of their knowledge and maturity than it is to teach one-on-one or children with very different backgrounds and at different stages in their development. A universal school entry age and the grouping of children in school by age is an institutional arrangement that makes school readiness a critical issue. If children are not ready for school at age 5, they may easily fall behind, generating the need for expensive remediation interventions. Moreover, a high proportion of children lacking school readiness may negatively affect the learning of children who are ready for school. The possible negative externality, together with the need to agree on a school entry age, provides a rationale for public policy intervention before children reach primary school.

The Policy Toolkit

Public policy should enhance children's lives from the time of their conception until well after they enter school. Before they begin the compulsory education process, children are molded mainly in their homes and in daycare centers. The challenge for public policy is to adopt an integral view of this development process (see Chapter 7).

Policymakers have at their disposal five main instruments to affect child outcomes and parental decisions: information and coaching (e.g., awareness campaigns, coaching mothers on breastfeeding), laws (e.g., parental leave, compulsory education at a given age), regulations (e.g., regulation of advertisements about baby formula, regulation of child-to-staff ratios in daycare centers), transfers (e.g., universal child transfers, tax credits, conditional cash transfers), and prices (e.g., subsidized childcare, free vaccination).

Governments may use a combination of these instruments to achieve their objectives (Carneiro and Heckman 2003). For instance, to ensure a well-educated population, they can make education compulsory at a given age, regulate class sizes and teaching standards, give parents a transfer conditional on taking children to growth and development check-ups and on school attendance, and provide free schooling. The combination of instruments should be dictated by the perceived difficulty of individuals and markets in achieving the stated objectives.

The government acts as the main or sole provider of services (e.g., childcare, education, health) in many areas crucial to the well-being of children in the early years. Given a fixed government budget, a key trade-off in the provision of these services is the relationship between quantity and quality. The government may understandably try to reach as many children as possible. However, with a fixed budget, serving more children implies less expenditure per capita. Many of the services provided by the public sector are experience goods (like the provision of daycare) and the government may have an incentive to provide low quality when this is hard to spot by consumers/voters. Clearly, this decision is not without consequences; it may not only waste money but potentially harm the well-being of children—particularly, those from the neediest sectors of society that cannot afford to obtain services elsewhere.

Child well-being results from a cumulative, nonlinear process of child development that encompasses four main areas: physical development, language/communication, cognitive skills, and socioemotional skills. This process of development does not unfold on its own, but is shaped by the experiences children accumulate at home, in daycare centers, and at school. Parents, relatives, other caregivers, teachers, and government all have a hand in shaping those experiences. Improving those experiences will shape children's lives and the face of the societies they live in for years to come. Clearly, child well-being matters for both ethical and economic reasons and public policy has a role to play in developing happy, healthy, and prosperous children.

2

A Report Card on Early Childhood Development

Child well-being is multidimensional. This chapter summarizes the evidence on the health, nutrition, cognitive, language, socioemotional, and motor development of young children in Latin America and the Caribbean. These measures are important in their own right, and because of their implications for long-term productivity and growth in the region. Where possible, comparisons across countries, changes over time, and differences within countries, especially by wealth or parental education—so-called socioeconomic gradients—are made to provide an added dimension to the description, and a clearer picture of the state of well-being of the region's children.

Just What the Doctor Ordered: Improved Child Health and Nutrition

In both developed and developing countries, low birth weight (less than 2,500 grams) has been associated with worse health and development outcomes in childhood, learning problems and poor performance in school, an increase in a number of chronic health conditions in adulthood and old age, and worse labor market outcomes.[1] Low birth weight is an indication of constraints in fetal nutrition (as can be caused by poor nutrition of the mother, infection, or smoking or drinking during pregnancy) or of prematurity (Kramer 1987, 2003).

Two recent papers report compelling evidence from Chile. The first of these (Bharadwaj, Eberhard, and Neilson 2014) finds that low birth weight (less than 2,500 grams) or very low birth weight (less than 1,500 grams) babies have test scores in math that are substantially lower in childhood and up to early adolescence. A companion paper (Bharadwaj, Løken, and Neilson 2013) exploits the fact that, in Chile (as is the case in many other countries), babies below the threshold for very low birth weight are eligible for special care in a neonatal intensive care unit. Babies whose weight was just below the cutoff (and who were therefore eligible for special care) were 4.4 percentage points less likely to die in their first year than those whose weight was just above the cutoff (and who were therefore ineligible for care). Moreover, between first and eighth grades, those whose weight at birth was just below the cutoff have test scores that are on average 0.15 standard deviations higher than those whose weight was just above. Taken together, these two papers with Chilean data make clear that low birth weight can have serious, negative consequences for child health and development, but that early intervention can mitigate these effects, at least in part.[2]

Box 2.1 Understanding Standard Deviations

Outcomes used to measure child well-being are not all in the same metric. Height is measured in centimeters and weight in kilograms. Test scores are measured in integers and each test has a different mean and standard deviation that is arbitrarily chosen by the test designers (e.g., the Peabody Picture Vocabulary Test [PPVT] has a mean of 100 and a standard deviation of 15). To express the myriad of measures into a common metric, researchers use a simple statistical technique. They subtract the mean from the observed outcome measure and divide this difference by the standard deviation of the distribution. These standardized measures all have a mean of zero and a standard deviation of one in the population.

People usually refer to differences in outcomes and gains from programs in terms of standard deviations. In a standardized variable a unit change in the outcome is equivalent to a change in one standard deviation. How can we interpret what a gain in one standard deviation implies? This very much depends on how the outcome variable is distributed in the population. If the distribution of test scores has a bell-shape (i.e., has a normal distribution), a gain of one standard deviation will take someone performing at the bottom 2.5th percentile of the distribution (where there are very few individuals in the population) to the 17th percentile. Because, there are more people concentrated toward the middle in a bell-shaped distribution (rather than uniformly distributed), a one standard deviation increase for someone at the 50th percentile produces a larger percentile gain than for someone at the bottom or top of the distribution.

There is also an often used convention in the psychology literature that classifies program gains of around 0.2 of a standard deviation as small, 0.5 as moderate, and 0.8 as large (Cohen 1969). This does not provide guidance for policy choice, however, as programs with small effects can also have lower costs (see McCartney and Rosenthal 2000). A thorough discussion of the cost-benefit analysis strategy for program choice is provided in Chapter 6.

Estimates of the proportion of all births that are low birth weight for Latin America and the Caribbean reveal large differences across countries (see Table 2.1). In Cuba and Chile, about 1 in 20 babies is born with low birth weight; in Colombia and Mexico, this proportion is about 1 in 10; and in Haiti, almost 1 in 4. For the region as a whole, 9 percent of babies are born with low birth weight, substantially below the level for countries in Africa (11–14 percent) and, especially, South Asia (28 percent). In some countries in Latin America and the Caribbean, the proportion of low birth weight babies has been increasing, especially among women with higher education levels. This result, which at first blush appears to be paradoxical, is a consequence of the fact that more premature babies who would have died in earlier years now survive (see Box 2.2 for evidence from Colombia).

Table 2.1   Low Birth Weight

Country	Percentage of children
Latin America and Caribbean	
Antigua and Barbuda (2011)	6
Argentina (2011)	7.2
Bahamas (2011)	11.6
Barbados (2011)	11.5
Belize (2011)	11.1
Bolivia (2008)	6
Brazil (2011)	8.5
Chile (2011)	5.9
Colombia (2012)	9.5

Continued

Table 2.1 Continued

Country	Percentage of children
Costa Rica (2012)	7.3
Cuba (2012)	5.2
Dominica (2011)	10.8
Dominican Republic (2007)	11
Ecuador (2012)	8.6
El Salvador (2011)	8.7
Grenada (2011)	8.8
Guatemala (2008–09)	11.4
Guyana (2009)	14.3
Haiti (2012)	23
Honduras (2011–12)	9.9
Jamaica (2011)	11.3
Mexico (2012)	9.15
Nicaragua (2011)	7.6
Panama (2011)	8.3
Paraguay (2009)	6.3
Peru (2011)	6.9
Saint Kitts and Nevis (2011)	10.4
Saint Lucia (2011)	10.1
Saint Vincent and the Grenadines (2011)	10.6
Suriname (2010)	13.9
Trinidad and Tobago (2011)	11.9
Uruguay (2012)	8.1
Venezuela (2011)	8.6
Regional averages (2009–13)	
Sub-Saharan Africa	13.05
Eastern and Southern Africa	11.26
West and Central Africa	14.18
Middle East and North Africa	—
South Asia	27.76
East Asia and Pacific	—
Latin America and Caribbean	9.02
CEE/CIS	6.12
Least developed countries	13.71
World	15.83*

Notes: Percentage of infants weighing less than 2,500 grams at birth. For Bolivia and Dominican Republic, data refer to years 2009–13. Such data are not included in the calculation of regional and global averages, with the exception of 2005–06 and 2007–08 data from India, Central and Eastern Europe and the Commonwealth of Independent States (CEE/CIS) .* Excludes China.

Source: Data and Analytics Section; Division of Data, Research and Policy, UNICEF. Basic Health Indicators 2010 for Paraguay; Colombia National Statistics System for Colombia; Demographic and Health Surveys (DHS) for Dominican Republic, Bolivia, Guyana, Honduras, and Haiti; Encuesta Nacional de Salud Materno Infantil (ENSMI) for Guatemala; Multiple Indicator Cluster Survey (MICS) for Suriname, Belize; Ministry of Health for Brazil, Argentina, Costa Rica, El Salvador, Cuba, Uruguay, and Nicaragua; National Institute of Statistics (INE) for Chile; National Institute of Census and Statistics (INE) for Chile; Other National Survey, National Institute of Public Health for Mexico; Pan American Health Organization (PAHO), Health Situation in the Americas: Basic indicators 2013 for Antigua and Barbuda, Bahamas, Barbados, Dominica, Grenada, Jamaica, Panama, Peru, Saint Kitts and Nevis, Saint Lucia, Saint Vincent and the Grenadines, Trinidad and Tobago; Sistema de Indicadores Sociales de Venezuela for Venezuela.

Box 2.2   Changes in Prematurity and Birth Weight in Colombia

The proportion of low birth weight babies has been on the rise in some countries in Latin America and the Caribbean. Figure B2.1 is based on vital registration data on all births in Colombia between 1998 and 2008. Panels a and b show that mean birth weight declined, and the proportion of babies with low birth weight increased between 1998 and 2008. The decline in birth weight is particularly sharp for babies born to women with university education—indeed, babies born to women with more education are now substantially more likely to be below the cutoff for low birth weight than those born to women with less education.

At first blush, this result appears to be paradoxical. Plausibly, however, it is a consequence of the fact that an increasing fraction of all births are preterm (births that occur before the thirty-eighth week of pregnancy), in particular among women with higher levels of education (see Figure B2.1, panel c). In the past, many of these "additional" low birth weight babies would have been miscarriages or would not have been born alive.

Figure B2.1   Weight at Birth, Colombia

a. Weight at Birth, according to Mother's Education

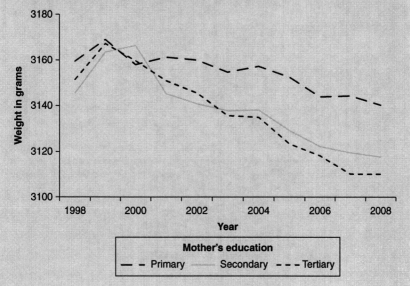

b. Proportion with Low Birth Weight, according to Mother's Education

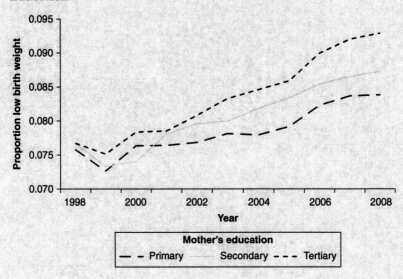

c. Proportion of Premature Births, according to Mother's Education

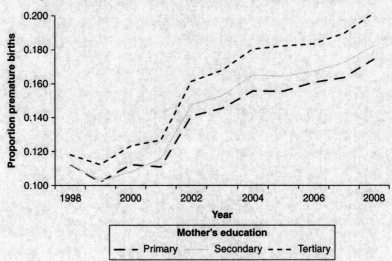

d. Changes in Proportion Low Birth Weight for Mothers with Tertiary Education

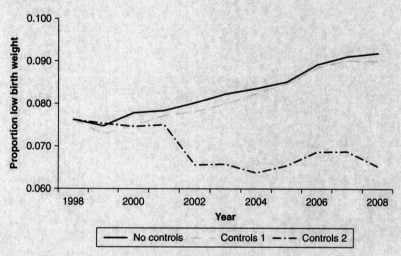

Source: Vital registration data, Colombia 1998–2008.

One way to test this is by controlling for prematurity, and seeing whether the increase in the proportion of low birth weight babies is still apparent. The results from this exercise can be found in panel d, for women with tertiary education (for whom the decline in birth weight over time is largest, as seen in panels a and b of the figure). Specifically, panel d includes three lines: A line with the average birth weight, without any controls; a second line, labeled "controls 1," which plots the decline in birth weight after accounting for possible changes in the age of the mother, whether the baby was delivered by C-section, and whether the birth is a multiple birth; and a third line, labeled "controls 2," which, in addition, controls for prematurity. A comparison of the three lines in the figure shows that, once prematurity is controlled for, the proportion of low birth weight babies born to mothers with tertiary education declines over time, by about 1 percentage point. In other words, the decline in birth weight for babies born to high-education mothers that is observed in Colombia between 1998 and 2008 can be fully accounted for by an increase in the proportion of births that are premature.

Birth weight is not the only measure of a newborn's health. Attending physicians or nurses also assess the newborn's heart rate, respiratory effort, muscle tone, reflex irritability, and color. This is the basis for the calculation of the APGAR score, generally assessed at one and five minutes after birth. The APGAR score ranges from 0 to 10. APGAR scores of 7 or higher are generally an indication that a newborn's health is good. Newborns with a score of 6 or lower, on the other hand, are substantially more likely to die in the neonatal period. This is the case even when the comparison is limited to babies of the same gestational age (Casey, McIntire, and Leveno 2001). Furthermore, using data from the United States, Almond, Chay, and Lee (2005) show that, controlling for family background and birth weight, low APGAR scores also predict poor health, lower cognitive ability, and an increase in behavioral problems at age 3.

For two years, 2008 and 2009, the vital registration data for Colombia includes a newborn's APGAR score. About 1 percent of newborns have an APGAR score of 6 or below at five minutes after birth. Babies born to women with only primary school education are significantly more likely to have an APGAR score of 6 or below than those born to women with university education (a difference of 0.18 percentage points), once gestational age and birth weight are controlled for. In sum, in Colombia, substantial inequalities can already be observed at birth. In some cases, as with birth weight, babies born to low-education women have better outcomes, while in others, as with the APGAR score, they have worse outcomes.

After birth, the most obvious measure of child welfare is also a tragic one: whether a child dies early on. The "infant mortality rate" is defined as the number of children who die before their first birthday, per 1,000 live births. Figure 2.1 summarizes changes in infant mortality between 1960 and 2010 for six countries that are broadly representative of what has occurred in the region: Brazil, Chile, El Salvador, Honduras, Jamaica, and Panama. Each panel corresponds to a different country. Each bar in a panel represents the infant mortality rate of that country in a given year. As with many social outcomes, it is useful to benchmark a country's performance relative to other countries with similar income levels. For example, was infant mortality in Brazil in 2010 higher, lower, or roughly the same as that of other countries with comparable income levels? To get a sense of this, next to each bar, a circle that represents the average infant mortality rate of all countries with a similar per capita GDP in that year is included (see Box 2.3 for methodological details).[3]

Figure 2.1   Infant Mortality per 1,000 Live Births

a. Brazil

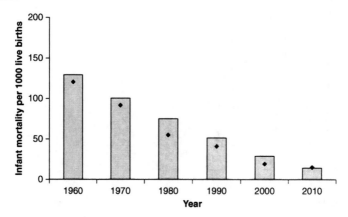

b. Chile

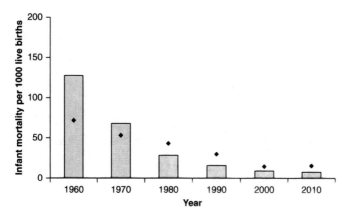

c. El Salvador

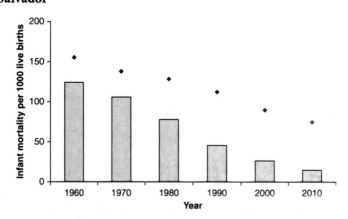

d. Honduras

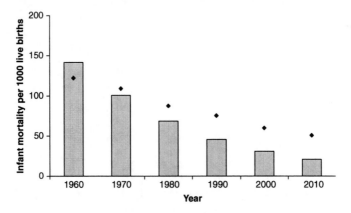

e. Jamaica

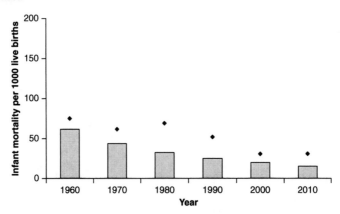

f. Panama

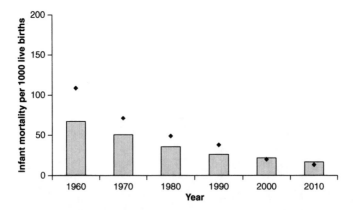

Source: World Development Indicators, Infant mortality rate (per 1,000 live births). Estimates developed by the UN Inter-agency Group for Child Mortality Estimation (UNICEF, WHO, World Bank, UN DESA Population Division). All values of GDP in PPP thousands of dollars (2005 International $) were taken from the Penn World Table.

Box 2.3   The Evolution of Infant Mortality Rates and Per Capita GDP

To see how the relationship between mortality and per capita GDP has evolved over time, nonparametric regressions of the infant mortality rate on GDP per capita were run, separately by decade, for a balanced panel of 79 countries for which these data are available for all six decades. Minor adjustments were made to the regression lines to ensure that the average difference between the observed mortality (the country points) and the predicted mortality (the regression line) is zero in every decade.

It is important to run these regressions separately by decade because medical technology, vaccinations, other public health measures (such as oral rehydration therapy) and the extension of clean water and sanitation all mean that infant mortality is lower in later decades at a given level of GDP. That is, in addition to movements along the curve (as the income of a country grows or, in some cases, contracts), there are downward shifts of the curves themselves over time.

Figure B2.2 focuses on one country, Honduras, which has made remarkable progress in reducing infant mortality. Each line corresponds to the relationship between the infant mortality rate and per capita GDP

Figure B2.2   Infant Mortality Rate and Per Capita GDP, Honduras, 1960–2010

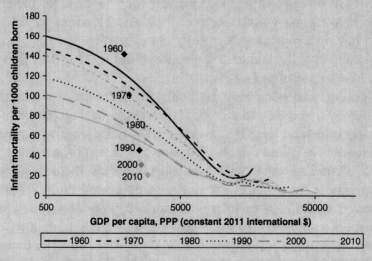

Source: World Development Indicators. Estimates developed by the UN Inter-Agency Group for Child Mortality Estimation (UNICEF, WHO, World Bank, UN DESA Population Division). All values of GDP in PPP thousands of dollars (2005 International $) were taken from the Penn World Table.

in a given year, and the points on the graph correspond to infant mortality in Honduras in those same years. The average infant mortality rate has fallen dramatically since 1960, especially at low income levels: A country with a per capita GDP level of $1,000 would, on average, have an infant mortality rate of 145 per 1,000 in 1960 but 80 per 1,000 in 2010. In 1960, Honduras had an infant mortality rate that was roughly 20 points above the level predicted by its GDP per capita. Since then, infant mortality in Honduras has fallen to levels that are considerably lower than those of other countries with similar income levels—in 2010, the infant mortality rate in Honduras was roughly 25 points below the regression line.

Infant mortality has declined dramatically in every country in the region. Over a 50-year period, 15 of the 17 countries in Latin America and the Caribbean with available data reduced infant mortality by 75 percent or more; three countries—Brazil, Chile, and Peru—reduced infant mortality by 90 percent or more.[4] Some countries, like Brazil, have had infant mortality rates that are roughly comparable to other countries with similar income levels throughout[5]; other countries, like El Salvador and Jamaica, have had lower mortality than other countries with similar income levels for the entire period[6]; yet other countries, like Chile and Honduras, have gone from having a mortality "surplus" to a mortality "deficit"[7]; finally, a few countries, like Panama, have moved in the other direction and now have excess infant mortality.[8]

To study socioeconomic gradients in mortality, it is necessary to work with household survey (rather than aggregate) data. The Demographic and Health Surveys (DHS) are nationally representative surveys of women of childbearing age that can be used to calculate a time series of the infant mortality rate (including among subgroups of the population), under some assumptions.[9] Table 2.2 summarizes differences in infant mortality for women of "high" education (complete secondary education or more) and "low" education (incomplete primary education or less) for countries that have recently fielded a DHS. It shows that, in the Dominican Republic, children born to low-education mothers are four times as likely to die in their first year as those born to high-education mothers;

Table 2.2   Infant Mortality Rate by Mother's Education

Country	Incomplete primary or less	Completed secondary or more
Bolivia (2004)	50.5	23.5
Colombia (2006)	23.8	12.5
Dominican Republic (2003)	39.9	11.1
El Salvador (2004)	13	10
Honduras (2008)	16.8	11.2
Peru (2008)	16.8	12.8

Note: Restricted to mothers between 25 and 37 years of age at the time of childbirth; five-year moving average; averages calculated for cells with at least 100 births.

Source: Demographic and Health Surveys (DHS), except for El Salvador; Encuesta Nacional de Salud Familiar (FESAL, 2008) for El Salvador.

in Bolivia and Colombia, children of low-education mothers are twice as likely to die in their first year. Maternal education gradients are much more modest in El Salvador, Honduras, and Peru.

To look further at within-country patterns in the evolution of infant mortality, an in-depth analysis of one country in the region, Peru, was carried out. Peru is an interesting case study of changes in infant mortality for a variety of reasons. First, it has collected high-quality DHS data since the mid-1980s. Second, it started off with very large disparities in infant mortality by (among other factors) place of residence, socioeconomic status, and ethnicity. An important question is whether the aggregate reductions in infant mortality in Peru were accompanied by a decline in within-country disparities.

Figure 2.2 analyzes the evolution of infant mortality for four population breakdowns. Panel a compares changes in infant mortality for women of "high" education (complete secondary or more) and "low" education (incomplete primary or less). In 1982, the infant mortality rate for children born to low-education mothers was more than twice as high as that for children born to high-education mothers (105 versus 50 deaths per 1,000 live births); by 2008, the infant mortality rate had declined to below 20 per 1,000 for both groups. This means that, over roughly a 25-year period, infant mortality for children born to women with incomplete primary education or less declined by more than 80 percent, which is equivalent to declines of more than 3 percent per year.

Figure 2.2   Population Breakdown of Infant Mortality, Peru

a. Infant Mortality by Mother's Education

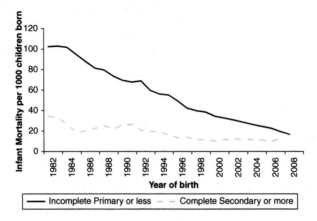

b. Infant Mortality by Mother's Ethnicity

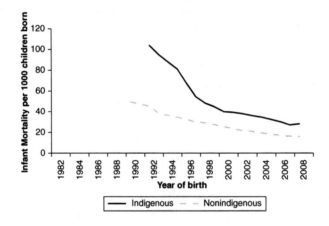

c. Infant Mortality by Mother's Age

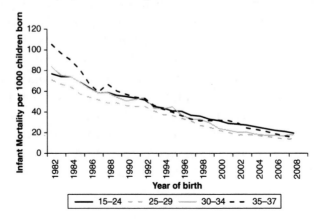

d. Infant Mortality by Infant's Gender

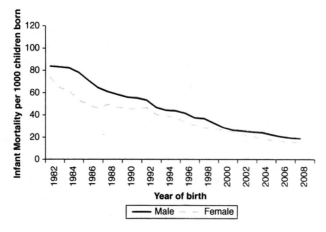

Note: Restricted to mothers between 15 and 37 years of age at the time of birth for panels b, c, and d, and to women 25–37 for panel a. 5-year moving average;, averages calculated for years with at least 100 births. For the ethnicity graph, the 1986, 1991 and 1996 DHS are excluded because data were not collected on ethnicity.

Source: Demographic and Health Surveys (DHS).

Panel b shows trends in the infant mortality rate for indigenous and nonindigenous mothers. (Ethnicity in Peru is defined on the basis of the respondent's mother tongue.) Data on ethnicity have been collected only in more recent surveys in Peru, so this time series can be constructed only from 1990 onward. The panel shows a dramatic reduction in infant mortality among the indigenous, especially in the 1990s. Between 1991 and 2008, a period of less than 20 years, the infant mortality rate of indigenous children fell by 75 percent—from approximately 100 deaths per 1,000 children born to 25 deaths.[10] To put the magnitude of these reductions in context, it is informative to compare them with declines in infant mortality among African Americans in the United States. It took the United States roughly 50 years, from 1935 to 1985, to reduce the infant mortality rate among African Americans from 80 to 25 deaths per 1,000 (Singh and van Dyck 2010); the same approximate reduction in the infant mortality rate among the indigenous in Peru was accomplished in less than 15 years, between 1995 and 2008.

Panel c shows that the reduction in infant mortality has affected mothers in all age groups, including younger mothers (whose children had substantially higher mortality rates in the first half of the 1980s, but not since then). Panel d shows that the infant mortality rate has fallen for boys and girls in more or less equal measure.[11]

In Peru, as in many other countries in Latin America and the Caribbean, the average age at which mothers have children has increased, total fertility has been falling, and births are more widely spaced, on average. To see how this might affect mortality, the observed changes in infant mortality can be broken down into changes in the characteristics of mothers and births, changes in the impacts of these characteristics on mortality rates, and an unexplained residual.[12] The results from these decompositions indicate that changes in characteristics, including the age of the mother, the number of older siblings a child has at birth, the number of months that separate her birth from the previous one, and whether the birth was a singleton or a multiple birth, account for only 7 percent of the decline in the infant mortality rate between the early 1980s and late 2000s in Peru. In other words, the changes associated with the demographic transition cannot by themselves explain much of the decline in infant mortality in Peru.[13]

Next, consider child height. Child height is important because although some children in any population will obviously be taller than others for genetic reasons, when the average stature of children in a population is low, it likely reflects a poor diet or frequent infections in childhood (including inflammation from asymptomatic infections, a phenomenon known as environmental enteropathy). This, in turn, can result in impaired cognitive development and, eventually, worse school outcomes, lower wages, and worse health status over the life cycle, including a higher incidence of chronic diseases in old age.[14]

Data on the height of young children have been collected regularly in many developing countries since the 1990s, including countries in Latin America and the Caribbean. Analysis of these data reveals large differences in the average stature of children in the region: A 4-year-old child is on average six centimeters taller in Chile than in Ecuador, and ten centimeters taller in Chile than in Guatemala.[15] Children have grown taller in some countries (in Honduras, Nicaragua, and Peru, 4-year-old children were on average two centimeters taller in 2012 than in 2000–01) but not in all (in

Panama, children were no taller in 2008 than in 1997, on average).[16] Adults, too, have generally been getting taller in Latin America, although, much as is the case with children, the degree to which this has occurred varies substantially across countries (see Box 2.4).

Box 2.4   Changes in Adult Stature

A number of economists, including the Nobel Prize winner Robert Fogel and Angus Deaton, as well as many nutritionists, including Reynaldo Martorell and Cesar Victora, have long argued that the average height of a population in adulthood can be a good marker of conditions in early childhood.[17] Historically, as nutrition has improved and childhood diseases have become much less prevalent, people have become much taller. For example, Deaton (2013) shows that European males have grown by roughly 1 centimeter per decade for over a century, so that the average male born in the 1980s is 12 centimeters taller than one who was born in 1860. Deaton also shows that in China, men and women are growing at roughly 1 centimeter per decade, while in India, men are growing at only half a centimeter per decade and women are growing at less than 0.2 centimeters per decade. He argues that Indians are short, and have been growing little over time, for a variety of reasons, including monotonous diets lacking in protein and fat, inadequate access to clean water, and poor sanitation. India has one of the highest rates of open defecation in the world and this, combined with high population density, results in a very poor disease environment. The preferential treatment of boys over girls in India likely accounts for the difference in their growth rates.

What about the height of adults in Latin America? The stature of adult women is measured in many of the surveys that are used to measure maternal and child health in the region, including the DHS. These data can be used to compare the stature of adult women across birth cohorts.[18] On average, across ten countries in the region where these data are available, women born in 1990 are about 2 centimeters taller than those born in 1960. However, this average hides important differences. In two countries, Brazil and Chile, women have on average been growing by more than 1.5 centimeters per decade, while in another six—Bolivia, the Dominican Republic, Guatemala, Haiti, Honduras, and Peru—women have been growing taller much more slowly, at less than 0.5 centimeters per decade.

Data on child height are also the basis for the calculation of chronic malnutrition. For this purpose, the height of a given child is compared to that of children in a reference population of well-nourished children.[19] If the height of a child is more than two standard deviations below the mean height of children of the same age and gender in this reference population, he or she is said to be stunted, or chronically malnourished.[20]

Figure 2.3 shows changes in chronic malnutrition for six countries that are broadly representative of what has occurred in the region: Bolivia, Guatemala, Haiti, Honduras, Mexico, and Paraguay. As in Figure 2.1, each panel includes bars corresponding to chronic

Figure 2.3   Chronic Malnutrition

a. Bolivia

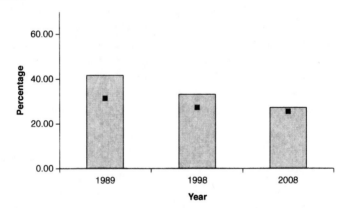

b. Guatemala

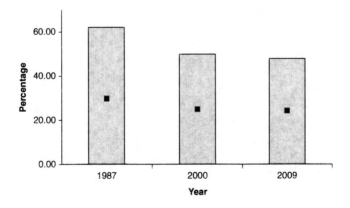

c. Haiti

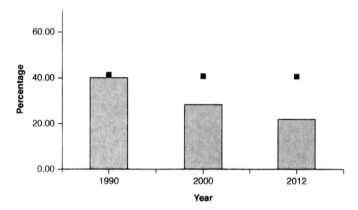

d. Honduras

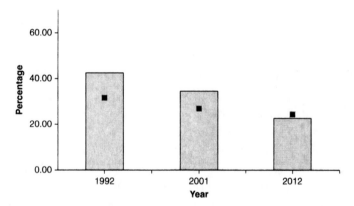

e. Mexico

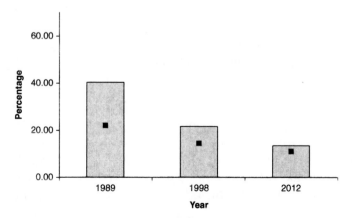

f. Paraguay

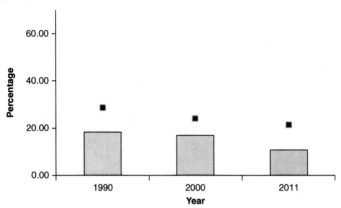

Source: World Development Indicators, World Bank. World Health Organization (WHO). All values of GDP in PPP thousands of dollars (2005 International $) were taken from the World Economic Outlook Databases (WEO).

malnutrition in a particular country and year, and circles for the average malnutrition in countries of the same income level. However, unlike infant mortality, data on malnutrition are only available beginning in the 1990s or 2000s for most countries, and are not available for exactly the same year in each country.

Many countries in the region have made a good deal of progress reducing stunting rates since the early 1990s. Over a 20-year period, stunting fell by approximately half in ten countries, and by more than 75 percent in Mexico. Most countries in the region now have stunting rates that are roughly comparable to, or substantially lower than, those found in other countries with similar income levels. Only Guatemala, which has one of the highest stunting rates in the world (48 percent), is a clear, negative outlier within the region.

As with infant mortality, it is also informative to look at differences within countries. Table 2.3 compares stunting rates for children of mothers with "low" education (incomplete primary education or less) and those of "high" education (complete secondary education or more) in 19 countries in the region. It shows that maternal education gradients are modest in some countries with overall low stunting rates, including in Brazil, Chile, and Trinidad and Tobago. In other countries, however, including Guatemala, Haiti, and Panama,

Table 2.3   Chronic Malnutrition, by Mother's Education

	Stunting	
Country	Incomplete primary or less	Completed secondary or more
Belize (2011)	24.6	10.5
Bolivia (2008)	36.7	11.8
Brazil (2009)	11.3	8.9
Chile (2012)	2.9	2.7
Colombia (2010)	20.9	8.6
Dominican Republic (2007)	13.7	7.4
Ecuador (2012)	39.6	18.3
El Salvador (2008)	26.5	11.8
Guatemala (2008)	59.5	13.7
Haiti (2012)	27	4.5
Honduras (2012)	35.8	7.5
Jamaica (2010)	—	6.3
Mexico (2012)	26.9	11.2
Nicaragua (2001)	34.9	8.7
Panama (2008)	35.1	7
Paraguay (2012)	12.9	6.3
Peru (2012)	37.3	8.5
Suriname (2011)	9	5.5
Trinidad and Tobago (1987)	5.8	4.8

Notes: For children aged 0–59 months, except for Chile and Trinidad and Tobago. In Chile, the sample refers to children aged 7–59 months, and in Trinidad and Tobago, the sample refers to children aged 3–36 months.

Source: Authors' calculations based on Demographic and Health Surveys (DHS) for Bolivia, Colombia, Dominican Republic, Haiti, Honduras, Peru, and Trinidad and Tobago; Multiple Indicator Cluster Survey (MICS) for Belize and Suriname; Pesquisa de Orçamentos Familiares (POF) for Brazil; Encuesta Longitudinal de la Primera Infancia (ELPI) for Chile; Encuesta Nacional de Salud y Nutrición (ENSANUT) for Ecuador; Encuesta Nacional de Salud y Nutrición (FESAL) for El Salvador; Encuesta Nacional de Salud Materno Infantil (ENSMI) for Guatemala; Survey of Living Conditions (SLC) for Jamaica; Encuesta Nacional de Salud y Nutrición (ENSANUT) for Mexico; Encuesta Nicaragüense de Demografía y Salud (ENDESA); Encuesta de Niveles de Vida (ENV) for Panama; Encuesta de Ingresos, Gastos y Condiciones de Vida (EIGyCV) for Paraguay.

children of less-educated mothers are more than five times as likely to be stunted as those of highly educated mothers. Also, there is a growing problem with the number of children who are overweight or obese, especially in some countries (including Bolivia, Chile, and Mexico) (see Box 2.5).

Box 2.5   Growing Weight Problems among Children

Childhood overweight and obesity is increasingly becoming a concern in a number of countries in Latin America and the Caribbean. Obesity in childhood has immediate consequences for child health and may also result in reduced self-esteem and increased depression. Moreover, between one-third and one-half of obese children become obese adults (Serdula and others [1993] is a review, cited in Rivera and others [2014]). It is well established that overweight and obesity are risk factors for non-communicable diseases in adulthood, including hypertension, type II diabetes, and cardiovascular diseases, among others.

A recent review by Rivera and his coauthors (2014) finds that the proportion of children under the age of 5 who are overweight has increased in a number of countries in Latin America. In Mexico, for example, the proportion overweight in this age group increased from 7.8 to 9.8 percent between 1988 and 2012.[22]

Table B2.1 focuses on the proportion of children under the age of 5 who are overweight or obese, by country, and by maternal education. It shows that the proportion overweight varies a great deal by country, from 3.6 percent in Haiti to 10.1 percent in Chile. In most countries, the rates of overweight and obesity are higher among children of mothers with more education. For example, in Colombia, 2.7 percent of children of "low"-education mothers are overweight, compared with 6.2 percent for children of "high"-education mothers; and in Peru, 0.8 percent of children of low-education mothers are obese, compared with 2.7 percent of children of high-education mothers.

Table B2.1   Overweight and Obesity by Mother's Education

Country	Prevalence of overweight (% of children under 5)	Overweight		Obesity	
		Incomplete primary or less	Completed secondary or more	Incomplete primary or less	Completed secondary or more
Belize (2011)	7.9	6.5	10	2.6	3.8
Bolivia (2008)	8.7	8.3	10.2	1.8	2.4
Brazil (2007)	7.3	—	—	—	—
Chile (2013)	10.1	—	—	—	—
Colombia (2010)	4.8	2.7	6.2	0.3	1.5
Dominican Republic (2007)	8.3	6.8	8.9	1.4	2.1

Continued

Table B2.1   Continued

Country	Prevalence of overweight (% of children under 5)	Overweight		Obesity	
		Incomplete primary or less	Completed secondary or more	Incomplete primary or less	Completed secondary or more
Ecuador (2012)	7.5	7.8	7.8	1.5	2.9
El Salvador (2008)	5.7	4.2	9.5	0.7	1.8
Guatemala (2009)	4.9	—	—	—	—
Haiti (2012)	3.6	3.5	7.1	0.8	0.9
Honduras (2012)	5.2	2.9	9.8	0.8	3.2
Jamaica (2010)	4	—	3.5	—	1.5
Mexico (2012)	9	8.3	9.5	2.7	2.1
Nicaragua (2006)	6.2	—	—	—	—
Panama (1997)	6.2	—	—	—	—
Paraguay (2005)	7.1	—	—	—	—
Peru (2012)	7.2	3.9	10.3	0.8	2.7
Suriname (2010)	4	—	—	—	—
Trinidad and Tobago (1987)	4	—	5.5	—	1

Notes: For children aged 0–59 months, except for Chile and Trinidad and Tobago. In Chile, the sample refers to children aged 7–59 months, and in Trinidad and Tobago, the sample refers to children aged 3–36 months.

Source: World Development Indicators (WDI) for prevalence of overweight (% of children under 5). For overweight and obesity by mother's education, the values reported are from own calculations based on Multiple Indicator Cluster Survey (MICS) for Belize; Demographic and Health Surveys (DHS) for Bolivia, Colombia, the Dominican Republic, Haiti, Honduras, Trinidad and Tobago, and Peru; Jamaica Survey of Living Conditions (JSLC) for Jamaica; Encuesta Nacional de Salud y Nutrición (ENSANUT) for Mexico; and Encuesta Nacional de Salud Familiar (FESAL) for El Salvador.

In sum, countries in Latin America and the Caribbean have made a great deal of progress in improving child health. The proportion of babies who are born with low birth weight is lower than in other developing regions. Also, the region has substantially reduced infant mortality and chronic malnutrition. Some simple statistics summarize the magnitude of the changes that have occurred in the past two decades. In each of three years, 1990, 2000, and 2010, roughly 10 million children were born in Latin America and the Caribbean.[21] Of these, 428,000 died before their first birthday in 1990, 270,000 in 2000, and 149,000 in 2010. Over a 20-year period, the likelihood that a child born in the region would die in her first year of life fell by almost two-thirds.[23] Similarly, in each of these three years, roughly 50 million children were under the age of five in Latin America and the Caribbean.[24] Of these 50 million children, 13.7 million were stunted in 1990, 10.2 million were stunted in 2000, and 7.5 million were stunted in 2010. Over a 20-year period, the likelihood that a child under the age of 5 in the region would be chronically malnourished has fallen by almost half. Despite these improvements, however, substantial socioeconomic gradients in infant mortality and, in particular, chronic malnutrition, persist in many countries.

The Gap between Rich and Poor: Cognitive, Language, Socioemotional, and Motor Development

In addition to health and nutrition, child development encompasses cognitive, language, socioemotional, and motor development (gross and fine). Data on these dimensions of child development have not been collected for nationally representative samples of children in a way that is comparable across countries and available at more than one point in time.[25] Indeed, there is no agreement on what is the "best" or even an "adequate" measure of language, cognitive, motor, or socioemotional development (see Box 1.4 in Chapter 1).[26] In practice, different researchers have used different instruments to measure these aspects of child development in the region.[27] In addition, there is no agreement about how to standardize the scores (see Box 2.6).

Box 2.6   The Debate over Standardization of Scores

In the literature on child development, there is a debate about whether it is preferable to use external or internal standardization to turn raw scores on a given test into measures that can be compared across children of different ages.

In external standardization, a table is used to convert raw measures into age-standardized scores. For example, the WHO Multicentre Growth Reference Study Group (2006) developed revised "growth tables." These tables, which are based on a sample of approximately 8,500 children in Brazil, Ghana, India, Norway, Oman, and the United States, are used to transform the height and weight of children at a given age into standardized z-scores. These z-scores, in turn, are the basis for the calculation of chronic malnutrition (stunting) and acute malnutrition (wasting) for populations all over the world.

No such consensus exists with regard to child language, cognitive, socioemotional, and motor development. Many tests include a table provided by the test developer to convert raw scores into age-standardized scores. However, the sample of children that was used to norm a test is often small. There is also a concern that the norms may not be culturally appropriate in some settings. For example, the TVIP (Test de Vocabulario en Imágenes Peabody), the Spanish-speaking version of the PPVT (Peabody Picture Vocabulary Test), a test that is widely used in evaluations in Latin America, was normed on relatively small samples of children of Mexican immigrants into the United States and on Puerto Rican children (1,219 and 1,488 individuals, respectively).

Internal standardization is an alternative approach. In internal standardization, a given raw score is normalized by subtracting the mean of children of the same age in the population where the test was applied, and dividing by the standard deviation of scores of children of the same age. This is often thought to be a more conservative approach because it does not rely on children from a different population. However, internal standardization makes it impossible to compare the scores of children from different samples—for example, to compare the language scores of children in Chile and Peru. Moreover, in dividing through by the standard deviation, a researcher is implicitly assuming that the observed standard deviation is a good measure of the true standard deviation or, at least, that the difference between the true and observed values is the same for children of different ages.

Unfortunately, this assumption may not always hold. When internal standardization is used, measurement error in child development will result in estimated socioeconomic gradients that are smaller than the true gradients. Suppose there is more measurement error in test scores for very young children—for example, because these children have more difficulty understanding a test, or the scores at these ages reflect a combination of tasks carried out by the children themselves (and observed by the enumerator) and reports from mothers. Under this circumstance, a researcher using internally standardized scores might conclude that socioeconomic gradients increase as children age—even though this could simply be a result of the correlation between measurement error and child age. Ultimately, the choice between external and internal standardization is not easy, and involves making a judgment call about the importance of various measurement problems.

The fact that child development specialists have not agreed on an appropriate test to measure the cognitive, language, socioemotional, and motor development of young children, and an appropriate reference population to transform raw scores into age-standardized scores, is a serious impediment to the measurement of child development deficits around the world and to the design and evaluation of effective policies.

Differences in the choice of tests and how they are standardized make comparisons across countries difficult. Nevertheless, two recent studies are exceptions. The first, an initiative known as PRIDI (the Spanish acronym for Regional Program of Indicators of Child Development), collected data using the Engle Scale, a new instrument developed for this purpose, on nationally representative samples of approximately 2,000 children in each of four countries: Costa Rica, Nicaragua, Paraguay, and Peru (Verdisco and others 2014). The Engle Scale, which was applied to children aged 24–59 months of age, measures child development in four domains: language and communication, cognitive, motor, and socioemotional development. Overall, comparing children in the richest and poorest quintiles in each country, there are large differences in language development (0.6 standard deviations, on average) and cognition (0.5 standard deviations, on average), and smaller differences in socioemotional development (0.3 standard deviations, on average) and motor skills (0.2 standard deviations, on average).[28] For the cognition and language and communication domains, the wealth gradients appear to increase substantially as children age.

The second study compares performance on the Test de Vocabulario en Imágenes Peabody (TVIP), the Spanish-speaking version of the Peabody Picture Vocabulary Test (PPVT), in the rural areas of five countries: Chile, Colombia, Ecuador, Nicaragua, and Peru (Schady and others 2015).[29] The TVIP is a measure of receptive vocabulary that has been applied to many samples in Latin America and elsewhere (see Box 2.7); among adults, it is generally considered to be a measure of verbal intelligence. The analysis shows there are steep socioeconomic gradients in TVIP scores in every country, ranging from 0.6 standard deviations in Colombia to 1.2 standard deviations in Ecuador.

Box 2.7 The Importance of Language

Many countries in Latin America and the Caribbean, including Chile, Colombia, Ecuador, Mexico, Nicaragua, and Peru, have collected data on receptive vocabulary at early ages using the TVIP (Test de Vocabulario en Imágenes Peabody), the Spanish-speaking version of the PPVT (Peabody Picture Vocabulary Test). The PPVT has been applied extensively in the United States, and translations of the PPVT have been applied in Cambodia, Ethiopia, India, Madagascar, Mozambique, and Vietnam, among other countries. The test has been extensively validated—a long list of references can be found at http://psychology.wikia.com/wiki/Peabody_Picture_Vocabulary_Test.

Early vocabulary has been shown to be strongly predictive of later school performance (Powell and Diamond 2012; Wasik and Newman 2009, among many other cites). Performance on the PPVT at early ages is associated with later school performance in many samples in the United States (Duncan and others 2007; Duncan and Magnuson 2011). Moreover, early vocabulary, as measured by the PPVT and similar tests, is also associated with wages and other labor market outcomes in adulthood in the United States and Great Britain (Case and Paxson 2008; Currie and Thomas 2001).

Schady (2012) uses a panel survey in Ecuador to show that TVIP scores at age 5 years are highly predictive of school performance in early elementary school. A 1 standard deviation increase in TVIP scores at age 5 is associated with 0.32 standard deviation increase in math and language scores three years later, and a decrease of 6.6 percentage points in the probability that a child is a year or more delayed in terms of her grade progression in school. As Schady points out, these associations are likely to be attenuated by measurement error—the "true" association between early vocabulary and school performance in Ecuador is likely to be larger. Although the PPVT and TVIP test only one dimension of early development, receptive language, it is a dimension that seems to be highly predictive of future outcomes.

There are also a number of country-specific studies with data from Colombia, Nicaragua, and Ecuador. These studies differ considerably in the age group of children who were analyzed; in the populations they cover (e.g., in their socioeconomic status); and in the tests that were applied, and how they were standardized. Despite these differences, the results from these studies are broadly consistent.

Two clear messages emerge. First, children in richer households have higher levels of cognitive and language development. A study of children aged 6–42 months in Bogotá, Colombia, uses the Bayley Scale of Infant Development to analyze gradients (Rubio-Codina and others 2015). The authors find that at age 42 months, children in the 90th percentile of the distribution of wealth have scores that are 0.7 standard deviations higher than those in the 10th percentile in language, and a full standard deviation higher in cognition. The evidence of wealth gradients is much weaker for the other domains of child development (gross and fine motor skills, and socioemotional development).

A study of children between 0 and 71 months of age in rural municipalities in Nicaragua analyzes gradients in a population that is sufficiently poor to be eligible for a targeted cash transfer program (Macours, Schady, and Vakis 2012). The authors apply an amended version of the Denver Developmental Screening Test, which measures four dimensions of child development (language, social-personal, fine motor, and gross motor), as well as a number of other tests for children 3 years and older. They find that the steepest socioeconomic gradients are observed in the language measure of the Denver, and in the TVIP.

Numerous papers study a population that is poor enough to be eligible for a cash transfer program in Ecuador (Paxson and Schady 2007, 2010; Schady 2011, 2012). Steep socioeconomic gradients are found in language, smaller gradients in memory, and no gradients in the incidence of behavior problems. Another study (Araujo and others 2014) uses data on 5-year-old children in the coastal area of Ecuador to analyze socioeconomic differences in executive function, calculated on the basis of tests of memory, attention, cognitive flexibility, and inhibitory control (see Box 1.2 for a definition of executive function). The authors report a difference in executive function of about 0.6 standard deviations between children whose mothers have incomplete primary education or less and those whose mothers have complete secondary education or more.

The second message from these studies is that gradients in cognition and language generally become larger as children age. In Bogotá, at age 18 months, the differences in language and cognition for children at the 10th and 90th percentiles of the distribution of wealth are approximately 0.4 standard deviations; at age 42 months, children in the 90th percentile of the distribution of wealth have scores that are 0.7 standard deviations higher than those in the 10th percentile in language, and a full standard deviation higher in cognition (Rubio-Codina and others 2015). In Ecuador, differences in the TVIP scores between children of mothers who themselves have high and low TVIP scores are modest at age 3 years but substantial at age 5 (Schady 2011). A plausible explanation for this pattern of results is that the effect of low socioeconomic status on child development is cumulative.

Are the patterns observed in the region unusual? In particular, are the socioeconomic gradients in Latin America and the Caribbean larger or smaller than those observed elsewhere? These are not easy questions to answer given the lack of comparability in the measures of child development used in different studies and countries. Nevertheless, some reasonable comparisons can be made, in particular with regard to receptive vocabulary, as the PPVT, its Spanish-speaking version (the TVIP), and translations of the PPVT into various languages have been applied in a number of developing and developed countries.

First, a direct comparison of socioeconomic gradients in receptive language between children in the United States and Ecuador suggests that the differences in vocabulary between richer and poorer households are larger in Ecuador (Paxson and Schady 2007).[30] Second, data from the Young Lives study suggests that socioeconomic gradients in receptive vocabulary are steeper in Peru than in India, Ethiopia, and Vietnam (López Boo 2014).

In sum, data from a number of studies in Latin America and the Caribbean show that there are substantial differences in child development within countries. Much as has been found in Australia, Canada, the United Kingdom, and the United States (Bradbury and others 2012; Waldfogel and Washbrook 2011), socioeconomic gradients in the region are steepest in language and cognitive development, and much less apparent for other outcomes, including socioemotional development and the incidence of behavioral problems. Differences in language and cognitive development between richer and poorer children appear early, and are generally more pronounced among older children, at least until these children enter the formal schooling system.

The Total Picture

What is known about the development of young children in the Latin American and Caribbean region? Overall, the region's children enjoy relatively good health and nutrition, especially when compared with conditions a few decades earlier. The proportion of babies that are born with low birth weight is lower than in other developing regions. Latin America and the Caribbean has made tremendous progress reducing infant mortality. Many countries in the region now have infant mortality rates that are comparable to, or lower than, those found in other countries with similar income levels. Children and adults in the region are becoming taller. A good deal of progress has also been made reducing stunting rates, although chronic malnutrition continues to be a challenge in parts of Central America and the Andean region, particularly among children in poor households and the indigenous.

The picture is less clear with regard to other dimensions of child development. Data are often lacking or are not comparable. Keeping these data limitations in mind, there appear to be steep socioeconomic gradients within countries in language and cognitive development. In contrast, and consistent with what is observed in richer countries outside the region, gradients are much less apparent in motor development (especially gross motor skills), socioemotional development, and the incidence of behavior problems.

Socioeconomic gradients in language and cognition are a concern because they are fundamental aspects of early school readiness. Indeed, panel data from the United States (Duncan and Magnuson 2011; Duncan 2011) and Ecuador (Schady 2012) suggest that children who begin school with adequate levels of early literacy and numeracy are much more likely to succeed in school. In this way, because poorer children in many countries in Latin America and the Caribbean are less likely to be school-ready than their better-off peers, inequality is transmitted from one generation to the next.

3

Family First

The family is the single most important determinant of child well-being. It matters in myriad ways. Parents decide what to feed their children and when to take them to the doctor. The home environment in which children are raised can be nurturing and warm, or harsh and cold. By talking to children, playing with them, reading or telling stories to them—or not—parents and other family members determine how much stimulation young children receive.

All these choices have profound and long-lasting effects on child development. This chapter discusses areas in which the home environment keeps many children in Latin America and the Caribbean from reaching their full potential. It then turns to the policies and programs that governments have put in place to influence the kinds of investments that parents and other caregivers make in young children.

The Family and Child Development

It All Begins with a Healthy Diet

Good nutrition is critical for adequate development, and this begins at conception (or earlier, as the nutritional status of the mother before pregnancy affects the development of the fetus). Global public health organizations recommend starting breastfeeding within an hour of birth and exclusive breastfeeding during the first six months of life (WHO 2015). Exclusive breastfeeding in the first months of life has been tied to reduced child mortality and improved child outcomes.[1] Breastfeeding may also strengthen the bond between mother and child (Papp 2014).

The differences across countries in Latin America and the Caribbean in the proportion of children who are exclusively breastfed for the first six months of life are large (see Table 3.1). In 10 out of 22 countries, the proportion of children exclusively breastfed is between 25 and 40 percent. However, exclusive breastfeeding rates are substantially higher in some countries, including Bolivia (60 percent), Peru (67 percent), and Chile (82 percent), and are very low in others, including the Dominican Republic (7 percent) and Suriname (3 percent). Figure 3.1 focuses on changes in breastfeeding rates between 2000 and 2012 for countries with multiple rounds of the Demographic and Health Surveys (DHS). In Bolivia and Peru, women in the first

Table 3.1   Exclusive Breastfeeding, Children 6 Months of Age or Younger

Country	Exclusive breastfeeding (%)
Argentina	32.7
Barbados	19.7
Belize	14.7
Bolivia	60.4*
Brazil	38.6*
Chile	84.5*
Colombia	42.7
Costa Rica	32.5
Cuba	48.6
Dominican Republic	6.7
Ecuador	40.0*
El Salvador	31.4
Guatemala	49.6
Guyana	33.2
Haiti	39.7
Honduras	29.7
Jamaica	23.8
Mexico	14.4
Nicaragua	30.6*
Paraguay	24.4*
Peru	67.4
Suriname	2.8
Uruguay	—

Note: Data refer to the most recent year available during the period 2009–13, with the exception of countries marked with a "*," where data refer to the most recent year available between 2001 and 2008.

Source: Data were taken from United Nations Children's Fund (UNICEF 2014); except for Chile (2006), where data were taken from Miguel Barrientos–Index Mundi–Chile–Health–Nutrition.

Figure 3.1   Median Exclusive Breastfeeding Duration, by Decade and Wealth Quintile

a. Bolivia

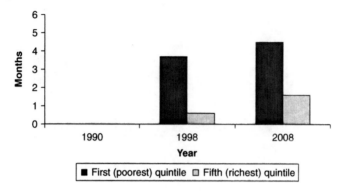

b. Colombia

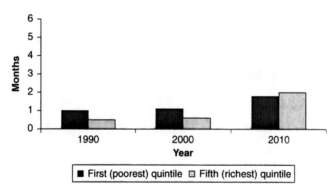

c. Dominican Republic

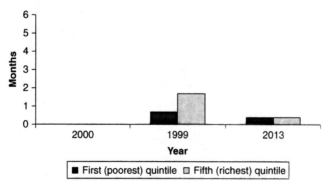

d. Haiti

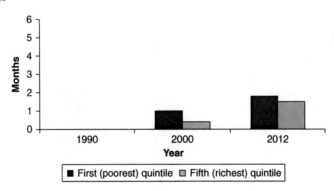

e. Peru

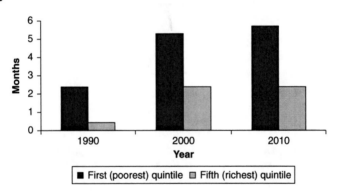

Note: Values reported refer to the last born.

Source: ICF International, 2012. Demographic and Health Surveys (DHS) Program STATcompiler.

(poorest) quintile exclusively breastfeed their children for more than twice as long as women in the fifth (richest) quintile. In Colombia, the Dominican Republic, and Haiti, on the other hand, there are no clear socioeconomic gradients in the duration of breastfeeding. The average duration of exclusive breastfeeding increased substantially in Bolivia, Colombia, and Peru, but not in the Dominican Republic.[2]

After 6 months of age, children should receive solid or semisolid foods, even if they continue to be breastfed. In most countries in Latin America and the Caribbean, food availability and overall caloric consumption are not issues. However, a very high proportion of overall caloric intake in many countries comes from cereals, roots, and tubers, especially among poor households. This is a concern because dietary diversity, not just the quantity of food, is important for adequate child growth and development at early ages (Aboud and Yousafzai 2015; Daelmans, Dewey, and Arimond 2009). In five countries, between 11 percent (Peru) and 31 percent (Guyana) of children between 6 and 23 months of age did not consume animal products (fish, meat, eggs) in the 24 hours preceding data collection (see Figure 3.2). The situation is direr in Haiti, where fully two-thirds of all children in this age group did not eat animal products. In some countries, there are also clear socioeconomic gradients. In Bolivia, for example, the probability that a child has been given animal products is 16 percentage points lower amongst the poorest households in the survey than among the richest ones.[3]

Figure 3.2 Percent of Children 6–24 Months Whose Parents Gave Them Animal Products in the Past 24 Hours, by Wealth Quintile

a. Bolivia

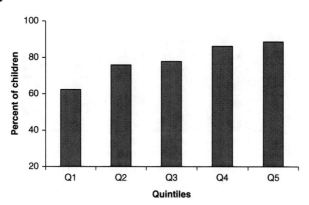

b. Colombia

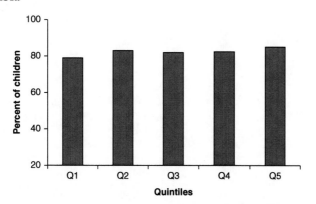

c. Dominican Republic

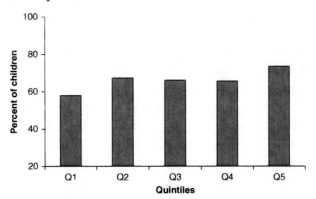

d. Guyana

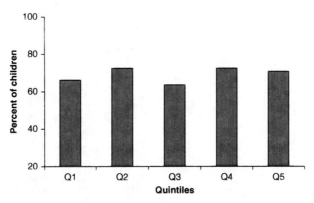

e. Haiti

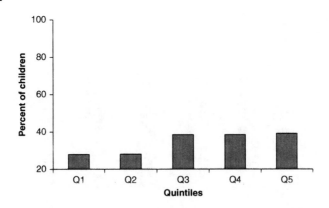

f. Peru

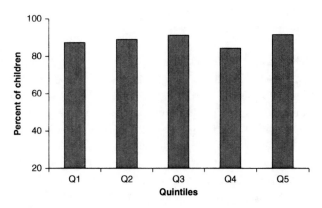

Note: Values refer to Bolivia (2008), Colombia (2010), Dominican Republic (2013), Guyana (2009), Haiti (2012), Peru (2012).

Source: Authors' calculations based on Demographic and Health Surveys (DHS).

A House Is Not a Home

To achieve their full development potential, young children should be raised in an environment that is warm and nurturing (Caldwell 1967). But how does one measure the warmth of a home or the quality of the interactions between young children and their parents? One approach relies on direct observation by trained enumerators. A popular instrument is the Home Observation for Measurement of the Environment (HOME) scale.

The overall HOME covers six domains (see Box 3.1 for details). Two of these domains—the responsiveness scale (which measures, e.g., whether parents responded to and encouraged children in a positive way) and the punitiveness scale (which measures, e.g., whether parents yelled at or hit children)—have been applied in a number of countries in the region, including Ecuador (Paxson and Schady 2007, 2010), Nicaragua (Macours, Schady, and Vakis 2012), a group of countries in the Caribbean (Chang and others 2015b), and Peru. The responsiveness scale ranges from 0 to 6; the punitiveness scale ranges from 0 to 5; and the "total" HOME score (for these two domains only) can take on values between 0 and 11. In each case, higher scores are indicative of *worse* parenting (less responsive, and more punitive). Importantly, there is evidence of a strong correlation

Box 3.1 The Home Observation for Measurement of the Environment Scale

The Home Observation for Measurement of the Environment (HOME) scale (Bradley 1993; Bradley and Caldwell 1977; Caldwell 1967; Caldwell and Bradley 1984) is designed to measure the nature and quality of a child's home environment. Different versions of the scale have been applied in a variety of settings since it was first proposed by Caldwell in 1967. The complete HOME scale for infants and toddlers has six domains: (1) *Emotional and verbal responsivity of parent* (also referred to as *Responsiveness*)—This measures, for example, whether the caregiver responds verbally to the child, praises her, and is physically affectionate. (2) *Acceptance of child behavior* (also referred to as *Punitiveness*, when reverse-coded)—This measures, for example, whether the caregiver yells at or hits the child during the interview. (3) *Organization of physical and temporal environment*—This measures, for example, whether the child's environment is physically safe and, when the main caregiver is away, whether care is provided by one of three regular substitutes. (4) *Provision of appropriate play materials*—This measures whether there are appropriate toys available for the child. (5) *Parental involvement with child*—This measures, for example, whether the main caregiver talks to the child while doing household work and keeps the child in visual range. (6) *Opportunities for variety in daily stimulation*—This measures, for example, whether the caregiver reads to the child and eats meals with her.

Different versions or subscales of the HOME have been applied in the region, including in Brazil (Grantham-McGregor and others 1998; Eickmann and others 2003), Chile (Lozoff and others 2010), and Costa Rica (Lozoff and others 1987). Paxson and Schady (2007, 2010) and Macours, Schady, and Vakis (2012) applied an adapted version of the *punitiveness* and *responsiveness* scales of the HOME in Ecuador and Nicaragua, respectively. These scales have also been applied more recently in an ongoing evaluation of a home visiting program in Peru, and in the Caribbean (Chang and others 2015b). Items in the punitiveness and responsiveness scales are measured by observation by enumerators (as opposed to reporting by mothers) during the course of a visit to the home for a survey (e.g., a survey to measure a child's development, which also asks questions of the mother, as was the case in both

Ecuador and Nicaragua). At the end of the household visit, enumerators complete a form with 11 questions:

Responsiveness:

1. Did the mother or father spontaneously say kind words or phrases to the children at least twice during the interview?
2. At least once, did the mother or father respond verbally to a child's vocalization?
3. At least once, did the mother or father tell the child the name of an object?
4. At least twice, did the mother or father spontaneously praise one of the children?
5. Did the mother or father convey positive feelings toward the children when they speak to or about them?
6. Did the mother or father caress or kiss one of the children at least once?

Punitiveness:

1. Did the mother or father yell at any of the children?
2. Was the mother or father annoyed with or hostile toward any of the children?
3. During the interview, did the mother or father hit any of the children?
4. During the interview, did the mother or father scold or criticize any of the children?
5. Did the mother or father forbid any of the children from doing something more than three times during the interview?

Each question received an answer of "yes" or "no." Following Paxson and Schady (2007, 2010), the responsiveness scale was reverse-coded, and higher values are an indication of "colder" parenting. In the case of the second scale, higher values are an indication of "harsh" or "punitive" parenting. The total HOME score for these two scales ranges from 0 to 11, with higher values corresponding to less responsive and harsher parenting.

between the HOME scores and children's mental development in a number of settings.[4]

There are socioeconomic gradients in the quality of the home environment in every country (see Table 3.2).[5] In rural Peru, the difference in the total HOME score between mothers with "high" education (complete secondary education or more) and those with "low" education (incomplete primary education or less) is 1.3 points (0.6 standard deviations). In rural Nicaragua it is 1.7 points (0.7 standard deviations). In Ecuador, where the data cover both rural and urban areas, this difference is smaller: 1 point (0.4 standard deviations). Moreover, in Ecuador, overall HOME scores are substantially lower (a better home environment) in rural than in urban areas (a difference of 0.2 standard deviations). In the three Caribbean countries (Antigua, Jamaica, and Saint Lucia), which are largely urban, there are not enough women with incomplete primary education or less to calculate a reasonable average for women in this group. However, in this sample, there is a difference of 0.6 points (0.3 standard deviations) between primary school graduates and secondary school graduates.

In a number of surveys, including the DHS and the Multiple Indicator Cluster Surveys (MICS), mothers are asked about the way in which they discipline their children, including whether they spank or hit them.[6] Researchers who study corporal punishment generally distinguish between "mild" corporal punishment, also referred to as spanking (striking a child on the buttocks or extremities with an open hand without inflicting physical injury), and "harsh" corporal punishment, also referred to as child abuse (including beating or hitting with an object, a closed fist, or striking a child on the face or torso) (see, e.g., Baumrind 2001; Gershoff 2002). Child development specialists agree that harsh corporal punishment of children results in lasting psychological damage, including elevated rates of mental health problems and aggression in adolescence and adulthood. No such consensus exists on the effects of spanking. Some researchers argue that spanking can be both effective and desirable, while others consider it ineffective and harmful (for competing views, see Baumrind [2001] and Straus [1994]).[7] In part, these debates reflect the difficulty of establishing causal effects (rather than simple associations or correlations) of corporal punishment on later outcomes (see Box 3.2).

Table 3.2 Socioeconomic Gradients in HOME Scores

	Ecuador: urban and rural (2005)			Peru: rural (2014)			Caribbean: Antigua, Jamaica, Saint Lucia, urban (2011/12)			Nicaragua: rural (2006)
	HOME				HOME			HOME		HOME
	Total	Cold	Harsh	Total	Cold	Harsh	Total	Cold	Harsh	Total
By wealth quintile										
First (poorest) quintile	2.77	2.27	0.5	3.08	2.49	0.59	3.04	2.41	0.63	4.42
Second quintile	2.45	2.09	0.36	2.71	2.2	0.51	2.65	2.26	0.39	3.90
Third quintile	2.19	1.88	0.31	2.58	2.07	0.5	2.52	1.99	0.53	3.71
Fourth quintile	2.02	1.77	0.24	2.26	1.81	0.44	2.40	2.03	0.38	3.67
Fifth (richest) quintile	1.94	1.74	0.19	2.03	1.6	0.43	2.50	1.78	0.72	3.45
Test Q1 = Q5	<0.01	<0.01	<0.01	<0.01	<0.01	0.01	0.09	0.01	0.64	<0.01
By maternal education										
Incomplete primary or less	2.83	2.46	0.37	3.07	2.39	0.69	—	—	—	4.07
Complete primary or incomplete secondary	2.39	2.03	0.36	2.48	2.04	0.44	2.99	2.35	0.64	3.53
Complete secondary or more	1.83	1.59	0.25	1.79	1.5	0.29	2.37	1.97	0.40	2.38
Test E1 = E3	<0.01	<0.01	0.011	<0.01	<0.01	<0.01	<0.01	0.01	<0.01	<0.01

Notes: The value for "cold" is the sum of the items for the responsiveness scale, reverse coded (so that higher values indicate a worse environment for each scale as well as for the total score). The HOME was assessed in the context of household surveys in all countries except in the Caribbean, where it was administered in health clinics. In the Caribbean, one of the questions in the harshness (or punitiveness) scale was not administered. (Question 5: "Did the mother or father forbid any of the children from doing something more than three times during the interview?"; see Box 3.1). In calculating the HOME punitiveness and total scores in the Caribbean sample, each household was given the average of the other 10 questions for this missing question. Also in the Caribbean, there were only three mothers with incomplete primary or less, so these three observations were excluded from the analysis.

Source: Author's calculations based on the data in Paxson and Schady (2007, 2010) for Ecuador; Macours, Schady, and Vakis (2012) for Nicaragua; own data for Peru and Caribbean.

Box 3.2   Harsh Corporal Punishment: How Much Does It Hurt?

It is relatively straightforward to establish associations between corporal punishment and a variety of outcomes, but establishing causal effects is substantially more complicated. Many papers use cross-sectional surveys that ask adults about current behaviors and outcomes, as well as about the incidence of various forms of corporal punishment in childhood (as in Afifi and others 2012, among many others). Other papers use longitudinal data that links the incidence of corporal punishment in childhood with learning or socioemotional outcomes later on (as in Berlin and others 2009, among many others). Many of these studies show that children who are reported to have been corporally punished have worse learning outcomes thereafter, have a higher incidence of mental health problems, and are more likely to be involved in criminal activity in adolescence and adulthood (see Gershoff 2002 for a meta-analysis of available studies).

It is not clear, however, whether these associations have a causal interpretation. Omitted variables are a serious concern, for at least two reasons. First, many studies find that children of lower socioeconomic status are more exposed to harsh parenting practices, including corporal punishment (Berlin and others 2009; Gershoff 2002, and the many references therein). However, socioeconomic status has effects on adult outcomes that are not mediated by parenting practices. The child development literature has generally tried to address this concern by controlling for various "confounders" (parental education, some proxy for household income), but these are unlikely to account for all the relevant variation. Second, there is individual (e.g., genetic) variability. Children who are more difficult (irritable, "fussy," or aggressive) are more likely to be corporally punished (Berlin and others 2009; Gershoff 2002). However, these children may be more predisposed to suffer from poor outcomes in adulthood for other reasons.

In both cases, associations between corporal punishment in childhood and poor outcomes in adulthood would likely overestimate causal effects. In addition, in research based on a single cross-section, there are concerns about recall error, and of possible correlations between current mental health status and the reporting of conditions in childhood.

In sum, while it is very likely that harsh corporal punishment has long-lasting, deleterious effects, robustly showing a causal effect of punishment on later outcomes is extremely difficult. The best evidence would likely come from an intervention that significantly reduced the incidence of harsh punishment, was implemented in a randomized fashion, and evaluated changes in parenting practices as well as child development outcomes.

Harsh corporal punishment is widespread in the region (see Figure 3.3). In four countries (Belize, Bolivia, Jamaica, and Saint Lucia), the incidence of harsh corporal punishment is 40 percent or more. In another four (Colombia, Peru, Suriname, and Trinidad and Tobago), it is close to, or above, 30 percent. In all countries there are maternal schooling gradients. In both Bolivia and Peru, for example,

Figure 3.3   Incidence of Harsh Corporal Punishment, by Country and Mother's Education

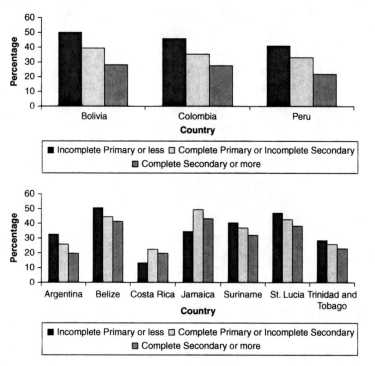

Source: Authors' calculations based on the data from Demographic and Health Surveys (DHS): Bolivia (2008), Colombia (2010) and Peru (2012); Multiple Cluster Surveys (MICS): Argentina (2011), Belize (2011), Costa Rica (2011), Jamaica (2011), Suriname (2011), St. Lucia (2011) and Trinidad and Tobago (2006).

a child of a mother with complete secondary school or more is only half as likely to be harshly punished as a child of a mother with incomplete primary school or less. In all countries boys are harshly punished more frequently than girls.

A True Story about Early Reading

In addition to having warm, nurturing, and stable interactions with their caregivers, young children need to have a home environment that stimulates the development of language and cognition. Children who are exposed to a greater number of words, for example, when parents talk to them, read to them, or tell them stories, develop a richer vocabulary early on.[8] A child's early vocabulary is highly predictive of performance on test scores in the early grades of primary school. Parents reading or telling stories to their children may also enjoy other benefits, including promoting attachment.

Data on the proportion of children who are read to at home are collected in a number of surveys in the region. Because these data come from a variety of sources, comparisons across countries must be made with a great deal of caution. However, the amount of stimulation that children receive within their home appears to vary a great deal across countries (see Table 3.3). For example, among countries that applied the MICS, the probability that a child is read to is 29 percentage points higher in Jamaica than in Costa Rica. Among countries that applied the PRIDI survey, this probability is 14 percentage points higher in Costa Rica than in Paraguay.

There are also steep socioeconomic gradients within countries. Children of mothers with less education are much less likely to be read to than children of mothers with more education in all Latin American countries except Guyana, where very few children are read to, regardless of their mothers' education. For example, in the four countries that conducted the MICS survey, children of mothers who have completed secondary school are 22–23 percentage points more likely to be read to than those of mothers who did not finish primary school in Argentina, Belize, and Costa Rica. By contrast, there are very modest maternal education gradients in reading in countries in the Caribbean—Antigua, Jamaica, St. Lucia, and Trinidad and Tobago.

Table 3.3 Maternal Education Gradients in Stimulation within the Home

Country	Year	Age in months range [10th, 90th percentiles]	N	Mean	Read books or look at picture-books with child		
					Incomplete primary or less	Complete primary or incomplete secondary	Complete secondary or more
Argentina (National)[a]	2011–12	[38, 57]	3,574	0.766	0.633	0.679	0.862
Belize (National)[a]	2011	[39, 57]	719	0.807	0.695	0.8	0.912
Chile (National)[b]	2012	[23, 73]	67,723	0.483	0.342	0.409	0.522
Colombia (Rural)[c]	2010	[6, 55]	1,535	0.437	0.34	0.46	0.577
Colombia (Urban)[c]	2010	[7, 53]	1,544	0.552	0.427	0.472	0.603
Costa Rica (National)[d]	2013	[28, 55]	1,556	0.621	0.577	0.578	0.701
Costa Rica (National)[a]	2011	[38, 57]	877	0.594	0.493	0.544	0.725
Ecuador (Coast Region)[e]	2012	[55, 66]	13,340	0.419	0.304	0.397	0.498
Ecuador (National)[f]	2012	[63, 74]	982	0.428	0.306	0.419	0.496
Ecuador (National)[g]	2005	[14, 75]	8,207	0.364	0.201	0.334	0.57
Guyana (National)[a]	2011	[38, 57]	907	0.235	0.19	0.252	0.216
Jamaica (National)[a]	2011	[38, 57]	666	0.888	—	0.867	0.91
Nicaragua (National)[h]	2014	[6, 64]	9,262	0.772	0.674	0.806	0.886
Nicaragua (National)[d]	2013	[28, 55]	1,681	0.504	0.348	0.551	0.621
Nicaragua (Rural)[i]	2006	[8, 73]	3,063	0.137	0.131	0.141	0.229
Paraguay (National)[d]	2013	[28, 54]	1,341	0.483	0.372	0.439	0.662
Peru (National)[d]	2013	[27, 56]	2,407	0.575	0.4	0.567	0.622
Peru (Rural)[j]	2013	[3, 22]	5,714	0.257	0.173	0.257	0.38
Peru (Urban)[k]	2013	[10, 23]	1,875	0.491	0.326	0.46	0.524

Continued

Table 3.3 Continued

Country	Year	Age in months range [10th, 90th percentiles]	N	Read books or look at picture-books with child			
				Mean	Incomplete primary or less	Complete primary or incomplete secondary	Complete secondary or more
St. Lucia (National)[a]	2012	[38, 57]	121	0.888	—	0.865	0.899
Suriname (National)[a]	2010	[38, 57]	968	0.568	0.434	0.575	0.726
Trinidad and Tobago (National)[a]	2008	[38, 57]	456	0.393	0.367	0.416	0.392
Caribbean[l]	2011–12	[19, 21]	499	0.95	—	0.942	0.956

Notes: For Chile, Colombia, and Ecuador, the question refers to any person, 16 years or older, who spent time reading to the child in at least one of the past seven days. For PRIDI surveys, the question refers to any person, 15 years or older, who spent time reading to the child during the past three days. For MICS, the question refers to any person, 16 years or older, who spent time reading to the child in the past three days. For Peru (rural and urban), the question refers to any person, 15 years or older, who spent time reading to the child at least once during the past seven days. For the Caribbean, the question refers to parents who spent time with their child reading "on a regular basis." The Caribbean sample only compares mothers with complete primary or incomplete secondary to mothers with complete secondary or higher.

Source: Authors' calculations based on the following surveys. [a] MICS: These surveys are meant to be nationally representative. [b] Encuesta Longitudinal de la Primera Infancia (ELPI): This survey is meant to be nationally representative. [c] Encuesta Longitudinal Colombiana de la Universidad de los Andes (ELCA): Urban sample representative of all but the richest 10 percent of population, rural sample representative for four geographic subregions. [d] PRIDI: These surveys are meant to be nationally representative. [e] Sample representative of children enrolled in kindergarten in coastal region of country. [f] Sample nationally representative of children enrolled in kindergarten. [g] Families eligible or almost eligible for the Bono de Desarrollo Humano cash transfer program. [h] Households representative for 31 municipalities targeted for the Amor Para Los Más Chiquitos parenting program. [i] Households representative for six rural municipalities targeted for the Atención a Crisis cash transfer program. [j] Households eligible for the Servicio de Acompañamiento a Familias (SAF) home visiting program in rural areas. [k] Households eligible for the Servicio de Cuidado Diurno (SCD) in urban areas. [l] Mothers with children aged 0–18 months attending well-baby clinics in Kingston-St Andrews region (Jamaica), St Lucia, and Antigua.

Government's Hand in Family Affairs

Children in Latin America and the Caribbean are raised in very different ways, depending on the country in which they are born, and the income and education levels of their parents. These differences and the early investments made by parents and others are critical in determining a child's life chances. Governments in the region have supported various kinds of programs to encourage families to invest more, or invest differently, in children. These interventions include programs that have sought to relax the household budget constraint by transferring cash to families, and those that have directly attempted to change parental behaviors and practices.

Relaxing the Purse Strings: Cash Transfers and Child Development

Chapter 2 showed that children in poorer households in the region have substantially lower levels of development, especially cognitive and language development, than children in richer households. Parents in poorer households invest less in their children. Fortunately, poverty among children in Latin America and the Caribbean has declined dramatically in the past decade (see Box 3.3).

Box 3.3   The Evolution of Childhood Poverty

Having more income does not improve child welfare per se. However, resources allow households to purchase more and better food; spend more on learning materials for children, such as books and toys; live in safer homes with fewer environmental risks for children; and, in some countries, use higher quality health, daycare, and education services. Poverty may also result in a higher incidence of stress and depression among a child's caregivers; this, in turn, has been linked to worse child development outcomes.

Poverty among children in the region has declined dramatically in the past decade, regardless whether poverty is measured with a poverty line of $2.5 or $4 per capita per day (see Figure B3.1). Focusing on the more stringent $2.5 line, childhood poverty has fallen by almost half.

Figure B3.1   Poverty Based on International Poverty Line for Children 0–5 Years Old

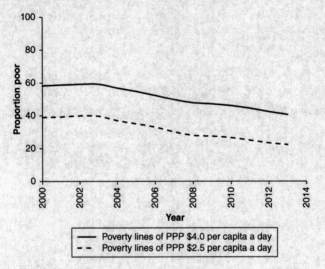

Note: Income adjusted with number of members. Nineteen countries were included: Argentina, Bolivia, Brazil, Chile, Colombia, Costa Rica, Dominica Republic, Ecuador, Guatemala, Honduras, Jamaica, Mexico, Nicaragua, Panama, Peru, Paraguay, Salvador, Uruguay, and Venezuela.

Source: Authors' calculations based on Inter-American Development Bank Harmonized Household Surveys.

In 2000, 41 percent of children lived in poverty, while in 2013 the comparable level was only 22 percent. Many countries can boast about this progress, including some in which poverty levels were initially very high (in Bolivia, poverty fell from 51 percent to 20 percent); and others where poverty levels were low (in Chile, poverty levels fell from 14 percent to 6 percent). Improvements occurred in large countries (in Brazil, poverty fell from 45 percent to 20 percent), as well as in relatively smaller ones (in Ecuador, poverty fell from 51 percent to 18 percent). The only important exceptions are Mexico and many of the countries in Central America (Costa Rica, the Dominican Republic, Honduras, and Guatemala), where declines in poverty have been very modest.

If the association between income and child development is, at least in part, causal, cash transfers made to poor households may improve child outcomes.[9] Many governments in the region have designed and implemented cash transfer programs targeted at poor households. These programs have wide coverage in some countries (including in

Brazil, Colombia, Ecuador, and Mexico) and can cost as much as half a point of GDP (Levy and Schady 2013). Some of these cash transfers are "conditional": they require households to engage in certain behaviors, like taking young children to preventive health check-ups or enrolling older children in school, in order to receive the transfers.

A number of cash transfer programs in the region have built in impact evaluations, often based on random assignment. The evidence on the effects of conditional cash transfers (CCTs) on child nutritional status is mixed (see Box 3.4), and has been summarized elsewhere (Fiszbein and Schady 2009; Lagarde, Haines, and Palmer 2009). Less is known about the impact of cash transfers on other domains of development, but two randomized evaluations report estimates of the impact of cash transfer programs on child cognitive and language development, among other outcomes.

Box 3.4   The Impact of Cash Transfer Programs on Child Nutritional Status

There are a number of evaluations of the effect of cash transfer programs on child health and nutritional status (in particular, height-for-age) in Latin America. The findings are mixed. In some cases, as with the PROGRESA-Oportunidades program in Mexico (Gertler 2004; Behrman and Hoddinott 2005; Rivera and others 2004) and the Red de Protección Social (RPS) program in Nicaragua (Maluccio and Flores 2005), there is evidence of positive effects on child height. In other cases, as with the Familias en Acción program in Colombia (Attanasio and others 2005), Bolsa Alimentacao in Brazil (Morris and others 2004), the PRAF program in Honduras (Hoddinott and Bassett 2008), the Atención a Crisis program in Nicaragua (Macours, Schady, and Vakis 2012), and the Bono de Desarrollo Humano program in Ecuador (Paxson and Schady 2010), the estimated effects are small and not significant at conventional levels.

Other evaluations have estimated the effect of cash transfer programs on iron-deficiency anemia. Here, too, the findings are mixed. Some evaluations report positive effects (as in Gertler [2004] for PROGRESA-Oportunidades in Mexico; and Paxson and Schady [2010] for the Bono de Desarrollo Humano program in Ecuador) whereas others find no effects (as in Hoddinott [2010], who discusses the evidence from RPS in Nicaragua and PRAF in Mexico). Of note, too, is that all of these evaluations focus on the short-term effects of cash transfer programs.

In Ecuador, the Bono de Desarrollo Humano (BDH) program made transfers equivalent to 10 percent of consumption for the mean recipient household. Transfers were not explicitly conditional on any prespecified behaviors (like health check-ups) for households with young children. Two studies consider the impact of the BDH program on child cognitive and language development in Ecuador. One study, which focused on children aged 12–35 months, found that the transfers increased the number of words young children could say, as reported by their mothers (Fernald and Hidrobo 2011). Another study, which focused on children aged 36–59 months, found that the transfers did not improve child outcomes among beneficiaries overall. However, transfers had a significant impact on cognitive and behavioral outcomes among children in the poorest households, with an effect size of 0.18 standard deviations (Paxson and Schady 2010).

In Nicaragua, the Atención a Crisis pilot program randomly assigned communities to one of three groups: a control group and two treatment groups, one of which received transfers that were substantially larger in magnitude (26 percent, rather than 15 percent of mean consumption).[10] Once again, transfers were not explicitly conditional. On average, the program improved the cognitive, language, and behavioral development of children 0–5 years of age by 0.12 standard deviations (Macours, Schady, and Vakis 2012).

The evaluation design in Nicaragua also allows for an analysis of the effects of bigger and smaller transfers. Comparisons between the two treatment groups show that overall consumption increased by much in the group that received the larger transfers, as expected. However, child development outcomes did not improve by much in this group, suggesting that something other than (or in addition to) the cash was at work. The Atención a Crisis program also changed various behaviors that are associated with better child outcomes (e.g., parents were more likely to tell stories, sing, or read to their children). Moreover, the changes in these behaviors are larger than what would be expected from the income transfer alone (Macours, Schady, and Vakis 2012).

In sum, rigorous evaluations show that cash transfers programs in the region have had positive, albeit modest impacts on child cognitive, language, and behavioral development, particularly when transfers are made to the very poorest households.[11] These results echo those

from developed countries.[12] The observed improvements in outcomes cannot be explained by the increase in income alone. Rather,
programs appear to have changed behaviors and spending patterns
in ways that benefited children. A key policy question is what characteristics of the BDH and Atención a Crisis programs account for
the changes in behaviors and expenditures that are observed.

Teaching Mom and Dad

Recipes for Better Feeding Practices
A striking characteristic of the region is the vast differences across
countries in breastfeeding rates. The reasons for these differences
are not well understood. However, a number of interventions have
been shown to be effective in increasing breastfeeding rates in some
settings, both inside and outside the region.

Some strategies are hospital based. The most convincing evidence on the effects of breastfeeding on a variety of outcomes (child
health, nutritional status, cognitive development) comes from a randomized control trial in Belarus (Kramer and others 2001, 2002,
2008). Maternity hospitals were randomly assigned to a treatment
group (in which mothers were encouraged to breastfeed using the
UNICEF/WHO Baby Friendly Hospital Initiative) and to a control
group (where no such encouragement took place). Exposure to the
intervention led to a substantial increase in breastfeeding rates and
less diarrhea among infants. There is also some evidence of program
effects on cognition, although these findings are less conclusive
(Der, Batty, and Deary 2008; Oster 2015).

Hospital-based strategies to increase breastfeeding do not reach
many mothers who give birth at home. The proportion of women
who give birth in a hospital or health center has increased substantially in many countries, as shown in Figure 3.4. However, home
deliveries are still frequent, particularly in some countries, and
among the poor and in rural areas. In Bolivia (2008) and Haiti
(2012), for example, 69 percent and 91 percent of all births to women
in the poorest wealth quintile, respectively, took place at home. Even
in middle-income countries in the region, a substantial proportion
of births among the poor still take place at home. In Colombia (2010)

Figure 3.4   Percentage of Women Who Gave Birth in a Health Facility, by Decade

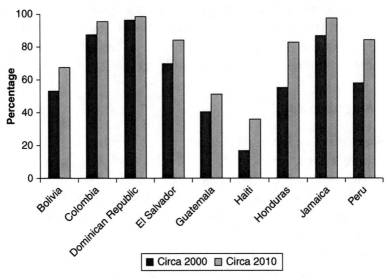

Note: For births in five years preceding the survey.

Source: ICF International, 2012. Demographic and Health Surveys (DHS) Program STATcompiler. Bolivia (1998, 2008); Colombia (2000, 2010); Dominican Republic (1999, 2013); El Salvador (2002, 2008); Haiti (2000; 2012); Honduras (2001, 2011); Jamaica (1997, 2008); Peru (2000, 2012).

and Peru (2012), 14 percent and 44 percent of all births to women in the poorest wealth quintile, respectively, are home deliveries. For these women, strategies that are not hospital-based are needed to encourage breastfeeding.

There is some encouraging evidence from within and outside the region that programs that rely on trained peer counselors can work. These were found to be successful in encouraging mothers to initiate and extend the duration of breastfeeding in periurban Mexico City (Morrow and others 1999). Similar findings have been reported in Burkina Faso, Uganda, South Africa (Tylleskär and others 2011), Bangladesh (Haider and others 2000), and India (Bhandari and others 2003).

Large-scale interventions with many components, all of which seek to encourage breastfeeding, have also been implemented in some countries. In Brazil, a multilevel behavioral change strategy that included the implementation of Baby Friendly Hospitals,

International Code of Marketing of Breast-Milk Substitutes, new clinical guidelines, multisectoral coordination, a review of maternity leave benefits, health staff training, peer counseling, and social mobilization through mass media campaigns has been credited with substantially increasing breastfeeding rates since 1975 (Rea 2003; Pérez-Escamilla and others 2012). However, by their very nature, the impact of these national, multicomponent strategies is hard to evaluate.[13]

Many countries in Latin America and the Caribbean have spent large amounts of resources on direct food distribution to poor households or on generalized price subsidies for some food items.[14] Relative to cash transfers of comparable value, food transfers are generally inefficient.[15] Food transfers may also contribute to overweight and obesity in childhood, a growing problem in Latin America and the Caribbean.

Programs that attempt to change feeding practices are more promising than those that only transfer food. There are a number of such programs in the region. Most are community-based initiatives that focus on promoting growth (e.g., the Atención Integral a la Niñez y a la Mujer en la Comunidad program, AINM-C, in Guatemala, and similar programs in other Central American countries). Home visitors measure height and weight and, based on the outcomes of this assessment, provide nutritional counseling. An alternative approach is to provide age-appropriate counseling independently of any anthropometric measurement, as happens in Mexico. The Mexican EsIAN (Estrategia Integral de Atención a la Nutrición) is a behavioral change strategy based on interpersonal communication provided at health services and in the community. It is delivered using the conditional cash transfer platform of PROSPERA and uses mass communication as a transmission mechanism for key messages.

Most programs that seek to change feeding practices in the region do not have credible evaluations of their impact, but there are exceptions. In Brazil, nutritional counseling delivered by doctors following the Integrated Management of Childhood Illness strategy (UNICEF/WHO) improved maternal practices and children's diets (Santos and others 2001). In Peru, an intervention in which health staff disseminated key nutrition messages and demonstrated how to prepare complementary foods to caregivers of young children increased the proportion of children who were fed nutrient-dense foods, and decreased the proportion of those who failed dietary requirements for energy, iron, and zinc (Penny and others 2005). As with programs that seek to boost breastfeeding, however, interventions based around health providers do not reach parents who do not make regular use of health services. In some cases, children in these households may be at the greatest developmental risk.

In sum, there is some evidence from inside and outside the region that it is possible to change child feeding practices. Programs that are successful share some important characteristics: they focus on changing behavior rather than just on delivering nutrition information, are culturally appropriate, coach the caregiver while he or she is trying new practices, and engage other family members and community leaders in the process.[16]

Improving the Home Environment

Feeding practices and nutritional status are not the only ways in which rich children differ from poor ones in Latin America and the Caribbean. There are also large differences in terms of their cognitive and language development, in the home environment, and in the amount of stimulation that children receive at home.

Parenting programs are one policy tool available to improve parenting practices. Three delivery models are common: home visits, group sessions, and clinic appointments. In the United States, there is a long tradition of home-visiting programs that seek to improve different aspects of the home environment for families with young children, and prevent child maltreatment and neglect. One of the best-known and most successful programs is the Nurse-Family Partnership program (see Box 3.5).

In Latin America and the Caribbean, parenting programs have focused mainly (although not exclusively) on early cognitive stimulation. This seems sensible given that the biggest developmental deficits among poor children are found in language and cognition, as shown in Chapter 2. A number of countries in the region have large programs, including Argentina (Programa Nacional Primeros Años), Brazil (Primera Infancia Melhor, PIM), Cuba (Educa a tu Hijo),

Box 3.5   The Nurse Family Partnership Program

In 2009, the Department of Health and Human Services in the United States launched the Home Visiting Evidence of Effectiveness review (Avellar and others 2014). Forty programs where service delivery was mostly achieved through home visiting were studied. The evaluation focused on programs whose stated objective was to affect at least one of following eight outcomes: child health; child development and school readiness; family economic self-sufficiency; linkages and referrals; maternal health; positive parenting practices; reduction in child maltreatment; and reductions in juvenile delinquency, family violence, and crime.

The review identified 17 out of the 40 programs evaluated as successful. (A successful program is one with proven success in at least one of the eight outcome domains, as demonstrated by a rigorous impact evaluation.) However, none of the programs showed impacts on reductions in juvenile delinquency, family violence, and crime. In addition, Avellar and others (2014) found that few home visiting programs significantly improved economic self-sufficiency (2 programs), coordination of resources and referrals (2 programs), maternal health (4 programs), and child maltreatment (6 programs).

A rigorously evaluated and well-known example of a home visiting is the Nurse Family Partnership (NFP), which currently operates in 32 states in the United States. This is a free, voluntary program that partners low income, first-time mothers with a registered nurse home visitor. A specially trained nurse visits the mother throughout her pregnancy (starting no later than the twenty-eighth week) and until the child is 2 years of age. Visits occur weekly for the first month after enrollment and then every other week until birth. After that, the frequency varies with age, from weekly to monthly visits. Home visits typically last around one hour. The average cost of NFP per family per year has been estimated at $4,100 (US Department of Health and Human Services 2011).

The objective of the programs is to improve pregnancy outcomes, child health, nutrition, and development, and to help mothers with family planning choices and work decisions. During the home visits, the nurse offers information and support to foster a better relationship between mother and child. The program explicitly promotes sensitive, responsive, and engaged caregiving.

The NFP has been evaluated through a series of randomized control trials that started in the late 1970s in the semirural town of Elmira

(New York), and continued in the city of Memphis (Tennessee) in the early 1990s and in Denver (Colorado) in the mid-1990s. Rigorous evaluations (Kitzman and others 1997, 2000; Olds and others 1986, 2000, 2002, 2007, 2014; Olds, Henderson, and Kitzman 1994) have found (in one or more sites): greater attendance to childbirth classes, more extensive use of nutritional supplementation programs, greater dietary improvements, fewer kidney infections, lower pregnancy-induced hypertension, fewer closely spaced subsequent pregnancies, and fewer subsequent pregnancies. Moreover, at age 2 years, children were seen in the emergency room less frequently and were less likely to be hospitalized with injuries or ingestions. At age 6, they had higher intellectual functioning and receptive vocabulary, fewer behavior problems in the borderline or clinical range, and were less likely to be classified as having emotional or behavioral problems. At age 9, they had fewer internalizing problems and dysfunctional attention. There are many other positive effects for the group of mothers and children at higher risk.

Ecuador (Creciendo con Nuestros Hijos), Mexico (Programa de Educación Inicial, PEI-CONAFE), Nicaragua (Amor Para los Más Chiquitos, APLMC), and Peru (Cuna Más). These programs vary in their scope, in the age range of the children that are the target group, and in the extent to which they focus on a particular group of households (e.g., the poor). The coverage of these programs varies substantially: Argentina, Cuba, Ecuador, and Mexico have the largest programs, covering between 350,000 and half a million children each. On the other hand, Brazil, Nicaragua, and Peru serve around 40,000 children each, while Chile, the smallest, serves less than 5,000 children.

Program costs per child also vary considerably, reflecting, in large measure, differences in the frequency of home visits or group sessions and in the qualifications (and therefore the remuneration) of the home visitors or group facilitators (Araujo, López Boo, and Puyana 2013).

Home visiting programs can significantly impact child development when the programs are of high quality and follow the prescribed curriculum. However, a recent study of the quality of six home visiting programs in Latin America and the Caribbean (Leer, López Boo, and Pérez Expósito 2014) suggests that home visitors are generally successful at establishing a warm, positive relationship with families and children, but much less successful at following the curriculum, activities, and behaviors established by the program. There is also compelling evidence of the impact of a number of parenting programs based on rigorous (often randomized) impact evaluations.

The most influential study of a home visiting program carried out in a developing country took place in Jamaica. Between 1986 and 1989, 129 malnourished children aged 9–24 months in the poorest neighborhoods in Kingston were randomly assigned to one of two conditions for two years: one group of children served as the control group, while the other group received a home stimulation intervention in which families were visited one hour a week by a community health worker. The health worker demonstrated play techniques to the mother using homemade toys, and encouraged her to practice them with the child during the week following the visit. The curriculum was structured, emphasized verbal interaction between mother and child, and taught concepts such as color, shape, size, number, and position.[17]

The results from this study are impressive. Twenty-four months after the intervention started, the researchers found large, positive effects on a number of child development outcomes for those who received the home visits (Grantham-McGregor and others 1991). In terms of cognitive development, children in the treatment group had scores about 0.8 standard deviations higher than those in the control group. A number of additional small-scale studies of home visiting programs in Jamaica (Gardner and others 2003; Powell and Grantham-McGregor 1989) also found positive impacts on child development, although the magnitude of the effect appears to fall sharply as the frequency of the home visits was reduced. Positive effects of home visits have also been reported in Brazil (Eickmann and others 2003) and Chile (Lozoff and others 2010).

One particularly noteworthy feature of the original Jamaican study is that it has followed participants into adolescence and early adulthood. Data from these follow-up surveys have shown that the effects of the intervention on cognitive development partially faded out over time: By the time they were 11 years of age, children in the treatment group had cognitive scores that were approximately 0.4 standard deviations higher than those in the control group. However, 20 years after the intervention, those who had received the stimulation intervention continued to have higher IQ and educational attainment, improved mental health (reduced depression and social inhibition), less violent behavior, and earnings around 25 percent higher than those in the control group (Gertler and others 2014; Walker and others 2011).

The results from the Jamaica study left unanswered a number of questions that are critical from the point of view of policy design. Could a similar intervention be delivered successfully by less-qualified community members who had been trained for this purpose? Could the results be replicated with somewhat larger numbers of children and home visitors? What are the important dimensions of context that determine whether this approach is generalizable? Could a comparable intervention be delivered effectively in groups or at health centers in order to reach a larger number of children?

Recent research from Colombia (Attanasio and others 2014, 2015) sheds light on some of these questions. In this study, 1,400 children between the ages of 12 and 24 months were randomly assigned to receive psychosocial stimulation through weekly home visits, or to a control group.[18] The curriculum from the Jamaican intervention was adapted to Colombia, and delivered by a group of community mothers eligible for the nationwide conditional cash transfer program, Familias en Acción. Home visitors were selected (or recommended) by prominent members of the local community, and received three weeks of training. They were supervised and trained by mentors with an undergraduate degree in psychology or social work hired for the project. Each mentor was responsible for 24 home visitors.

The study found that home visits increased cognitive and receptive language development by 0.26 and 0.22 standard deviations, respectively, and improved the quality of the home environment (Attanasio and others 2014). However, the program was most effective among children who had higher levels of development at baseline and among children of mothers who had higher skills, as proxied by their schooling levels, vocabulary, and IQ (Attanasio and others 2015).

Although the sample size in Colombia was substantially larger than that in the original Jamaican study, it too is best thought of as a pilot, implemented by researchers with a careful, controlled design. Less is known about the effects of programs implemented at scale. One exception is a study from Ecuador that evaluated home visits carried out by nongovernmental or community organizations, funded by the Fondo de Desarrollo Infantil (FODI). Home visitors followed guidelines developed by FODI. These guidelines focused on warm, responsive parenting, and enriching activities for the child. The modality of the intervention depended on the age of the child: individual for children 35 months and younger, and group-based for children ages 36 months and older. Visits lasted an hour each and were weekly.

The intervention was not assigned randomly. However, because the budget for the program was limited, and FODI followed a formula to score proposals and determine eligibility, it is possible to compare children covered by proposals that were just funded (the "treatment" group) with those that just missed receiving funding (the "control" group). Estimates of the impact of the FODI home visits based on this evaluation strategy suggest substantial effects on child development. Twenty-one months after the beginning of the intervention, children in the treatment group had better language (0.4 standard deviations), memory (0.6 standard deviations), and fine motor skills (0.9 standard deviations) than those in the control group (Rosero and Oosterbeek 2011).[19]

A recent randomized evaluation of a parenting program in clinics in the Caribbean also sheds light on alternative modes of delivery. The intervention used group delivery at five routine visits for children between 3 and 18 months of age, while mothers waited to see the nurse. The use of media combined with demonstration of age-appropriate activities was a key element of the intervention (see details in Box 3.6). Substantial benefits to children's cognition and mother's parenting knowledge were found (Chang and others 2015b). This suggests that a combination of home visits and group meetings may be a cost-effective way of delivering parenting services (Grantham-McGregor and others 2014; Aboud and Yousafzai 2015).

Box 3.6   A Hybrid Parenting Intervention in the Caribbean

A recent randomized evaluation in Jamaica, St Lucia, and Antigua sought to determine the effects of a pilot program on mothers' parenting styles, stimulation provided in the home, maternal depressive symptoms, and children's language and psychomotor development. The program consisted of home visits combined with a health center–based approach to parental training (Chang and others 2015b).

A parent training package was delivered in clinics while mothers waited to see the nurse. No additional staff was required in this health center intervention, which included short, locally made videos with parents and their children demonstrating positive interactions to promote development. The mothers shown on the films were of similar social background to the majority of women in the clinics, which may have helped mothers see the relevance of the behaviors and activities. The health center intervention was implemented for children from age 3 to 18 months.

The videos were reinforced by child development messages. At each one of five visits, nurses gave out message cards and play material (two books and one three-piece puzzle were given at visits at 9, 12, and 18 months of age). Community health aides (CHAs) were trained to discuss the messages and demonstrate activities. Each clinic was provided with a toy box and CHAs gave mothers opportunities to practice activities with their children. A supervisor oversaw the CHAs' work in the clinic once a month to ensure the intervention was delivered as planned and provided further coaching support to the CHAs. She also verified that the nurses were giving out message cards and materials.

The intervention showed important benefits for children's cognition (effect sizes of 0.38 standard deviations). The change observed in mothers' parenting knowledge (effect sizes of 0.40 standard deviations) suggests that the mothers remembered the messages delivered. A cost-benefit calculation was conducted, and the most conservative analyses found benefit cost ratios of 5.3 (Chang and others 2015a). This hybrid model—with both home and health center–based training—is promising because it has the potential to reach large numbers of children.

In addition to parenting programs targeted at infants and toddlers, there are other programs that work with parents and others to improve child cognition and language (e.g., reading programs). Evidence from developed countries suggests that these programs can have some success (see Box 3.7), although the fact that many parents of poor children in Latin America and the Caribbean themselves have limited skills (e.g., those that are illiterate or have very little schooling) may be an important constraint in some settings.

Box 3.7   The Beauty of a Bedtime Story

Cognitive stimulation interventions that foster play between parents and children provide opportunities for the development of vocabulary in the first two years of life. What other strategies are available to further foster language development at home in the preschool years? One option is shared-reading practices: a parent reading a picture book with a toddler or a teacher reading a book to a class of preschoolers.

There are relatively few studies about the impact of shared reading interventions in developed countries (National Early Literacy Panel 2008). In some interventions, parents receive age-appropriate books and are trained to promote an active role of children in book-reading by asking them questions and providing feedback. There is encouraging evidence of moderate effects of these interventions on vocabulary of preschool and kindergarten children in relatively small randomized control trials.[20] No robust evaluations have been found of programs at scale. Moreover, most research has been conducted in developed countries, predominantly with English-speaking children (Dickinson and others 2012). The paucity of research in developing countries (for an exception, see Vally and others 2014 on South Africa) is likely to be related to parental difficulties fostering the development of their children's vocabulary when their own vocabulary is limited.

There are also a number of evaluations of interventions that focus on increasing reading and literacy during summer holidays when children from low socioeconomic background tend to lose ground on literacy achievement with respect to their more affluent peers—a phenomenon that has been described as "Summer Loss."[21] Researchers speculate that this setback is partly explained by lack of voluntary reading of low socioeconomic background children over the summer. A series of relatively large randomized control trials of summer reading programs have been carried out. The evidence from these studies suggests that it is possible to obtain modest gains in literacy by implementing summer voluntary reading programs. Their effectiveness can be enhanced by engaging parents and teachers in the process (White and others 2014).

Successful parenting programs share a number of characteristics. Home visitors and group facilitators establish a relationship of trust with the mothers (and in some cases fathers) of the children that are targeted by the intervention; there is a clear, guiding philosophy for what the intervention is trying to accomplish, and the staff understands it well; in the case of programs that seek to improve early stimulation, home visitors and facilitators work with parents during the session on a set of structured activities and encourage them to continue these activities between sessions; and staff receives considerable training and close supervision and mentoring.[22]

A Place for Government at the Family Table

Traditionally, policymakers in developing countries have regarded the family as being largely outside the realm of public policy. In this view, raising children is the business of parents, not governments, at least until children begin formal education. This view is only partially correct, at best.

Certainly, parents should continue to be the central actors shaping the lives of young children. But parents can make decisions that are not optimal for child development for a variety of reasons. Parents may have low incomes and be credit-constrained, and so be unable to purchase goods and services that are beneficial for child development. They may have discount rates that are higher than those that are socially optimal. They may not know the benefits of certain behaviors (e.g., the benefits of breastfeeding); may not know how to implement them (e.g., how to discipline children without harsh physical punishment); or may not be capable of performing certain tasks (e.g., an illiterate mother cannot read to her child). Under any of these circumstances, investments in child development will be lower than is socially desirable, or the wrong sorts of investments will be made. Shaping the environment in which parents make decisions about investments in young children is an appropriate— indeed, a necessary—role for public policy.

Cash transfer programs have had some success improving child development in Latin America and the Caribbean. However, cash transfer programs have mostly focused on health, nutrition, and access to school. Poor children particularly lag behind in terms of cognitive and language development, and in these domains, the impact of cash transfers has been modest.

The impact of cash transfers on child development has been driven, at least in part, by behavioral changes among recipients that cannot be explained by the cash alone. But little is known about the reasons for these behavioral changes. Possibly, the fact that transfers are made to women is important.[23] Possibly, too, the fact that households are encouraged to spend the transfer on children (even in the absence of any explicit "conditions") may lead households to mentally "earmark" transfers for children, as would be suggested by behavioral economics.[24] Cash transfer programs could be redesigned to have a larger impact on child development outcomes if these issues were better understood.

Poor child nutrition continues to be a challenge in some countries in the region, particularly among children in poor households, in rural areas, and among the indigenous, and especially in Central America and the Andean region. A program of protein supplementation in early childhood in Guatemala had substantial positive impacts on adult outcomes.[25] Interventions that have focused on nutrition education, are hands-on, and are well-adapted to local circumstances have been effective in changing feeding practices in a number of developing countries (Dewey and Adu-Afarwuah 2008; Imdad, Yakoob, and Bhutta 2011), although the effects they have had on child development are generally small (Aboud and Yousafzai 2015).

The biggest promise, but also the biggest uncertainty, surrounds programs that directly seek to improve parenting practices. Changing behaviors is hard. Changing behaviors about something as intimate and personal as child rearing practices is even harder. In spite of this, parenting programs have had large impacts in some settings (Aboud and Yousafzai 2015; Howard and Brooks-Gunn 2009). The long-term impacts of early stimulation in Jamaica on educational attainment, IQ, participation in criminal activities, and wages are remarkable (Gertler and others 2014; Walker and others 2011).

The two biggest challenges facing parenting programs in Latin America and the Caribbean (and in other developing regions) are scale and creating mechanisms to identify those families that are most at risk. The strongest results on parenting programs, discussed earlier, come from small, carefully controlled pilots.[26] Replicating these findings at scale will involve creating a human resource system that provides staff with professional development, coaching, and close supervision, as well as reasonable compensation. Otherwise, staff will be poorly motivated, and turnover will be high. In turn, this will compromise trust, continuity, and fidelity of implementation, and result in no meaningful relationship with families, and no impact on child development.

Parenting programs should be targeted at children and families who are most at risk. But identifying at-risk families and having them participate in a parenting program is not straightforward. In some cases, the challenge is developing the capacity to deliver services in very remote, rural areas. In other cases, the main concern is self-selection. Parents who are concerned and interested in learning about effective parenting styles and strategies are, almost by definition, better parents than others. Parents who are engaged in behaviors that are most harmful to child development may be most difficult to bring into a parenting intervention. Interventions for particularly at-risk children will require more skilled and better-trained staff, but the returns to effective programs for these groups are likely to be especially high.

Developing effective, at-scale parenting programs that reach at-risk children is difficult because it is not what the public sector traditionally knows how to do. It does not involve constructing infrastructure (unlike, say, expanding the coverage of preschool), and it does not involve delivering the same service to a large population (unlike, say, a cash transfer program). Rather, it involves painstaking work in which social workers or others trained for this purpose seek to build a relationship of trust with families, and encourage them to do certain things that they would not necessarily do on their own, but which are known to have large impacts on child development.

Establishing an effective parenting program at scale involves taking the long view. It requires a government to commit to a process of design, trial, evaluation, and redesign—all the while building up the human capacity to more effectively deliver a high-quality service.

The fact that rigorously evaluated parenting programs in the region have had large, positive effects on child development—and on the adults these children eventually become—suggests that this is an investment the region can ill afford not to make.

4

Daycare Services: It's All about Quality

Daycare services (daycare) refer to services that offer childcare outside the family home for young children, particularly children who are not yet of an age to be covered by the formal school system. Many governments in Latin America and the Caribbean have subsidized or directly provided daycare.

Providing daycare generally has two objectives: enabling mothers to work and improving child development. This chapter discusses the coverage and quality of daycare services in Latin America and the Caribbean and the impacts they have had on child development.

Daycare, in Numbers

Daycare services reach more than 3.1 million children through over 114,000 providers in Latin America and the Caribbean, according to a study of 36 of the largest daycare programs in the region (Araujo, López Boo, and Puyana 2013).[1] Table 4.1 summarizes the proportion of children from birth to 3 years of age in daycare, separately for urban and rural areas, in seven countries where these data are available: Brazil, Chile, Colombia, Ecuador, Guatemala, Nicaragua, and Uruguay.[2] The data reveal dramatic increases in the use of daycare in some countries. In Brazil and Chile, the proportion of children in daycare doubled in the past decade, and in Ecuador it increased sixfold. In Brazil, Chile, Colombia, and Ecuador, between one-fifth and one-third of all children between the ages of 0 and 3 are in daycare. In Nicaragua—and especially in Guatemala—coverage is much lower. In all countries except Ecuador, the proportion of children who attend daycare is substantially larger in urban than in rural areas.

Table 4.1   Enrollment in Center-Based Daycare Services (in %)

Country	2000			2010		
	National	Rural	Urban	National	Rural	Urban
Brazil	11.7	4.5	13.3	21.2	9.4	23.5
Chile	11.4	3.4	12.6	26.1	15.7	27.5
Colombia	—	—	—	—	13.5	34
Ecuador	3.7	2.8	4.3	23.2	23.1	23.3
Guatemala	1	0.5	2.1	1.2	0.5	2.2
Nicaragua	8	6.5	9.3	7.6	7.4	7.7
Uruguay	21.7	5.4	22.9	35.1	20.7	37.7

Note: — = not available.

Source: Authors' calculations based on Pesquisa Nacional por Amostra de Domicilios (PNAD), 2002, 2012, for Brazil; Encuesta de Caracterización Socioeconómica Nacional (CASEN), 2000, 2011, for Chile; Encuesta Longitudinal Colombiana de la Universidad de los Andes (ELCA), 2010, for Colombia; Encuesta de Condiciones de Vida (ECV), 1997–98, 2013–14, for Ecuador; Encuesta Nacional de Condiciones de Vida (ENCOVI), 2000, 2011, for Guatemala; Encuesta de Medición de Nivel de Vida (EMNV), 2001, 2009, for Nicaragua; and Encuesta Continua de Hogares (ECH), 2006, 2013, for Uruguay.

The coverage of daycare services is extensive in many countries in the region. But who uses daycare, particularly services that are publicly provided or financed? In answering this question, two considerations are particularly important: the age of children and the socioeconomic status of their families.

Child age is an important consideration for many reasons. For one, at young ages, when the immune system is developing, children are much more vulnerable to infections and disease than when they are somewhat older. This means that health and sanitation conditions and protocols are particularly critical in daycare provided to the youngest children.

Another reason that child age is an important factor is the process of child development. The strong consensus from many disciplines is that it is critical for young children to develop a strong, affectionate tie with at least one primary caregiver. In the fields of psychology and child development, this idea goes back to the pioneering work of Bowlby (1958) and Ainsworth (1969), and is often referred to as Attachment Theory. Having a strong bond with at least one adult allows children to learn to regulate their feelings, establish a sense of security as they explore their surroundings, and develop trust.

Bowlby and others argued that the first two years of a child's life (perhaps especially the period between 6 and 18 months) are particularly important for the formation of these relationships between a child and a primary caregiver. Full-time daycare of low quality can disrupt the process of attachment formation between young children and their primary caregivers.

Finally, child age is important because the cost of providing care of comparable quality is substantially higher for very young children (especially infants) than for somewhat older ones. The higher cost arises because acceptable child-to-caregiver ratios are much lower for younger children. For example, the American Academy of Pediatrics (2005) recommends a ratio of one caregiver for every three children aged 0–11 months, and a ratio of one caregiver for every eight children aged 4–5 years. Lower child-to-staff ratios are desirable for younger children because caregivers in smaller groups have more time to interact with each child. Moreover, they can help in reducing the transmission of disease and improve safety. On this count alone, the cost of providing high-quality daycare for an infant is almost triple that of a preschooler.[3]

Figure 4.1 focuses on changes over time in the coverage of daycare in Brazil, Chile, Ecuador, Nicaragua, and Uruguay.[4] It shows that daycare use is substantially higher for somewhat older children.

Figure 4.1   Enrollment in Center-Based Daycare Services

a. Brazil

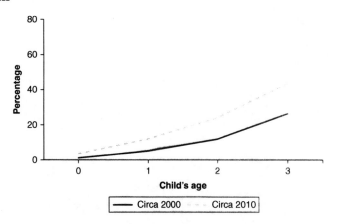

b. Chile

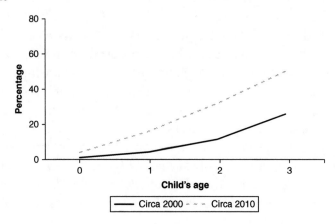

c. Colombia

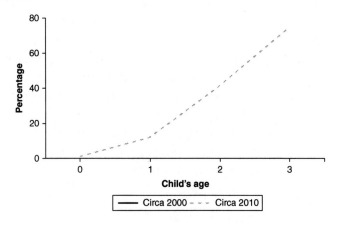

d. Ecuador

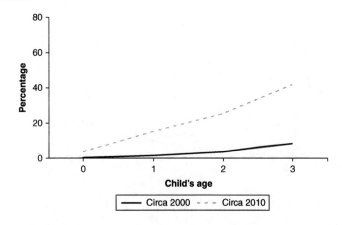

e. Nicaragua

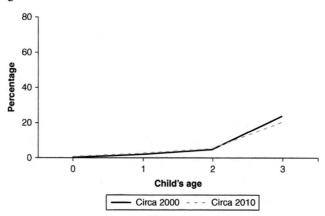

f. Uruguay

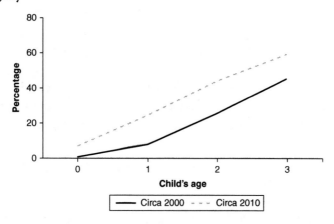

Source: Author's calculations based on Pesquisa Nacional por Amostra de Domicilios (PNAD) 2002, 2012 for Brazil; Encuesta de Caracterización Socioeconómica Nacional (CASEN) 2000, 2011 for Chile; Encuesta Longitudinal Colombiana de la Universidad de los Andes (ELCA) 2010-Urban area; Encuesta de Condiciones de Vida (ECV) 1997–1998, 2013–2014 for Ecuador; Encuesta de Medición de Nivel de Vida (EMNV) 2001, 2009 for Nicaragua; and Encuesta Continua de Hogares (ECH) 2006, 2013 for Uruguay.

However, daycare use over the past decade has increased among both older and younger children.

The socioeconomic status of children who attend daycare is important for two reasons. One reason is that most public daycare services in the region are free or heavily subsidized. There is, therefore, a redistributive element to public daycare, and understanding who benefits from the implicit transfer is important.

The second reason that the socioeconomic status of families is important is that the impact of daycare on child development depends on the
quality of daycare *relative* to the quality of care that a child in daycare
would have received if daycare had not been available or if parents had
chosen not to make use of it. This is often referred to as the "counterfactual." For most children in the region, the counterfactual to daycare
is care by parents, other relatives (sometimes minors) at home, or informal care by neighbors or others. Little is currently known about the
quality of care in these counterfactual environments in the region.

Chapter 3 presented compelling evidence that the home environment for young children in richer households is more supportive of
child development in a variety of ways. Children in wealthier households are more likely to receive nutritious foods, more likely to be read
to and to receive early stimulation, and more likely to have warm, supportive parenting than those in poorer households. If the daycare provided is of high quality, moving a poor child from home care to daycare
will improve her environment more than moving a rich child would.

Figure 4.2 focuses on differences in daycare enrollment between
mothers with "high" levels of education (complete secondary school
or more) and "low" levels of education (incomplete primary school
or less).[5] In all countries except Ecuador, daycare use is higher

**Figure 4.2   Enrollment in Center-Based Daycare Services, by Mother's
Education**

a. Brazil

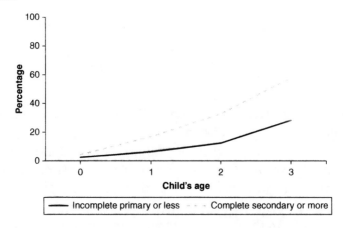

b. Chile

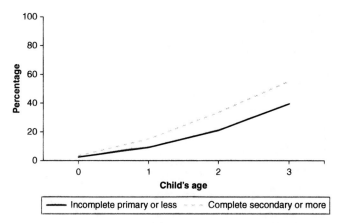

c. Colombia

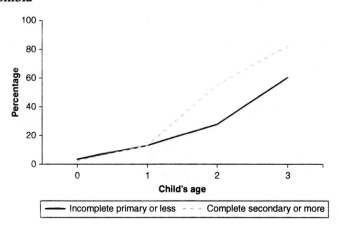

d. Ecuador

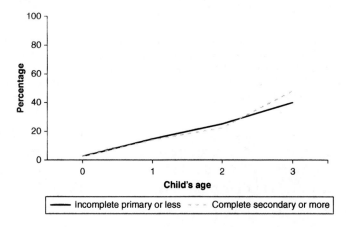

e. Nicaragua

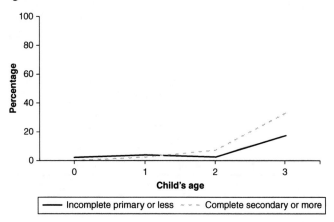

f. Uruguay

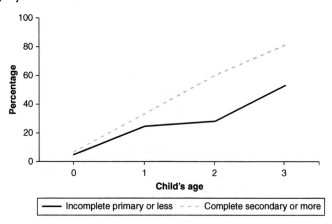

Source: Author's calculations based on Pesquisa Nacional por Amostra de Domicilios (PNAD) 2002, 2012 for Brazil; Encuesta de Caracterización Socioeconómica Nacional (CASEN) 2000, 2011 for Chile; Encuesta Longitudinal Colombiana de la Universidad de los Andes (ELCA) 2010-Urban area; Encuesta de Condiciones de Vida (ECV) 1997–1998, 2013–2014 for Ecuador; Encuesta de Medición de Nivel de Vida (EMNV) 2001, 2009 for Nicaragua; and Encuesta Continua de Hogares (ECH) 2006, 2013 for Uruguay.

among women with higher education levels. In Brazil, Colombia, and Uruguay, these differences are large. At 3 years of age, the likelihood that children will use daycare services is at least 20 percentage points higher for children of high-education mothers than for children of low-education mothers.

The household survey data for most countries does not distinguish the type of daycare that is used, including whether it is public or private. Fortunately, there are exceptions. In Chile, Colombia, and Ecuador, respondents are asked not only whether their children are attending daycare, but also the type of provider.

Table 4.2 summarizes these findings separately for children of high-education and low-education mothers, limiting the sample to children in daycare. High-education mothers are much more likely to use private services than low-education mothers in all three countries.[6] However, even among children of high-education mothers, most are in public daycare. (For example, in Chile in 2011, among women who use daycare, 96 percent of low-education women and 72 percent of high-education women use public daycare.)[7] In Chile and Ecuador, where these values are available for more than one point in time, the biggest expansion in daycare in the past decade has been in the public sector.

Table 4.2 Use of Public and Private Daycare, by Maternal Education

Country	Year	Type of daycare service	Public (%)	Private (%)
Chile	2000	Incomplete primary or less	73.8	26.2
		Complete secondary or more	24.1	75.9
		Total	39.3	60.7
	2011	Incomplete primary or less	96.4	3.6
		Complete secondary or more	71.5	28.5
		Total	77.1	22.9
Ecuador	1997–98	Incomplete primary or less	81.8	18.2
		Complete secondary or more	44.3	55.7
		Total	65.8	34.2
	2013–14	Incomplete primary or less	91.5	8.5
		Complete secondary or more	63.3	36.9
		Total	86.8	13.2
Colombia	2010	Incomplete primary or less	100	0
		Complete secondary or more	67.2	32.8
		Total	74.3	25.7

Source: Author's calculations based on Pesquisa Nacional por Amostra de Domicilios (PNAD), 2002, 2012, for Brazil; Encuesta de Caracterización Socioeconómica Nacional (CASEN), 2000, 2011, for Chile; Encuesta Longitudinal Colombiana de la Universidad de los Andes (ELCA), 2010, Urban area; Encuesta de Condiciones de Vida (ECV), 1997–98, 2013–14, for Ecuador; Encuesta de Medición de Nivel de Vida (EMNV), 2001, 2009, for Nicaragua; and Encuesta Continua de Hogares (ECH), 2006, 2013, for Uruguay.

In sum, the use of daycare services, particularly public daycare, has increased dramatically in some countries in the region. Daycare use is higher among high-education than among low-education mothers. It is also higher among older children than among younger children, but has increased for children of all ages, including for infants and young toddlers.

A Not-So-Pretty Picture of Daycare Services

The provision of daycare in Latin America and the Caribbean can be broadly mapped into one of two models of operation: community and institutional.

The community model relies heavily on the community for space and labor. Caregivers are community mothers, and care is provided in their homes or in a community building that has been made available for this purpose. The scale is small: each provider (a mother or a group of mothers) generally serves no more than 30 children. Children are often in a single mixed-age group that can include infants, toddlers, and preschoolers. The program pays the community mother a subsidy per child to cover the costs of food and to remunerate her. However, the community mother is not formally employed by the program. Formally or informally, parents might be asked to pay a fee for the service. Traditionally, community models require little of their caregivers in terms of qualifications such as schooling and pre-service training. Caregivers have few if any opportunities for professional development. Community models often depend on a government agency responsible for children and families or a ministry of social development. Examples of this type of model can be found in Guatemala and Colombia (Hogares Comunitarios), Peru (Cuna Más, formerly Wawa-Wasi), and Nicaragua (PAININ).

The institutional model operates through larger centers that have been exclusively built (or adapted) for the purpose of daycare. Given the larger size of the centers, children are frequently grouped into classrooms by age. Provision might be carried out directly by the program or subcontracted to third parties. Caregivers are generally required to have a technical or vocational degree in early childhood education. They have an employment relationship with the program and receive employment benefits. Under this model, parents might also be asked to pay a fee. Institutional models are more common in the Southern Cone (Argentina, Chile, and Uruguay) and in Mexico. Given that institutional daycare models rely on educators, they often have a formal link with (or depend on) ministries of education.

The community modality of daycare became very popular in many countries in the region in the 1980s. However, in the past decade, countries like Colombia and Peru have significantly reformed their community daycare services. For example, Colombia offers in-service training to professionalize caregivers (community mothers), and passed a reform to ensure they would have a formal contract and receive a minimum wage and employment benefits. Peru is phasing out the service provided in private homes. Instead, it is moving all children and caregivers to community spaces that have been adapted and equipped for this purpose. Colombia, Ecuador, and Peru are investing substantially in infrastructure to expand the coverage of institutional services.

The impact of attending daycare on child development depends critically on its quality. But what is high-quality daycare? Love, Schochet, and Meckstroth (1996, cited in Blau and Currie 2006) describe it in the following way:

> (In high-quality care) caregivers encourage children to be actively engaged in a variety of activities; have frequent, positive interactions with children that include smiling, touching, holding, and speaking at children's eye level; promptly respond to children's questions or requests; and encourage children to talk about their experience, feelings, and ideas. Caregivers in high-quality settings also listen attentively, ask open-ended questions and extend children's actions and verbalizations with more complex ideas or materials, interact with children individually and in small groups instead of exclusively with the group as a whole, use positive guidance techniques, and encourage appropriate independence.

As this description suggests, many elements determine the quality of daycare. In practice, however, a distinction is often made between the structural and process dimensions of quality.

Structural dimensions of quality refer to the presence (or absence) of resources that can facilitate the interactions that should take place in a learning environment. They include aspects related to infrastructure (space, lighting, furniture, and equipment); elements related to health, sanitation, and safety (health protocols, emergency procedures); the characteristics of educators and caregivers (their pre-service and in-service training, experience, salaries); and the characteristics of the group of children under their responsibility (size, age range, caregiver-to-child ratios).

Process dimensions of quality refer to the elements of daycare that directly impact a child's day-to-day experience, learning, and development. They focus on the implementation of the curriculum (if one is available) and, in particular, on the frequency, types, and quality of interactions between children and their caregivers, between children and their peers, and between caregivers and parents.

Different approaches have been taken to measuring quality in prekindergarten and daycare, both in developed and in developing countries. One approach focuses on measuring a set of "minimum standards" that providers should meet. For example, in the United States, the National Institute for Early Education Research (NIEER) has proposed a National Quality Standards Checklist (Barnett and others 2003, 2004). This checklist focuses on structural quality, including the qualifications that teachers and caregivers have; whether they receive in-service training; class sizes and the child-to-caregiver ratio; whether there are screening and referral services; and whether meals are provided.

Alternatively, quality can be measured by direct observation at the daycare center. One family of instruments widely used for this purpose includes the Infant and Toddlers Environment Rating Scale (ITERS-R) (Harms, Cryer, and Clifford 1990); the Early Childhood Environment Rating Scale (ECERS-R) (Harms and Clifford 1980; Harms, Clifford, and Cryer 1998); and the Family Child Care Environment Rating Scale (FCCERS-R) (Harms and Clifford 1989).[8] ITERS focuses on center-based care for infants and toddlers (0–29 months old). ECERS focuses on center-based care for preschoolers (30–59 months old). FCCERS focuses on infants, toddlers, and preschoolers (0–59 months) in family childcare contexts. The instruments assess seven aspects or dimensions of care: space and furnishing, personal care routines, listening and talking, activities, interactions, program structure, and parents and staff. Scores are assigned to each dimension. They range from 1 to 7, with a score of 1 being inadequate quality, 3 being minimal quality, 5 being good quality, and 7 being excellent quality.

Another instrument is the Classroom Assessment Scoring System (CLASS) (Pianta, La Paro, and Hamre 2008a; La Paro, Hamre, and Pianta 2012; Hamre and others 2014), which measures one key aspect of process quality: the nature of the interactions between children and their teachers or caregivers (see Box 4.1). Scoring is on a 1–7 scale, with scores of 1–2 reflecting poor quality, 3–5 reflecting medium quality, and 6–7 reflecting high quality. For infants and toddlers, the CLASS measures the quality of interactions in two domains: Emotional and Behavioral Support, and Engaged Support for Learning.

Other tools, such as the Knowledge of Infant Development Inventory (KIDI) (MacPhee 1981), focus on caregivers' factual knowledge of child rearing practices, child development processes,

---

Box 4.1   The Classroom Assessment Scoring System

The Classroom Assessment Scoring System (CLASS) observation tool was developed by researchers at the University of Virginia to evaluate the quality of teacher-student interactions that predict child academic and social outcomes in daycare, preschool, and primary school classrooms. The CLASS measure provides a validated and reliable common metric to describe how teachers use the materials they have available to them and how they interact with their students (Pianta, La Paro, and Hamre 2008a).

The CLASS addresses the fact that as children grow and develop, the complexity and nature of their interactions with caregivers and teachers also change. There are age-appropriate versions of the instrument for infant, toddler, preschool, and kindergarten through third grade (K-3) classrooms. While the CLASS for toddlers and infants describes two broad domains of effective teacher-student interactions (Emotional and Behavior Support and Engaged Support for Learning), the CLASS for preschool and K-3 separates interactions into three domains (Emotional Support, Classroom Organization, and Instructional Support).

Each domain contains a number of dimensions that focus on a particular aspect of effective teacher-student interactions important to academic and social success. As an example common to all age versions of the instrument, Positive Climate is one of the dimensions found within the Emotional and Behavior Support or Emotional Support domains,

Figure B4.1 The Classroom Assessment Scoring System, Preschool and K-3

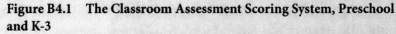

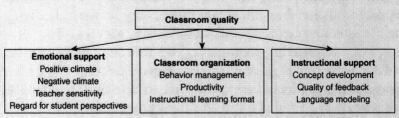

depending on the version of the instrument. Positive Climate is defined as the "the emotional connection between teachers and students and among students and the warmth, respect, and enjoyment communicated by verbal and nonverbal interactions" (Pianta, La Paro, and Hamre 2008a, p. 23). "Physical proximity," "peer assistance," "social conversation," "smiling," "verbal affection," "eye contact," "respectful language," and "evidence of cooperation and sharing" are the kinds of indicators that CLASS observers take into account when scoring a classroom under the Positive Climate dimension. Figure B4.1 depicts the domains and dimensions found in the CLASS preschool and K-3 versions.

For children of all ages, CLASS scores measure the extent to which that dimension is characteristic of the classroom. Scores range from 1 (minimally observed) to 7 (frequently observed). (Scores for the Negative Climate dimension are reversed.) Observation can begin with the start of the school day, or at any predetermined time arranged with the teacher. Classroom observations are completed by highly trained and certified observers and are done over four or more 20-minute cycles. The CLASS has also been approved and validated for use with videotaped classroom observations.

The CLASS has also emerged as a powerful professional development tool, helping teachers identify and model the types of interactions known to improve children's emotional and cognitive development.

and infant norms of behavior. Specifically, on the KIDI, respondents are read 58 statements about children, and are asked to choose between "agree," "disagree," and "not sure."

What is the quality of daycare in Latin America and the Caribbean? A useful starting point to answering this question is an in-depth study of quality in a nationally representative sample of 400 public daycare centers of the Centros Infantiles del Buen

Vivir (CIBV) program in Ecuador (Araujo and others 2015). CIBV subcontracts daycare services to communities, local governments, and grassroots organizations. The services are targeted to children 0–3 years of age, although in practice a large proportion of users are older than 3. Unlike most childcare services in Latin America, this program operates in both urban and rural areas. Caregivers are required to have a secondary school degree, but in practice compliance with this requirement is far from perfect. They are hired by the organization that acts as provider and are paid the minimum wage. Fifty percent of centers surveyed reported charging parents a fee, although this is not permitted by the program guidelines. All centers are required to have a professional in the role of center coordinator, with tertiary-level credentials. When the data for the study were collected in 2012, the CIBV program operated through 3,800 centers, serving 118,000 children.

The CIBV data reveal that caregivers have very little knowledge of child development. The average caregiver answered 31 of the 58 questions on the KIDI correctly. Simple random guessing would have resulted in 29 correct responses, which gives an indication of how low these caregivers scored.

More comprehensive measures also paint a discouraging picture of quality in CIBV centers. Figure 4.3 focuses on the ITERS. Because policymakers in the region (and elsewhere) frequently pay more attention to the physical infrastructure of a center than to other dimensions of quality, two panels are presented in the figure. Panel a focuses on one dimension of the ITERS—space and furnishings—which is a measure of the physical infrastructure of the center. Panel b presents the average on the other six dimensions of the scale, which are a combination of indicators of "process" and "structural" quality. The median center in Ecuador has a score of approximately 2 on space and furnishings, and a score of 1.5 on the composite of the other dimensions; both are in the "inadequate quality" range. Even the best-performing centers have very low levels of quality. A center at the ninetieth percentile has a score of 3 on space and furnishings (minimal quality), and a score of 2 on the composite of the other dimensions (inadequate quality).

Figure 4.4 presents comparable results for the CLASS. On the Emotional and Behavioral subscale, which is important for children's

Figure 4.3   The Infant and Toddlers Environment Rating Scale Measures of Daycare Quality, Ecuador

a. Space and Furnishing

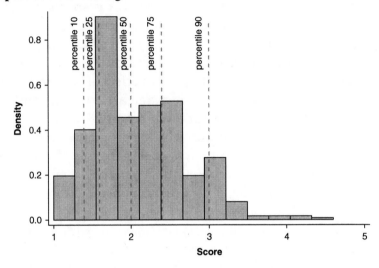

b. Other Dimensions of Quality

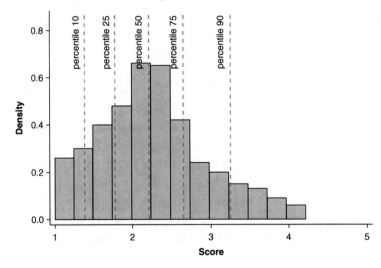

Source: Araujo and others (2015).

Figure 4.4 The Classroom Assessment Scoring System Measures of Daycare Quality, Ecuador

a. Emotional and Behavioral Support

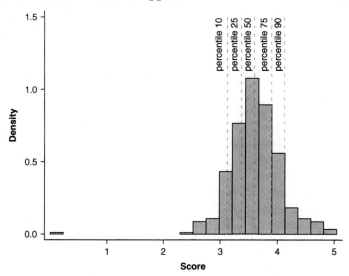

b. Engaged Support for Learning

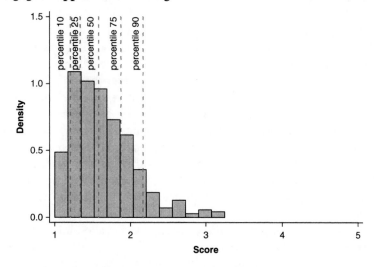

Source: Araujo and others (2015).

socioemotional development, most centers fall into the mid-range of quality. On the Engaged Support for Learning subscale, which is important for cognitive and language development, virtually all of the centers have poor quality. Centers with lower structural quality in Ecuador generally have worse process quality (see Box 4.2).

Box 4.2   Structural and Process Quality of Daycare in Ecuador

Recent research from the United States suggests that structural measures of quality, including those measured in checklists like those proposed by the National Institute for Early Education Research (NIERR), are only weakly correlated with process quality and child development outcomes (Mashburn and others 2008). However, given the much lower levels of structural quality of daycare observed in Latin America and the Caribbean, it is not clear whether this result carries over to the region. One way of analyzing this is by seeing whether, on average, measures of structural quality are correlated with scores on the Infant and Toddlers Environment Rating Scale (ITERS) and the Classroom Assessment Scoring System (CLASS).

In Ecuador, the Centros Infantiles del Buen Vivir (CIBV) program guidelines require caregivers to be secondary school graduates. In practice, just over two-thirds (68 percent) of all caregivers meet this criterion. The CIBV also requires maximum ratios of 8 children per adult (for children younger than 24 months of age) to 12 children per adult (for children 24 months and older). In practice, there appears to be considerable variation in child-caregiver ratios. At the 10th percentile of the distribution, there are 6 children per adult, at the median there are 9, and at the 90th percentile there are 12 children per adult. (Children of different ages are frequently in the same classroom, so it is not easy to determine whether the program is complying with its own guidelines.) There is also considerable variation in the experience of caregivers, from 0 years at the 25th percentile (i.e., caregivers for whom this is the first year working with children) to 2 years at the median, and to 8 years at the 90th percentile.

Table B4.1 reports conditional associations between quality, as measured by the ITERS or the CLASS, and caregiver education, experience, and child-adult ratios in the CIBV program in Ecuador. It is important to keep in mind that these values may not have a causal interpretation; other reasons may explain why classrooms with fewer children per caregiver and caregivers with more experience and education have better quality (as measured by the ITERS and the CLASS).

Table B4.1   ITERS, CLASS, and Characteristics of Teachers and Daycare Centers in Ecuador

	ITERS				CLASS			
Caregiver has completed secondary school	0.26* (0.13)			0.30** (0.13)	0.26** (0.11)			0.29** (0.11)
Caregiver has 3+ years of experience		0.02 (0.12)		0.09 (0.12)		0.10 (0.12)		0.14 (0.12)
Child-adult ratio			−0.05** (0.02)	−0.05** (0.02)			0.01 (0.03)	−0.00 (0.03)
R-squared	0.016	0.000	0.018	0.040	0.014	0.002	0.000	0.018

Notes: All regressions include canton fixed effects. N is 403 daycare centers. Robust standard errors corrected for clustering at the canton center in parentheses. *** $p < 0.01$, ** $p < 0.05$, * $p < 0.1$.

ITERS = Infant and Toddlers Environment Rating Scale; CLASS = Classroom Assessment Scoring System.

Source: Authors' calculations based on the data in Araujo and others (2015).

The table shows that some, but not all, measures of structural quality are associated with better scores on the ITERS and CLASS. ITERS and CLASS scores are between 0.26 and 0.30 standard deviations higher in classrooms in which the caregiver has a secondary school degree than in those where the caregiver does not. ITERS scores (but not CLASS scores) are also better in classrooms where there are fewer children per caregiver. For every additional child per caregiver, the ITERS score goes down by 0.05 standard deviations. In other words, halving the number of children per caregiver from 12 to 6 is associated with an improvement in scores of 0.30 standard deviations. On the other hand, having a caregiver with more experience does not predict quality, as measured by the ITERS or the CLASS.

The analysis of the CIBV program in Ecuador suggests that the quality of daycare services is very low. But is Ecuador unusual relative to other countries in the region? Apparently not. The largest public daycare program in Peru, Cuna Más, and public daycare provided by the Crecer Bien Para Vivir Bien program in Potosí and Chuquisaca, Bolivia, are also of very low quality. Table 4.3 reports the median and the score of the classroom at the 90th percentile of the distribution of quality in the two programs. On the ITERS, the median center

Table 4.3   Quality of Daycare Services in Bolivia and Peru

	Bolivia, CBPVB		Peru, Cuna Más	
	Median	90th percentile	Median	90th percentile
ITERS				
Total	*1.3*	*1.8*	*3.6*	*4.8*
Space and furnishing	1.2	1.8	3.4	4.8
Personal care routines	1.1	1.2	3.2	5.5
Listening and talking	1.3	3	3.3	5.3
Activities	1.2	1.7	2.9	3.8
Interaction	1.4	2.8	5	6.8
Program structure	1.1	1.3	4	6
Parents and staff	1.3	2.2	2.8	3.6
CLASS				
Total	—	—	*3.1*	*3.6*
Emotional and behavioral support	—	—	*3.9*	*4.4*
Positive climate	—	—	3.4	4.1
Negative climate	—	—	6.9	7
Teacher sensitivity	—	—	3.3	4
Regard for child perspectives	—	—	3.1	3.8
Engaged support for learning	—	—	*1.8*	*2.3*
Behavior guidance	—	—	3	3.5
Facilitation of learning and development	—	—	2.5	3
Quality of feedback	—	—	1.3	1.8
Language modeling	—	—	1.5	2.1
KIDI				
Caregiver	—	—	23	26
Educator–coordinator	—	—	26	30
Observations		100		602

Notes: ITERS = Infant and Toddlers Environment Rating Scale; CLASS = Classroom Assessment Scoring System, KIDI = Knowledge of Infant Development Inventory. — = not available.

Source: Bolivia data from the baseline survey of the impact evaluation of the Crecer Bien para Vivir Bien (CBPVB); Peru data from the baseline survey of the impact evaluation of Cuna Más 2013 (Servicio de Cuidado Diurno). Both studies were conducted by Inter-American Development Bank staff.

in the Bolivian sample had a score of 1.3, and a center at the 90th percentile of quality had a score of 1.8 (inadequate quality). In Peru, the median center had a score of 3.6 (minimal quality) and a center at the 90th percentile of quality had a score of 4.8 (good quality). The CLASS scores for Peru are also discouraging, in particular on the

Engaged Support for Learning dimension. Even the best-performing centers in the sample had a score of 2.3 (poor quality) on this measure, showing that children are not provided with an environment conducive to promoting their cognition and school readiness skills.

In Colombia, the ITERS, ECERS, and FCCERS have also been used to measure the quality of care provided by the Hogares Infantiles and Centros de Desarrollo Infantil (the institutional modalities of public daycare), and the Hogares Comunitarios (the community modality of daycare) (Bernal 2014). In all three programs, the quality of the care is very low, ranging from 1.7 to 2.1 for the institutional modality of daycare, to 2.3 for the community modality. In Chile, a study of 63 daycares in the province of Concepción found that the average score on the ITERS was 3.2, in the range of minimal quality (Herrera and others 2005). Moreover, 68 percent of all the daycares had quality in the 1–2 (inadequate) range. Finally, a study of daycare (crèches) in Brazil measured the quality of care in six cities: Belém, Campo Grande, Florianópolis, Fortaleza, Rio de Janeiro, and Teresina (Verdisco and Pérez Alfaro 2010). The study used the ECERS but, because initial piloting suggested that the overall scores would be very low, the scores were redefined on a 1–10 (rather than 1–7) scale, with 1–3 being classified as "inadequate," 3–5 classified as "basic," 5–7 classified as "adequate," 7–8.5 as "good," and 8.5–10 as "excellent" quality. On this amended 10-point scale, the average care provided in the seven cities in the sample ranged from 2.2 ("inadequate") to 3.9 ("basic").

In sum, the quality of daycare in many countries in the region, as measured by direct observation of centers, is very low. This is the case in countries that primarily provide daycare through the community modality (like Colombia and Peru), those that use the institutional modality (like Brazil and Chile), and those where the service is a mixture of both modalities (like Ecuador).

The Impact of Daycare on Child Development: No Small Matter

The literature on the effects of daycare on child development in developed countries is large. There is convincing evidence from the United States that providing intensive, high-quality daycare to children from very disadvantaged backgrounds can have dramatic effects on their development and life chances. However, the strongest evidence comes from small pilot programs rather than from at-scale programs.

One program in the United States that has been very carefully evaluated is the Abecederian Program. Abecederian provided eight hours of very high-quality daycare, year-round, from birth through 5 years of age, implementing a structured curriculum that emphasized language, emotional regulation, and cognitive skills, and low child-to-caregiver ratios. All participants were socioeconomically disadvantaged: on average, only one of every four households had both parents living in it. Most mothers were high school dropouts and had an average IQ of 85. A careful evaluation, based on random assignment to a "treatment" and "control" group was built into the Abecederian program.

At age 4, children who received the Abecederian intervention had cognitive scores that were 0.74 standard deviations higher than those in the control group. As children aged, program effects on cognition faded out. Nevertheless, at age 15, those who had received the intervention in early childhood continued to outperform those who had been randomly assigned to the control group by 0.37 standard deviations on cognition, and by a similar amount on standardized tests of reading and math achievement (Campbell and others 2002). At age 21, beneficiaries were 23 percentage points more likely to be attending a 4-year college (Barnett and Masse 2007). In their mid-thirties, children who had received the Abecederian intervention had significantly lower risk factors for cardiovascular disease (e.g., they had lower blood pressure) than those who had been randomly assigned to the control group (Campbell and others 2014).

Most of the studies on the effects of daycare in at-scale programs in high-income countries (including Canada, Denmark, and the United States) find that daycare has positive effects on child cognitive development for children from disadvantaged backgrounds. Many studies, however, also report negative effects of daycare attendance on socioemotional development and child behavior, particularly full-time daycare for young children.[9]

What about the evidence from Latin America and the Caribbean? Within the region, credible evaluations of the impacts of daycare on child outcomes are scarce. Two papers evaluate the impact of community-based care in Bolivia (a program known as Proyecto Integral de Desarrollo Infantil, PIDI) (Behrman, Cheng, and Todd 2004) and in Colombia (the Hogares Comunitarios program) (Bernal and Fernández 2013).[10] At the time they were evaluated, both programs provided full-time daycare and food to children in the home of a community mother. The community mothers who served as caregivers received minimal training, and each was responsible for about 15 children. The annual cost of the program per child was estimated to be $516 in Bolivia and $430 in Colombia.

Both evaluations suggest that daycare had a positive, if modest, effect on child development: about 0.2 standard deviations. The impacts are driven by positive effects among somewhat older children (roughly 4 years of age or older). Among younger children, the program effects are generally not significant, and in some cases they are wrong-signed (indicating that the program led to worse outcomes).

In Ecuador, the Fondo de Desarrollo Infantil (FODI) subsidized daycare provided by approved nonprofit or community organizations.[11] All organizations seeking to receive a subsidy from FODI were required to prepare a proposal. FODI scored and ranked all proposals using a formula and funded those that were most highly ranked until the budget of the program for that year was exhausted. If funded, the organization received $488 per child from FODI and was expected to provide full-time daycare (52 weeks per year, 5 days per week, 8 hours per day) using a curriculum developed by the program.

Rosero and Oosterbeek (2011) estimate that FODI had no effect on child motor and social development. However, the effects of the program on cognitive and language development are negative and statistically significant (about 0.3 standard deviations, on average), implying that children who attended FODI were substantially worse off than those who did not attend. Mothers of children who attended daycare were also less likely to provide responsive parenting.

Two studies evaluate reforms to the Hogares Comunitarios program in Colombia. The first (Bernal forthcoming) evaluates an effort to provide substantial in-service training and a degree in child development to the community mothers who were acting as caregivers. It involved almost 2,500 hours of instruction (compared to the 40 hours of training that the community mothers had previously had as a prerequisite to being declared eligible as caregivers). Topics covered included child health, nutrition and development, developmental milestones, and appropriate educational and stimulation practices at different ages. Training appears to have improved the quality of daycare, as measured by the FCCERS, and had a positive impact on some measures of child cognitive development.

The second study (Bernal and others 2014a) evaluates a key aspect of the reform of daycare services in Colombia. Beginning in 2007, the government began a program of constructing large centers serving between 150 and 300 children each. The size of these new centers permitted children to be grouped by age, as is recommended in the child development literature. Initially, the reform contemplated hiring a professional educator for every 25 children, and hiring the community mothers as assistants. In practice, however, many of the community mothers simply became caregivers in the new centers. In addition, each center included three professional staff specialized in health and nutrition, socioemotional support, and pedagogical support, respectively. Specialized staff was also employed for cooking and cleaning (tasks that had previously been carried out by the community mother). Construction of each center cost $1 million, on average. Relative to the community service it replaced, the cost of the service in these large centers more than tripled, to $1,500 per child per year (excluding the initial investment in infrastructure).

A convincing evaluation was built to estimate the impact of replacing community daycare with daycare provided in the new centers. The evaluation showed very disappointing results. Some measures of structural quality improved (most obviously, the quality of the infrastructure). However, process quality, as measured by the FCCERS, ITERS, and ECERS scales, was no better in the new centers than in the Hogares Comunitarios. Indeed, on a number of dimensions, including routines and activities, the relationship between caregivers and children, and the relationship between caregivers and parents, the new centers had lower quality than the Hogares Comunitarios.

Most disappointingly (but perhaps not surprisingly, given the fact that process quality did not improve), children in the large centers did not experience any consistent improvements in nutrition, cognitive development, or socioemotional development, relative to those who stayed in the Hogares Comunitarios.[12]

In sum, there are only a handful of evaluations of the impact of daycare services on child development in Latin America and the Caribbean. All these evaluations have some methodological limitations, and none of them meets the gold standard of a randomized trial with high levels of compliance.[13] Nevertheless, the main message from these evaluations is clear: full-time daycare in the region is generally of low quality and does not consistently improve child development, especially among the youngest children.

Sketching Out Policy

More young children now attend publicly provided or subsidized daycare (public daycare) in Latin America and the Caribbean than ever before. The primary goal of publicly provided daycare in many countries in the region was to facilitate the entry of women into the labor force. To some extent, daycare has accomplished this goal, although the magnitude of the impact depends on the extent to which public daycare crowds out private daycare that was already available.[14]

From the point of view of child development, the critical issue is whether the daycare that is provided is of a higher quality than the counterfactual care that children would have received if public daycare were not available. Little is known about this counterfactual. However, the most salient characteristic of the public daycare that is currently available in the region is its very low quality. It seems unlikely that daycare of such low quality would improve child outcomes. The results from a handful of impact evaluations of programs in the region confirm that the benefits of this daycare for children are uncertain at best.

Some developed countries provide generous support for daycare. In these countries, a large proportion of children aged 0–2 years are in formal care, including in Denmark (63 percent), Iceland (56 percent),

Norway (42 percent), and Sweden (45 percent). However, in these countries, daycare is of high quality: daycare workers almost invariably have a postsecondary degree in early childhood education and are highly trained (Ruhm 2011). Other developed countries provide only minimal support for daycare. Instead, these countries rely on a combination of tax breaks or subsidies for families with young children and generous mandated parental leave benefits. In these countries, the proportion of children aged 0–2 years who are in formal daycare is generally very low, including in Austria (11 percent), Germany (14 percent), and Switzerland (less than 10 percent) (Ruhm 2011). In some countries in Latin America and the Caribbean, in particular those where the size of the informal sector is relatively small, mandating paid parental leave, or increasing the length of time that is covered, may make sense (see Box 4.3).

Box 4.3   Mandated Parental Leave

Many developed countries support families with young children by mandating paid leave for parents. Most studies using data from a variety of countries have found that paid parental leave reduces child mortality and morbidity (Ruhm 2000; Tanaka 2005). Some studies also find that expansion in parental leave improves child development. For example, an increase in paid and unpaid maternal leave entitlements in Norway in the late 1970s is estimated to have led to a 2 percentage point decline in high school dropout rates and a 5 percent increase in wages at age 30 (Carneiro, Løken, and Salvanes 2015). However, estimates for leave expansions in Germany (Dustmann and Schönberg 2012) and Canada (Baker and Milligan 2010) do not find significant effects.[15]

Whether policies of mandated leave are feasible and desirable in Latin America and the Caribbean is a difficult question because of the large proportion of workers (more than 50 percent in most countries) in the informal sector, where such mandated leave could not be enforced.[16] Funding is also a concern because mandated benefits are not cheap—in the Nordic countries (Denmark, Iceland, Norway, Sweden), the costs average between 0.5 and 0.8 percent of GDP (Ruhm 2011)—and because mandated leave could affect the choice between formal and informal work, depending on how it is financed.[17]

In practice, many countries in Latin America and the Caribbean are likely to continue to provide or subsidize daycare in the fore-seeable future. But major changes are necessary if daycare is to be beneficial (or at least not harmful) for the children who use it. In thinking about these changes, it is useful to distinguish between daycare in rural and urban areas.

In rural areas, population densities are low and qualified educators are scarce. It is not clear what a cost-effective daycare service of reasonable quality looks like in this context. If the service in rural areas continues to be primarily of the community modality, giving community mothers in-service training, coaching, and better supervision may hold some promise.

In urban areas, population density is high, and the differences in child development between children in rich and poor households are large. In this setting, priority should be given to the most disadvantaged children. These may be children from very poor households, or children who are at particularly high risk (e.g., in families with domestic violence, child abuse, or drug use). For these children, the alternative to daycare—the counterfactual—is an environment that is not supportive of child development. They are most likely to benefit from high-quality daycare services. Credible evaluations of model programs like the Abecederian in the United States show that high-quality daycare targeted at very disadvantaged children has the potential to transform their lives.

High-quality care is child focused. Child-to-caregiver ratios are low, as is staff turnover. As a result, caregivers know the children in their care well, and can establish close, emotionally stable relationships with them. Caregivers are professionals, use rich language, and provide learning opportunities that are cognitively stimulating. In practice, very few children in Latin America and the Caribbean receive daycare services with these characteristics.

High-quality care is not cheap. The average annual cost of the Abecederian program was approximately $18,000 per child (in 2013 dollars). In Colombia, the aeioTU program, which seeks to provide high-quality care to poor children, costs $1,870 per child per year, roughly four times the cost of the basic daycare that is provided in many of the large-scale programs in the region (in particular those that operate with a community modality). Substantially improving the quality of care means that, at a given budget, daycare could only be provided to a much smaller number of children in the region than is currently the case.

If high-quality public daycare services are primarily targeted to the poor, more families will turn to other forms of care. This raises the question whether private, not-for-profit, or informal providers of daycare should be accredited, regulated, and a minimum standard of care enforced. There is no simple answer to this question. Accreditation is a way of providing parents with (limited) information about the quality of care. This is useful because it is hard for parents to accurately assess quality—daycare, like hospital care, car repair, and a variety of other services, is an "experience good," with substantial information asymmetries between providers and consumers. However, accreditation and minimum standards are no panacea. In some countries in Latin America and the Caribbean, the capacity of the public sector to accurately assess, monitor, and enforce quality standards are an issue. Moreover, standards will raise average prices of formal daycare and push low-quality providers out of the market, leaving poor households with fewer choices. Some poor households will not be able to afford the higher-quality, regulated care and will turn to the completely unregulated market (e.g., care by a neighbor or family member). In some cases, this quality will be of even lower quality than the formal care it has replaced, so that children could be made worse off by the regulation (Hotz and Xiao 2011).

The biggest challenge for countries in the region is finding the right balance between quality and coverage in public daycare. In many countries in the region, the participation of women in the labor market is low. Helping women enter the labor force is an important goal for governments for a variety of reasons. It will increase economic growth and may reduce disparities between men and women. Daycare may encourage some women who would not otherwise have been employed to work. However, low-quality care will not benefit children, and may actually harm them. The benefits from the increased employment of women may, therefore, come at the expense of child development. The costs, in terms of more behavioral problems among children, worse schooling outcomes, and, eventually, worse mental health and lower productivity in adulthood, may be substantial.

For a given budget, there is a potential trade-off between daycare programs that offer extensive coverage, substantial effects on female labor supply, but few benefits for children, and those that have limited coverage, modest effects on female labor supply, but substantial benefits for the children who use the service. The surge in the supply of public daycare in the region in the past decade and the very low quality of these services suggest that governments need to focus much more on improving the quality of daycare than they have done to date.

5

Early Schooling: Teachers Make the Difference

School enrollment in the early grades is close to universal in Latin America and the Caribbean, but the quality of education is generally poor. As a result, many children in the region learn little in their first years of formal schooling. Since early education is considered vital for economic and social progress, the region's failure in this area is of great concern.

The lack of cognitive (and other) skills of Latin American and Caribbean workers is frequently cited as a major reason behind the low economic growth rates of the region (Hanushek and Woessmann 2012). Policymakers are generally aware of the poor performance of secondary school students from Latin America on the Program for International Student Assessment (PISA) tests. However, skill formation is a cumulative process. It is hard to learn in late childhood and adolescence without a solid foundation. Fixing the problem of low quality in secondary school may do little for learning outcomes if the same is not done for the quality of schooling in the early years.

Early School Enrollment: A Regional Success

By and large, young children in Latin America and the Caribbean attend school. Figure 5.1 plots the proportion of children enrolled in school between 1990 and 2014 in six countries: Brazil, Chile, Honduras, Jamaica, Mexico, and Panama.[1] Changes in these countries are broadly representative of those that have taken place throughout the region. The solid line focuses on children aged 6–9.

Figure 5.1   School Attendance, 1990–2014

a. Brazil

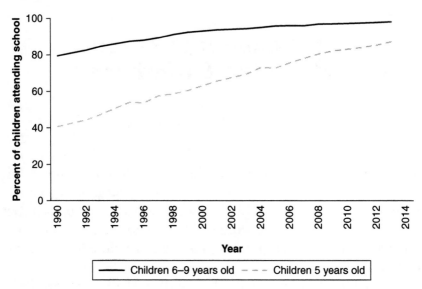

b. Chile

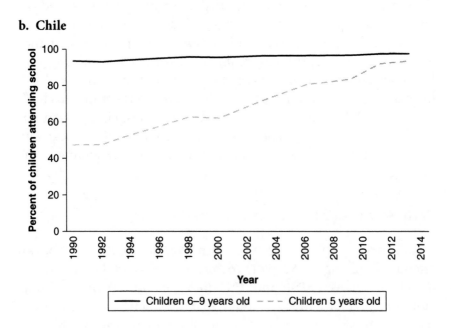

c. Jamaica

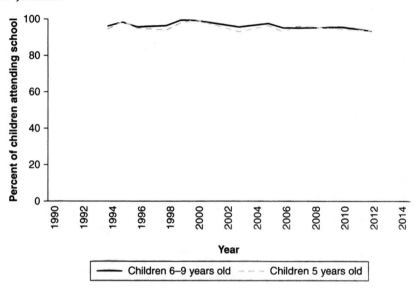

d. Honduras

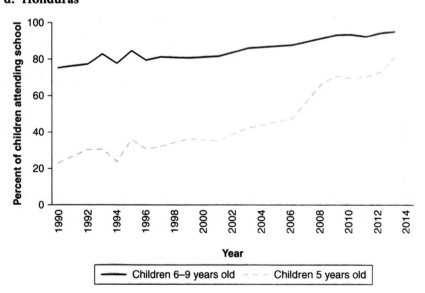

e. Mexico

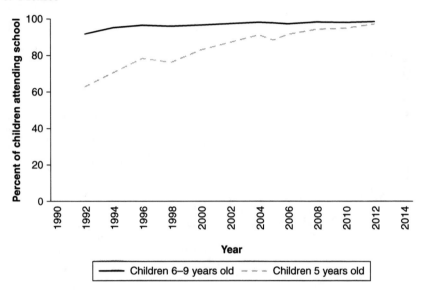

f. Panama

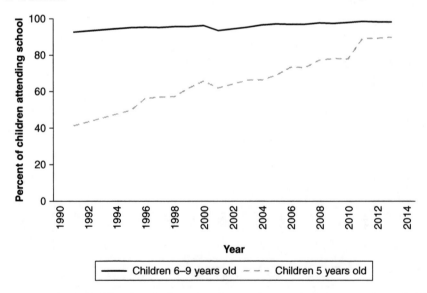

Source: Authors' calculations based on Inter-American Development Bank Harmonized Household Surveys.

For children who start school on time and do not repeat grades, this corresponds to enrollment in roughly first through third or fourth grade of primary school, depending on the exact birth date.[2] In virtually every country in the region, including the poorest ones, school attendance for children aged 6–9 years is universal or very close to universal. In many countries, this has been the case since at least the early 2000s.

Good evidence from the region, particularly from the Southern Cone countries, shows that children who attend pre-primary school are better prepared to learn in later grades. Argentina implemented a large program to expand the coverage of pre-primary education between 1993 and 1999. Children who benefited from this expansion in coverage performed better on mathematics and Spanish achievement tests in third grade. One year of pre-primary school increased children's test scores by 0.23 standard deviations. Children who attended pre-primary school also demonstrated superior participation skills, such as attention, effort, class participation, and discipline, as reported by their teachers (Berlinski, Galiani, and Gertler 2009).

In Uruguay, pre-primary school attendance for children 4 and 5 years old resulted in a significant, positive effect on the number of years of schooling completed. By age 15, children who had attended some pre-primary school were 27 percent more likely to be in school than their peers who did not, and had on average completed 0.8 more years of schooling (Berlinski, Galiani, and Manacorda 2008).[3]

The dashed line in Figure 5.1 shows that many countries in the region have made a sharp push to extend the coverage of education for 5-year-olds.[4] Moreover, wealth gradients in enrollment have declined substantially. For example, in Chile, the difference in the proportion of 5-year-olds attending school between the first and fifth wealth quintiles fell from 29 to 5 percentage points between 2000 and 2013; in the Dominican Republic, it fell from 33 to 7 percentage points; and in Panama it fell from 45 to 15 percentage points (Table 5.1). Increasingly, the enrollment gap in kindergarten between the rich and the poor is closing, much as it did in the first grades of primary school in earlier decades.

Table 5.1   School Attendance, by Wealth Quintile

| Country | Difference between richest and poorest quintiles (percentage points) | | | |
| | 5-year-old children | | 6- to 9-year-old children | |
	2000	2013	2000	2013
Argentina	16	5	2	0
Bolivia	30	31	9	1
Brazil	35	13	9	2
Chile	29	5	4	0
Colombia	33	13	9	1
Costa Rica	36	28	4	2
Dominican Republic	33	7	7	5
Ecuador	21	8	5	1
El Salvador	52	35	25	7
Honduras	42	26	20	4
Mexico	21	4	5	2
Panama	45	14	4	2
Paraguay	23	30	9	2
Peru	36	12	3	3
Uruguay	16	5	2	0

Note: When data for 2000 or 2013 were not available, data from the nearest year were used. For 2000, data from 2001 were used for Brazil, Costa Rica, Honduras, Nicaragua, and Paraguay. For 2013, data from 2012 were used for Mexico and Nicaragua. Data for Uruguay correspond to urban areas only.

Source: Authors' calculations based on Inter-American Development Bank Harmonized Household Surveys.

A Low Score in Learning Outcomes

Although young children in Latin America and the Caribbean go to school, many of them appear to learn very little. Data on test scores in the first grades of pre-primary and primary school are scarce, and (as with child development) comparability is an issue. Only two countries in the region—Chile and Honduras—participated in the 2011 application of the Trends in International Mathematics and Science Study (TIMMS) of fourth grade students, and only two countries—Colombia and Honduras—participated in the 2011 application of the Progress in International Reading Literacy Study (PIRLS) of fourth grade students.

It is not possible to credibly benchmark early learning outcomes of children in Latin America and the Caribbean relative to other countries outside the region. However, a large number of countries in Latin America have participated in a regional test of language and math applied to third graders in Latin America in 2007 (Segundo Estudio Regional Comparativo y Explicativo, or SERCE) and 2013 (Tercer Estudio Regional Comparativo y Explicativo, or TERCE). These data can therefore be used to compare the learning outcomes of young children in different countries in the region.

There are substantial differences in math test scores across countries in 2013, as is shown in Table 5.2.[5] Chile, Costa Rica, Uruguay, and Mexico performed relatively well; the Dominican Republic, Nicaragua, Paraguay, and Panama did not. Third graders in Chile, the top performer, posted scores that were 0.9 standard deviations higher, on average, than children in the Dominican Republic, the country with the lowest average scores.[6]

SERCE and TERCE are, by construction, comparable in their difficulty. This makes it possible to analyze changes in a country's

Table 5.2   Math Test Scores, by Country and Year

	SERCE (2007)	TERCE (2013)
Argentina	0.03	0.22
Brazil	0.03	0.27
Chile	0.19	0.55
Colombia	−0.01	0.13
Costa Rica	0.25	0.39
Ecuador	−0.18	0.16
Guatemala	−0.29	0.01
Mexico	0.21	0.33
Nicaragua	−0.18	−0.10
Panama	−0.25	−0.04
Paraguay	−0.09	−0.08
Peru	−0.17	0.22
Dominican Republic	−0.69	−0.35
Uruguay	0.26	0.34

Notes: All scores have been redefined as standard deviation units of the 2007 score. SERCE = Segundo Estudio Regional Comparativo y Explicativo; TERCE = Tercer Estudio Regional Comparativo y Explicativo.

Source: Authors' calculations based on data from SERCE and TERCE.

performance over time. Test scores have increased in all countries, but the magnitude of these changes varies widely. In Peru, Chile, the Dominican Republic, and Ecuador, test scores have increased by 0.3 standard deviations or more. In Paraguay, Nicaragua, Uruguay, Mexico, Costa Rica, and Colombia, improvements have been more modest: 0.15 standard deviations or less.

Countries also vary in the proportion of the total variation in TERCE test scores that is accounted for by differences across and within schools. The cross-school component explains almost half of the variability in test scores in Panama, Paraguay, and Peru. Conversely, the cross-school component is much smaller—about one-quarter—in Chile, Costa Rica, and Mexico. This finding suggests that policies to raise the learning outcomes of the lowest-performing students that target specific schools, rather than children within schools, are more likely to be effective in some countries (such as Peru) than in others (such as Chile). Box 5.1 presents a methodological discussion of how these cross- and within-school components can be estimated.

Box 5.1   The Variance in Test Scores: Is It the Child or the School?

From a policy point of view, it is important to know whether the variation in test scores in early primary school in a country results primarily from the fact that some schools have lower average scores than others or, rather, from differences between children within the same school. A decomposition of the variance in test scores into across-school and within-school components attempts to answer this question. Such a calculation was carried out using the 2013 TERCE (Tercer Estudio Regional y Comparativo), a regional test applied to third graders in Latin America in 2013.

In its simplest form, this decomposition can be calculated by a regression of test scores in a country on school fixed effects. The R-squared in this regression measures the between-school variance in test scores. The R-squared in these regressions was about 0.5 in Panama, Paraguay, and Peru, but only about 0.25 in Chile, Costa Rica, and Mexico. However, sampling error may be a problem for these "naïve" estimates of the across- and within-school components of the variance. This is because the number of schools and of children tested per school varied a great deal across countries in TERCE.

The robustness of the results from the basic decomposition (in particular, the relative ranking of countries) to the presence of sampling error was tested in two ways. In one approach, a new sample was created. By construction, this new sample had exactly the same number of schools and the same number of children per school, in each country. Specifically, schools with eight or fewer tested children (the value at the 25th percentile for the sample as a whole) were discarded, and a sample of 158 schools (the number of schools in the country with the fewest schools in the sample, Colombia) and 9 children per school was randomly chosen in every country. (The sample for each country has exactly 1,422 children.) One hundred iterations of this procedure were carried out, regressions of test scores on school fixed effects were run in each sample, and the average R-squared for these 100 iterations was calculated. Using this procedure, Peru, Panama, and Colombia (rather than Paraguay) were estimated to have the highest across-school variance, while Chile, Costa Rica, and Mexico were estimated to have the lowest across-school variance, as before.

The second approach was inspired by the literature on teacher value added (see Box 5.2). In this literature, it is standard to calculate the variance of teacher effects. It has long been recognized, however, that sampling error tends to overstate the true variance of teacher effects. Specifically, $V_o = V_t + V_e$, where V_o is the observed variance, V_t is the true variance, and V_e is the variance of the measurement error. One approach to correcting the observed variance is to estimate the variance of the measurement error using an Empirical Bayes procedure.[7] The same approach can be used to correct the variance of school (rather than teacher) effects for sampling error in TERCE. When the variance is uncorrected, the three countries where the school effects explain the largest fraction of the total variance in test scores are Paraguay, Peru, and Honduras; these are also the countries in which differences across schools explain the largest fraction of the total variance after the Empirical Bayes correction. Similarly, when the variance is uncorrected, the three countries where the school effects explain the smallest fraction of the total variance in test scores are Chile, Costa Rica, and Mexico; these are also the countries in which differences across schools explain the smallest fraction of the total variance after the Empirical Bayes correction.

In sum, no matter how the variance is decomposed, there are some countries, like Peru, where a great deal of the variation in child test scores is driven by differences across schools, and others, like Chile, where much more of this variation is driven by differences across children in the same school.

Data on the socioeconomic characteristics of children and their parents collected in SERCE and TERCE are limited and are missing for many children. Better data to study wealth gradients in learning outcomes are available in three country-specific tests: the Cerrando Brechas study of kindergarten students in 2012 in Ecuador, the Exámenes de la Calidad y el Logro Educativos (EXCALE) of first graders in 2011 in Mexico, and the Evaluación Censal de Estudiantes (ECE) of second graders in 2010 in Peru.

To analyze socioeconomic gradients in math scores, children in Cerrando Brechas, ECE, and EXCALE were sorted into quintiles of the national distribution of wealth in each country.[8] These results, reported in Table 5.3, show that the richest children scored 0.5 standard deviations higher than the poorest children in Ecuador and Mexico, and a full standard deviation in Peru.[9] Table 5.3 also shows that in Ecuador and Peru boys have higher scores than girls, while the reverse is true in Mexico.

Table 5.3   Wealth Gradients in Math Scores

	Cerrando Brechas (Kindergarten, Ecuador)	EXCALE (first grade, Mexico)	ECE (second grade, Peru)
Second quintile	0.069	0.070	0.100***
	(0.042)	(0.064)	(0.018)
Third quintile	0.159***	0.202***	0.458***
	(0.052)	(0.063)	(0.022)
Fourth quintile	0.296***	0.384***	0.712***
	(0.055)	(0.060)	(0.023)
Fifth quintile	0.532***	0.524***	0.996***
	(0.070)	(0.045)	(0.031)
Girl	−0.036**	0.061*	−0.057***
	(0.017)	(0.032)	(0.013)
R-squared	0.022	0.063	0.110
Observations	14,243	6,776	60,646

Notes: Coefficients and standard errors (in parenthesis). Units are in standard deviations. Children in the first (poorest) wealth quintile are the omitted category. Standard errors clustered at the school level. *** $p < 0.01$, ** $p < 0.05$, * $p < 0.1$.

Source: Authors' calculations based on Cerrando Brechas test of kindergarten students in 2013 in Ecuador, the Exámenes de la Calidad y el Logro Educativos (EXCALE) of first graders in 2011 in Mexico, and the data for the Evaluación Censal de Estudiantes (ECE) of second graders in 2010 in Peru.

It is also possible to estimate socioeconomic gradients in early learning outcomes in Jamaica. Samms-Vaughan (2005) analyzes the evolution of test scores using a (relatively small) sample of approximately 250 children; these children were followed from pre-K to third grade. Samms-Vaughan compares the performance of children on the Reading, Spelling and Arithmetic subscales of the Wide Range Achievement Test (WRAT) in households that are asset-rich and asset-poor. At pre-K age, the mean difference between those in the high- and low-asset groups was between 0.6 and 0.8 standard deviations; by third grade, socioeconomic gradients had widened considerably, to between 1.0 and 1.3 standard deviations.[10]

In sum, the evidence makes clear that learning outcomes in Latin America and the Caribbean are poor, especially in some countries, and among children from households that are poorer and where parents have less schooling.

Grading Classroom Quality

The fact that children are enrolled in school but many of them appear to learn very little suggests that the quality of early schooling is a serious problem in the region.[11]

Classroom quality is a complex, multifaceted construct, but (much as is the case with the quality of daycare, discussed in Chapter 4) it can be separated into two discernible components: structural and process quality. Structural quality focuses on features of the classroom experience such as the environment, the nature and level of teacher training and experience, adoption of certain curricula, class size, and student-teacher ratios. Process quality, on the other hand, refers to a student's direct interactions with resources and opportunities in the classroom. This includes the ways teachers implement lessons, the nature and quality of interactions between adults and students or between students and their peers, and the availability of certain types of activities.

Structural Quality: A Lesser Factor

Some studies in the United States have found that lower child-to-teacher ratios in the early grades improve child learning outcomes. The best known of these studies is Project STAR in Tennessee, an intervention that randomly assigned children in kindergarten through third grade to "small" (13–17 students per teacher) or "large" classes (22–25 students). Children in the smaller classes outperformed those in the large classes in the short run (Krueger 1999), although some of these effects faded out as children became older (Krueger and Whitmore 2001). Remarkably, Chetty and others (2011) find that children randomly assigned to smaller classes outperform those in larger classes on a number of measures of adult performance, including college attendance, roughly two decades later.

Nevertheless, these results do not appear to be the norm. Reviews of hundreds of interventions in the United States conclude that the evidence that these structural features have a direct impact on children's academic achievement or social development is mixed (Hanushek 2003; NICHD Early Child Care Research Network 2002).

These findings have been corroborated with research on developing countries. Murnane and Ganimian (2014) review 115 well-designed impact evaluations of educational interventions in over 30 lower- and middle-income countries, and conclude that learning outcomes were not consistently improved by better materials, classroom technology, flexible education funding grants, or smaller class sizes, unless the day-to-day interactions of children and teachers were also targeted. Kremer, Brannem and Glennerster (2013) arrive at a similar conclusion.[12]

Process Quality: The Real Test

When adults are sensitive and responsive to children's cues and needs, children begin to learn and develop (National Scientific Council 2012). As children enter formal schooling, interactions among teachers and students in the classroom begin to play a critical role in development.

How students spend time: A key component of process quality is how students spend their classroom time. A growing body of literature indicates that the extent to which students are engaged in educationally focused activities in the classroom predicts academic and social outcomes. Specifically, when instruction is targeted to a specific skill, that particular skill is developed (NRP 2000; Snow, Burns, and Griffin 1998). For example, language and literacy instruction is related to greater skill gains in language and literacy (Piasta and others 2012), while greater emphasis on math and science is associated with greater skills gains in math and science (Clements and Sarama 2011; Sarama and Clements 2009). Within the social and emotional domain, teachers who model explicitly and teach about emotions help students develop knowledge about emotions and regulation (Denham, Bassett, and Zinsser 2012).

Several large-scale studies in the United States have carefully studied how time is spent in the classroom (Early and others 2005; Hamre and others 2006; La Paro and others 2009). These studies generally conclude that a substantial amount of time in most classrooms is spent on noninstructional activities such as routines and transitions.

Results from Latin America and the Caribbean present a similar picture. Bruns and Luque (2015) report the results from the application of the Stallings Classroom Snapshot instrument (Stallings 1977) in more than 15,000 classrooms in six countries in Latin America and the Caribbean (Brazil, Colombia, Honduras, Jamaica, Mexico, and Peru).[13] Figure 5.2 reproduces some important results from their research. On average, only between 50 and 65 percent of time in the classroom in the six countries is spent on instruction, well below the Stallings good practice benchmark of 85 percent. This means that, even in the best-performing countries in the region, a full day of instruction is lost per week, relative to the good practice benchmark. In every country in the region, between 8 and 14 percent of time is lost because teachers are physically absent from the classroom altogether (e.g., arriving late or leaving early), or are engaged in social interactions with other adults (e.g., chatting at the classroom door). Thus, in a 200-day school year, students on average miss 20 full days of instruction. Even when a teacher is spending time on instruction, it is comparatively rare for all of the students in the classroom to be engaged; more often than not, more than half the children are not paying attention and are disengaged or bored (Bruns and Luque 2015).

Figure 5.2   How Teachers Spend Their Time in the Classroom

a. Proportion of Time Spent on Different Classroom Activities

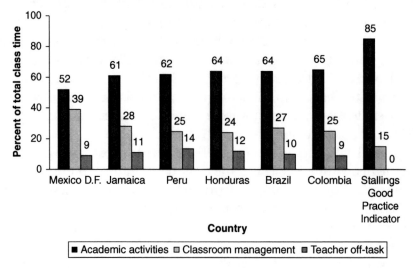

b. A Breakdown of Teacher Time Off-Task

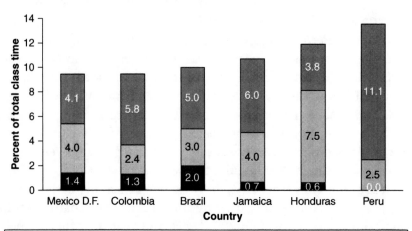

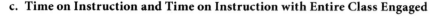

c. Time on Instruction and Time on Instruction with Entire Class Engaged

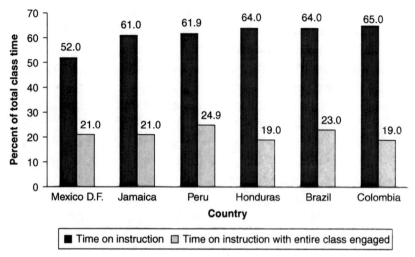

Source: Bruns and Luque (2015).

The quality of teacher-child interactions: Over the past two decades, researchers in the United States have focused on another key aspect of students' classroom experience—the elements of teachers' interactions that promote positive development. This body of work considers the moment-to-moment learning experiences students have with their teacher and peers. A number of studies have found that the quality of students' interactions with one another and with their teachers is more important for their achievement on evaluations of academic preparedness than aspects of structural quality.[14]

Given this growing body of evidence that the quality of teacher-child interactions matter for students' development, more recent work has focused on articulating a clear framework of what effective interactions look like. Building on previous descriptions of quality teaching (Brophy and Good 1986; Eccles and Roeser 2005), the Teaching Through Interactions framework (Hamre and Pianta 2007) has become a widely used and accepted model for understanding and measuring the quality of teacher-child interactions. It is aligned with a classroom observation tool, the Classroom Assessment Scoring System (CLASS) (Pianta, La Paro, and Hamre 2008b), used in much of the research in this area (see Box 4.1). The Teaching Through

Interactions framework describes three domains of interactions that have strong theoretical and empirical backing: emotional support, classroom organization, and instructional support.

Emotional support: In classrooms with high levels of emotional support, teachers and students have positive relationships and enjoy spending time together. Teachers are aware of, and responsive to, children's needs, and prioritize interactions that place an emphasis on students' interests, motivations, and points of view. In classrooms with low levels of emotional support, teachers and students appear emotionally distant from one another, and there are instances of frustration in interactions. Teachers seldom attend to children's need for additional support and, overall, the classroom follows a teacher's agenda with little opportunity for student input. Many studies from the United States have found associations between the teachers' provision of emotionally supportive interactions in the classroom and students' social-emotional development.[15]

Classroom organization: In highly organized classrooms, teachers are proactive in managing behavior by setting clear expectations; classroom routines allow for students to get the most out of their time engaged in meaningful activities; and teachers actively promote students' engagement in those activities. In less organized classrooms, teachers might spend much of their time reacting to behavior problems; classroom routines are not evident; students spend time wandering or not engaged in activities; and teachers do little to change this. When teachers manage behavior and attention proactively, students spend more time on-task and are better able to regulate their attention (Rimm-Kaufman and others 2009). Students in better organized and managed classrooms also show larger increases in cognitive and academic development (Downer and others 2010).[16]

Instructional support: In classrooms with high levels of instructional support, a teacher promotes higher order thinking and provides quality feedback to extend students' learning. At the low end, rote and fact-based activities might be common, and students receive little to no feedback about their work beyond whether or not it is correct. In these classrooms, teachers do most of the talking or the room is quiet. The quality of instructional support provided in a classroom is most consistently linked with higher gains in academic outcomes, such as test scores.[17]

Although the three domains of teacher-student interactions are conceptually distinct, and can be measured separately, it is frequently observed that teachers who excel in one domain also excel in the other two. For this reason, when taken together, the behaviors associated with higher levels of emotional support, classroom organization, and instructional support can be described as "Responsive Teaching" (Hamre and others 2014).

Though students learn and develop more in classrooms with higher quality teacher-child interactions, few students actually experience these types of interactions in the early years of school. For example, in the United States, emotional support and classroom organization are typically of only moderate quality in primary classrooms, and instructional support is moderate to low.[18] A recent study using data from Finland finds qualitatively similar results (Salminen 2013).

There is a small, but growing body of evidence from Latin America on teaching practices in the early grades, with a focus on the interactions between teachers and students. Cruz-Aguayo and others (2015) report the results from the application of two instruments that measure different aspects of classroom quality in a sample of 78 kindergarten, first-grade, and second-grade classrooms in three countries in Latin America: Brazil, Chile, and Ecuador. The first instrument is the SNAPSHOT (Ritchie and others 2001), which (like the Stallings) focuses on the activity that is happening within a classroom at a given moment.[19] The second instrument that was used is the CLASS. In addition to these two instruments, data were collected on some aspects of structural quality, including student-teacher ratios.

The results from the SNAPSHOT suggest that the bulk of instructional time in all three countries involved students working on a whole group activity (e.g., students sitting at their desks and copying teacher-provided sentences from the chalk- or white-board, or reproducing letters) or individually (e.g., students working on identical pages in their workbooks). Typically, children sat at small desks, with all desks facing the front of the classroom. Students rarely worked collaboratively in small groups. In some classrooms in all three countries, no activity occurred during much of the time, and students were provided little or no direction.

The results from the CLASS, summarized in Figure 5.3, indicate that in all three countries, scores on the Emotional Support and Classroom Organization domains of the CLASS were in the midrange, while scores on Instructional Support were consistently very low, especially (but not only) in Ecuador.[20] Similar patterns were found in a nationally representative sample of kindergarten classrooms in Ecuador (as reported in Araujo and others 2014). Like others (Bruns and Luque 2015), Cruz-Aguayo and others (2015) also emphasize that students' classroom experiences frequently were very different across classrooms within the same school.

Leyva and others (2015) assess time use and the quality of teacher-student interactions, as measured by the CLASS, and the association between these dimensions of process quality and student outcomes, in a sample of 91 public prekindergarten classrooms in Chile. A substantial amount of time was spent on noninstructional activities, such as eating snacks, transitions, and recess.[21] Higher

Figure 5.3   The Classroom Assessment Scoring System Domain Scores, Brazil, Chile, and Ecuador

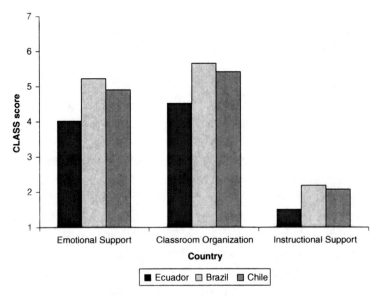

Source: Cruz-Aguayo and others (2015).

levels of instructional support were associated with larger gains on one of the three tests of language and early literacy, and one of the two tests of executive function.

One of the best-designed studies on the effects of teacher quality and the classroom environment on child learning outcomes is Araujo and others (2014), who study a sample of 454 public kindergarten classrooms in the coastal area of Ecuador. The paper begins by discussing the difficulty of credibly identifying the effects of better teachers, or better teaching practices if students are assigned to teachers on the basis of unobserved characteristics. The study avoids this problem by randomly assigning an entering cohort of approximately 15,000 kindergarten students in 202 schools, all of which had at least two kindergarten classes, to teachers. Compliance with the random assignment was very high at 98 percent.

During the school year, Araujo and others (2014) collected very rich data on teachers and students. They used the CLASS to measure the quality of interactions between teachers and students in the classroom. They also collected additional information on teachers, including whether they were tenured or worked on a contract basis; their years of experience in the teaching profession; their intelligence, as measured by the Wechsler Adult Intelligence Scales (WAIS-IV); their personality, as measured by the Big Five personality inventory; teacher executive function; and a variety of characteristics about teachers and their environments when they were children. At the end of the year, they collected 12 separate tests of child learning, including four tests each of early literacy, early math, and executive function.

Based on this careful design, Araujo and others (2014) first show that a child randomly assigned to a teacher at the 95th percentile of the distribution of quality learns, on average, 0.18 standard deviations more than a child assigned to an average teacher. In terms of magnitude, this effect is comparable to that found in a randomized evaluation of a program that gave cash transfers equivalent to about 10 percent of household expenditures to extremely poor households in Ecuador (0.18 standard deviations, as reported by Paxson and Schady [2010]), and to estimates of the impact of a year of pre-primary education in Argentina (0.23 standard deviations, as reported by Berlinski, Galiani, and Gertler [2009]).[22] The effects are also similar to those reported in the literature on teacher effects in the United States (as summarized in Hanushek and Rivkin [2012]).

Moreover, the same teachers improve child learning outcomes in all domains (language, math, executive function) and these teachers improve the learning outcomes of all children in a classroom (those with higher and lower baseline levels of development, those whose parents have more or less education, and those in households with higher or lower levels of wealth) by roughly the same amount. As the authors put it "a rising tide" (in this case, random assignment to a better teacher) "lifts all boats" (in this case, improves the learning outcomes of all children).

To what extent do different teacher characteristics or behaviors affect child learning in kindergarten? Much as is the case in the United States, very inexperienced teachers (teachers with three or fewer years of teaching experience) produce less learning: a child randomly assigned to a "rookie" teacher, defined in this way, learns on average 0.16 standard deviations less than a child assigned to a more experienced teacher. (Above three years, there are no returns to experience in terms of child learning outcomes.) Whether a child is assigned to a tenured teacher or to one who works on a contract basis does not affect her learning gains. Smarter teachers, as measured by the WAIS-IV, produce more learning, but the effects are small.[23] None of the personality traits measured by the Big Five (neuroticism, extraversion, openness, agreeableness, and conscientiousness) is significantly associated with more or less student learning. Similarly, a teacher's score on a test of executive function and various measures of her early environment (such as her parents' education) do not predict student learning. On the other hand, teacher-student interactions, as measured by the CLASS, are strongly predictive of child learning outcomes (Araujo and others 2014).

Lessons for Policy

In most countries in Latin America and the Caribbean, enrollment in the first grades of primary school is essentially universal, and the proportion of children who go to kindergarten (including children from poor households) is rising rapidly. It is not unreasonable to assume that, much as happened with enrollment in primary school, enrollment in kindergarten will no longer be a challenge for most countries in the region in the foreseeable future.

What is a challenge for the region is quality—particularly process quality. There is clear, consistent evidence that the quality of the education many children receive is poor, and does not prepare them well for schooling in later grades or for life generally.

Some problems seem to be common to many countries and most classrooms. Too much time is spent on rote learning, with the teacher talking or writing things on the blackboard and children repeating them or copying them down. Children generally do not work in groups on tasks that stimulate creative thinking or develop higher-order critical faculties. However, in many other respects, teachers—often, teachers in the same school, teaching comparable children—vary tremendously in their effectiveness.

Why are many teachers in Latin America and the Caribbean so much less effective than others? Is it mainly a problem of skills because practical tools that focus on teaching practices are not emphasized in pre-service and in-service training? Or is it mainly a problem of incentives because teachers in the region are generally not rewarded for better performance? These are important questions, as the likely effects of alternative policies depend on the reasons for the low performance of many teachers in the early grades in the region.

If teachers lack skills, professional development may help. Professional development can improve classroom practices and child learning outcomes. However, most professional development programs for teachers in the region are ineffective. They are theoretical rather than hands-on; they do not give teachers practical tools that help them become better teachers; and they are generic, rather than focused on a particular teacher's strengths and weaknesses.

Multiple studies from the United States show that teachers who receive coursework and personalized coaching on effective teaching practices can change their daily interactions with children in ways that have meaningful consequences for student learning and development.[24] The challenge is to find models for countries in the region that are effective, and can be taken to scale. This will require careful design and implementation, and rigorous evaluation, preferably based on random assignment. With very few exceptions, this evidence has been lacking in the region.

It may also be, however, that some teachers do not exert enough effort. Under these circumstances, teacher pay for performance may help. Experimental and quasi-experimental evidence from the United States presents a mixed picture about the effectiveness of teacher pay-for-performance.[25] In developing countries, results have been more positive. Merit pay programs significantly improved learning outcomes in India (Muralidharan and Sundararaman 2011), Israel (Lavy 2002, 2009), and Mexico (Behrman and others 2015), although this evidence is largely about somewhat older children.

A number of countries and cities in the region, including Brazil (with Pernambuco) and Chile (with the Sistema Nacional de Evaluación del Desempeño, SNED), give rewards to teachers or schools (or both) that produce particularly large learning gains. However, in all countries in Latin America and the Caribbean the vast majority of a teacher's pay is determined by the number of years in service, and her contractual status (whether tenured or not).

Economists are generally more enthusiastic about pay for performance than educators. One question is what it is that teachers should be rewarded for. Most pay for performance schemes reward teachers on the basis of calculations of value added. Value added is a measure of the average increase in learning that takes place among plausibly comparable students assigned to different teachers (see the discussion in Box 5.2).

Box 5.2   Teacher Value Added

Estimating a teacher's value added is one way of measuring her effectiveness. Value added focuses on the learning gains among students taught by a teacher in a given grade. For example, to compare the value added of three teachers teaching first grade in different classrooms in the same school, one would estimate the average increase in child development or test scores between the end of kindergarten and the end of first grade, separately for children in each classroom. This is an estimate of the value added of each teacher. To see how much better one teacher is than another, one would also calculate the mean increase for all first graders in that school. The difference between the learning gains of children in one teacher's classroom and the average learning gains across all three first grade teachers in that school would be an estimate of her relative effectiveness.

The estimation of teacher value added has been popular among economists since the pioneering work by Hanushek (1971) and Murnane (1975). In part, this work, and much that followed, was a response to a consensus among researchers that, although there were large differences in the effectiveness of teachers, the observed characteristics of teachers, including their experience, contractual status, and credentials, explained very little of these differences. By focusing directly on child learning outcomes, measures of value added sidestep the focus on teacher characteristics. This is both the strength and the limitation of this measure. If the assumptions that are necessary for estimates of value added to have a causal interpretation hold, then value added focuses directly on what really matters: child development or learning outcomes. But the assumptions may not always hold, and estimates of a teacher's value added are silent about what it is that one teacher does that makes her more effective than another.

The most important assumption in estimating value added is related to the unobserved characteristics of children. Children are not generally assigned to classrooms at random. Headmasters know which teachers are more effective than others. A headmaster who seeks to equalize outcomes within a school might assign the most difficult children to the best teachers. If the information that the headmaster uses to make these assignments is not adequately "controlled for," the true value added of the best teacher would be underestimated (because she received the most difficult students). Conversely, better teachers may have more bargaining power, and a headmaster who would like to retain the best teachers in a school might give those teachers easier children. In this case, the true value added of the best teacher might be overestimated (because she received easier students). Parents—particularly parents who are most aware of and interested in their children's learning—may also exert pressure to have their children in one or another classroom. But these parents are likely to have unobserved characteristics that themselves have an impact on learning gains, regardless of the teacher their children are assigned to. This too would introduce biases.

Because all the relevant characteristics of teachers and students cannot be measured, estimates of value added make one critical assumption: that whatever may be the differences in the children assigned to one or the other teacher, they are captured by the "baseline" measure of learning or development (which, generally, is learning outcomes at the end of the previous grade). Put differently, estimates of value added assume that any difference in learning *gains*, as opposed to learning *levels*, can be attributed to teachers—especially when the comparison is limited to children taught by different teachers within the same school.

A great deal of research has gone into testing this hypothesis. An influential paper by Rothstein (2010) used rich data from North Carolina to show that *future* teachers predict *earlier* learning gains. This is an indication that teachers and children were not matched with each other at random, and that the characteristics of teachers and children that determined the match may bias estimates of value added. More recent work by Chetty, Friedman, and Rockoff (2014), however, argues that estimates of teacher value added are a good indication of that teacher's effect on learning, uncontaminated by possible differences across students. For example, in one set of estimates, the authors focus on teachers who change schools. Headmasters in one school may have different objectives than those in another school, and the student population may vary a great deal between schools. Even so, when a teacher with a positive value added changes schools, the value added in the school she leaves goes down, and the value added in the school she joins goes up, by proportionately the same amount, on average. This suggests that a teacher carries her "value added" with her, and this is largely independent of the school, headmaster, or student body.

Another concern with estimates of value added is that, even if they are causal, these estimates appear to vary a great deal for the same teacher from one year to the next. Part of that variation may be because some teachers are more effective at teaching a particular group of students, and the composition of their classroom varies from one year to the next—even if this is by chance alone. It may also be that teachers have a particularly good or bad year. Finally, measurement error of various sorts will tend to dampen the correlation of estimated value added for a given teacher in different years. Put differently, the same teacher may be equally effective in one year and the next, but measurement error will make it appear as if her effectiveness has changed across years.

Rewarding teachers on the basis of value added is attractive because it focuses on what matters—learning—rather than on what does not matter—observable teacher characteristics. Pay for performance could also have other advantages. In Latin America, teachers do not appear to be underpaid overall, relative to other white-collar occupations (such as office workers). However, the distribution of teacher wages is compressed at the top, relative to that of workers in similar occupations, suggesting that the most effective teachers are getting paid too little to keep them in the profession (Mizala and Ñopo 2012). A steeper salary scale, with pay increases and promotions depending in part on teacher performance, may help to bring more talented people into the teaching profession.[26]

Nevertheless, rewarding teachers on the basis of calculations of value added is not simple. Some concerns are practical. Calculating value added is data intensive. If, for example, teachers in first through third grade are to be rewarded on the basis of value added, it would be necessary to apply tests at the end of kindergarten, first, second, and third grade to all students every year.[27] Moreover, value added is a noisy measure of teacher quality, as can be seen by the fact that estimates of value added for the same teacher can vary considerably from one year to the next (Araujo and others 2014 for Ecuador).

Other concerns are related to possible behavioral responses by teachers to the introduction of high-stakes testing. Pay for performance on the basis of value added could encourage teachers to cheat, teach to the test (rather than emphasizing learning more broadly), or focus on particular groups of students (e.g., those who are just below a given proficiency cutoff). Some of these issues can be mitigated with a careful design of the details of the pay for performance scheme (Neal 2011). Alternatively, it would be possible to reward teachers for classroom behaviors that predict learning, rather than test scores, although this approach also has important limitations.[28]

Estimates of teacher value added could also be used to identify teachers who, year after year, produce very little learning and development among the children in their classrooms. If, after receiving high-quality in-service training, these teachers continue to underperform, serious consideration should be given to dismissal or early retirement.[29] Dismissing teachers is controversial and politically difficult, but the stakes in terms of possible improvements in child learning and subsequent outcomes are very high. Reasonable estimates for Ecuador, which build on calculations for the United States (Hanushek 2009, 2011; Kane and Staiger 2002b), suggest that replacing the lowest-performing 10 percent of kindergarten teachers with average teachers would raise the wages of all affected cohorts by roughly 1.6 percent (see Box 5.3).

Box 5.3   How Much Does Teacher Effectiveness Matter?

Research from the United States estimates that replacing a low-performing teacher (a teacher at the 10th percentile of the quality distribution) with an average teacher would boost the lifetime income of each child in that class by approximately $40,000, which, for a class of 25 children, is equivalent to an increase in total earnings of close to $1 million (Hanushek [2009, 2011] and Kane and Staiger [2002a] provide estimates of comparable magnitude).

Are these results relevant for Latin America and the Caribbean? Estimates like these always involve making a number of assumptions, but some simple calculations suggest that the value of improving the effectiveness of the lowest-performing teachers (or replacing them with other teachers) in the region may also be substantial. Holding years of schooling constant, a 1 standard deviation increase in literacy skills in Chile has been estimated to increase average wages by 15 percent (Hanushek and Zhang 2006). In Ecuador, simulations suggest that replacing the lowest-performing 10 percent of kindergarten teachers with average teachers would increase mean learning outcomes in kindergarten by 0.11 standard deviations (Araujo and others 2014).[30] If the increase in learning carries over from kindergarten to adulthood, and if the estimates from Chile can be used to approximate the labor market returns in Ecuador, then replacing the lowest-performing 10 percent of kindergarten teachers with average teachers would result in an increase in wages of all affected cohorts by roughly 1.6 percent per year. Moreover, if the increase in teacher quality motivates children to stay in school longer, as seems plausible, then there would be an additional benefit because children acquire more schooling.

Improving quality is more difficult than increasing access. There is no one-size-fits-all policy for all countries. Nevertheless, a judicious combination of monetary incentives for outstanding teacher performance; innovative programs of in-service training, coaching, and mentoring; and dismissal for teachers who are persistently low performers holds promise in many settings.

6

More Bang for the Buck: Investing in Early Childhood Development

Spending resources on early childhood may be one of the best investments a government can make. To begin with, the earlier the government invests in a child, the longer the country has to reap the benefits. Moreover, the rate of return to some investments may be lower if made later in life (e.g., it may be hard to achieve gains in IQ after a certain age). Finally, investments in early childhood development generate potential ripple effects on investments made later on; in other words, the returns to investment in human capital are higher if investments were made in the early years. Also, disparities in child development outcomes are present before children enter primary school. Public investment in early childhood can be a powerful equalizing force. Do government spending priorities reflect these opportunities? How can governments in Latin American and Caribbean countries maximize the returns to investments in early childhood development?

Under 5 and Underserved: Government Spending on Early Childhood Development

While more spending does not always go hand-in-hand with better outcomes, public budgets reveal government priorities. Historically, investing in children has been an important goal for governments in the region, but until recently, the focus has not been on early childhood (age 0–5 years).[1]

Public spending on children (age 0–12 years) increases with age (Table 6.1). Countries in the region spend only 0.4 percent of GDP on average on early childhood (age 0–5 years), compared to 1.6 percent of GDP on average on middle childhood (age 6–12 years). In some countries, only 10 percent of the budget for children is allocated to early childhood (ages 0–5). Spending on early childhood services and programs in the region makes up less than 6 percent of total social spending (i.e., spending on education, health, housing, and social protection).

On average, governments in Latin America and the Caribbean spend about $300 per child per year on early childhood, in contrast to $1,000 on middle childhood, but these sums vary widely. The governments of higher-income countries in the region tend to spend more on early childhood than their lower-income counterparts. Yet patterns also vary among countries with similar income levels. Among the richer countries, for example, public spending per child on early childhood ranges from $253 in Peru to $882 in Chile.

Table 6.1 Public Expenditure on Children by Age Group, Early and Middle Childhood

Country	GDP in $ per capita	Expenditure in $ per child		Expenditure as percent of GDP	
		Ages 0–5	Ages 6–12	Ages 0–5	Ages 6–12
Chile	15,732	882	2,608	0.5	1.7
Brazil	11,208	641	2,179	0.5	2.3
Mexico	10,307	488	1,041	0.6	1.4
Colombia	7,826	402	844	0.6	1.6
Peru	6,660	253	464	0.4	0.9
Dominican Republic	5,826	58	451	0.1	1.1
Jamaica	5,290	127	848	0.3	2.1
Guatemala	3,478	83	305	0.4	1.7
Nicaragua	1,851	21	226	0.2	2.0
Average	*7,575*	*328*	*996*	*0.4*	*1.6*

Notes: Data on expenditure and GDP are in current dollars for 2012 except for Colombia, which are for 2011.

Source: Author's elaboration based on Alcázar and Sánchez (2014), World Development Indicators, and ECLAC.

Box 6.1   Gaps in Budget Data

Calculating government expenditures on children on a cross-country basis is a complicated task involving methodological decisions and data limitations. Following Alcázar and Sánchez (2014), this chapter used a three-step procedure to estimate public expenditures in nine Latin American and Caribbean countries between 2004 and 2012. First, public social spending on children from age 0 to 12 years was defined as a composite estimate of expenditures on education (preschool and primary) and social programs, including daycare, parenting programs, conditional cash transfers, and in-kind benefits. Second, expenditure data from budget reports and directly from budget offices and the relevant sectoral ministries were used. Third, the *Government Finance Statistics Manual 2001* served as a guide to select budget classifications and construct estimates of public social spending on children.

The data collection exercise faced several limitations:

- *Public access to budget information.* Peru is the only country of the nine reviewed here that has online access to an integrated financial management system providing disaggregated information that allows for identifying social expenditures benefiting children.
- *Expenditures at the subnational level.* The availability of budget information on social expenditures at subnational levels is limited in some countries, particularly in Mexico.
- *Health expenditures.* Health expenditures are not included in the estimates of public social spending on children due to weaknesses in the quality and availability of budget information on the health sector in most selected countries, except for Chile and Peru.

Tracking the overall level of public expenditures on children is an important task for governments that are concerned about the well-being of children. Peru has made significant progress in the use of public management instruments that facilitate the monitoring of budget execution on children. In 2008, Peru gradually implemented performance-based budgeting (PBB), starting with five pilot strategic programs and involving all levels of government. By 2014, 41 percent of the overall budget was formulated under PBB. Additionally, Peru's integrated financial management system and performance monitoring system of PBB programs, called Resulta, promotes budget transparency and accountability.

Source: Alcázar and Sánchez (2014).

Public spending in Jamaica is twice as high or even more than its regional peers with similar per capita incomes. While income is certainly important, it is not the only driver in the allocation of public spending. For example, Guatemala boasts the largest allocation to early childhood development relative to its overall social spending envelope. Thus, there is room for changing policy priorities and shifting more resources to early childhood.

Public spending on early childhood is not only low relative to investments in middle childhood, but also with respect to spending on all other age ranges, particularly the elderly who receive pensions and other transfers against risks linked to old age. For instance, even though Chile, Guatemala, and Peru have very different population profiles, they share similar patterns in terms of the distribution of spending over the life cycle. These countries all spend between seven and nine times as much on the elderly as on children aged 0–5, measured on a per capita basis (Figure 6.1).[2]

The composition of public spending on early childhood also varies in the region (see Table 6.2). Expenditure on early childhood development comprises preschool and various social programs. The top three social programs that reach children during the early years are preschool, daycare, and conditional cash transfer (CCT) programs. In general, preschool spending is highest, at almost 0.2 percent of

Figure 6.1   Per Capita Public Spending by Age Group and Age Composition

a. Chile

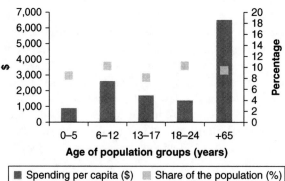

b. Guatemala

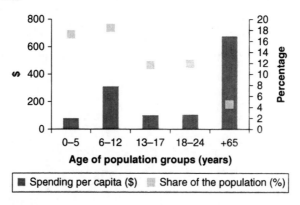

c. Peru

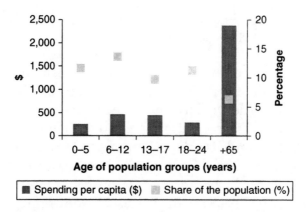

Source: Authors' calculations based on Alcázar and Sánchez (2014) and ECLAC.

GDP in the region, while daycare spending amounts to less than 0.1 percent of GDP. Parenting programs receive the smallest allocation of the overall budgets.[3]

Some countries spend more on preschool than daycare, including Guatemala, Mexico, and Peru. Other countries allocate more public resources to daycare than preschool, such as Chile and Colombia. Public daycare programs are not offered in Jamaica, but there is almost universal coverage of preschool education. Conditional cash transfers and school feeding programs for early childhood are offered in all countries included in the table (except for CCT, in Nicaragua). Budgets for both programs vary across countries, but levels are below 0.1 percent of GDP.

Table 6.2   Public Expenditure on Early Childhood by Program (% of GDP)

	Parenting (0–5 years)	Daycare (0–5 years)	Preschool (3–5 years)	School feeding (4–5 years)	CCT (0–5 years)
Chile	0.00	0.25	0.10	0.06	0.05
Colombia	0.06	0.19	0.20	0.03	0.07
Dominican Republic	n.d.	0.03	0.02	0.01	0.05
Guatemala	0.00	0.02	0.29	0.02	0.09
Jamaica	n.d.	n.d.	0.21	0.03	0.01
Mexico	0.00	0.02	0.40	n.a.	0.06
Nicaragua	0.03	0.06	0.03	0.04	n.d.
Peru	0.02	0.02	0.26	0.06	0.05
Average	*0.02*	*0.08*	*0.19*	*0.04*	*0.05*

Notes: n.d. = no data; n.a. = not applicable. Data are for 2012, except for Colombia, which are for 2011. The ages for the target children's groups are presented within parentheses in column titles.

Source: Author's elaboration based on Alcázar and Sánchez (2014).

Finally, it is important to place Latin American and Caribbean regional early childhood public expenditure in a broader comparative perspective. The Organisation for Economic Co-operation and Development (OECD) presents several early childhood development indicators in its Family Database. Based on two specific components of spending—the share of pre-primary and daycare spending in GDP—Latin America and the Caribbean spends less than half the OECD average (0.7 percent). In contrast to Nordic countries, where early childhood investments exceed 1 percent of GDP and daycare services account for more than half the total, the share of daycare spending in general is much lower in the region, although exceptions like Chile, Colombia, and Nicaragua stand out (Figure 6.2).

Public Spending Trends: On the Way Up

Even though early childhood public spending remains low in relative terms, investments have increased significantly over the past decade across the region. For example, Chile, the Dominican Republic, and Guatemala spent between two and four times as much in 2012 as at the beginning of the 2000s on a per child basis. Preschool spending and conditional cash transfer programs have expanded in most countries, accompanied to a lesser extent by daycare and parenting programs.

Figure 6.2 Public Expenditure on Daycare and Pre-primary (Percent of GDP)

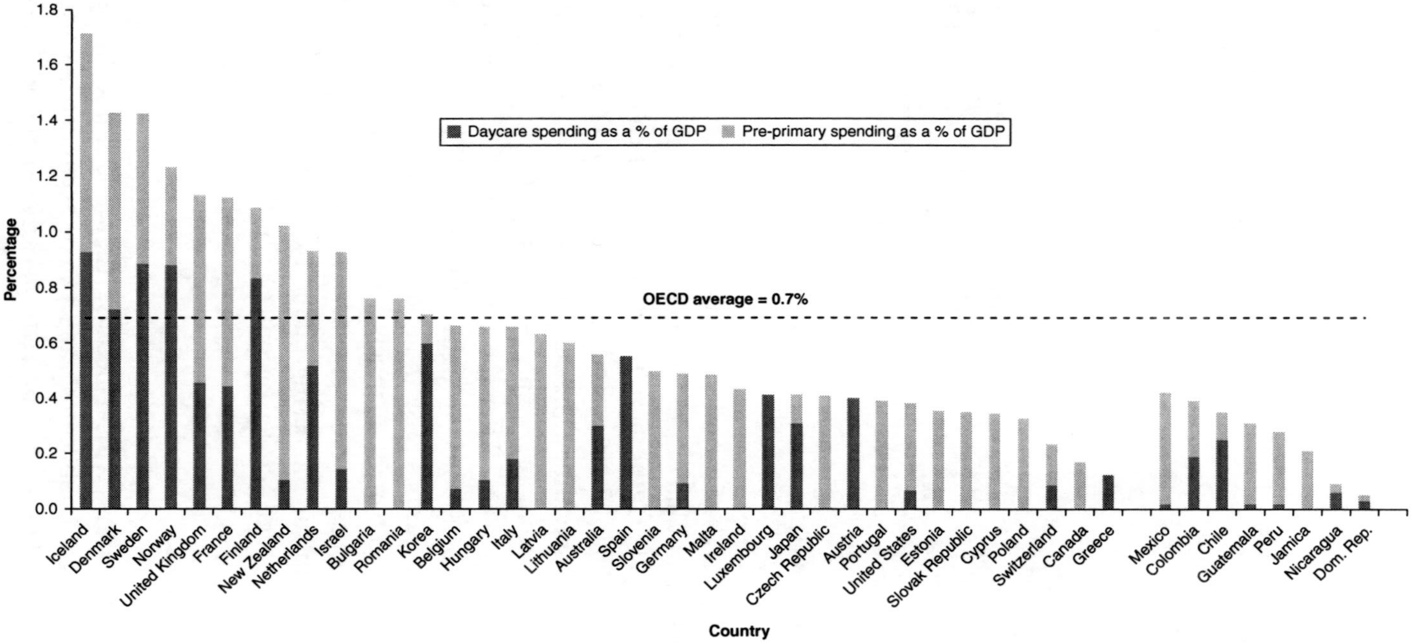

■ Daycare spending as a % of GDP   ▨ Pre-primary spending as a % of GDP

OECD average = 0.7%

Source: Authors' calculations based on Alcázar and Sánchez (2014) and OECD.

Figure 6.3   Per Child Early Childhood Spending, 2004–12 (Annual Percentage Growth)

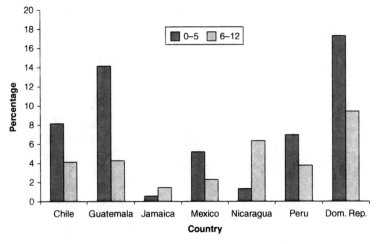

Source: Authors' calculations based on Alcázar and Sánchez (2014) and ECLAC.

On a regional basis, total early childhood public spending per capita grew at an annual rate of 7 percent per year in real terms between 2004 and 2012 (Figure 6.3). In particular, expenditures expanded during the 2008–09 crisis, and in general grew at faster rates than overall social spending. The case of Nicaragua is illustrative: early childhood spending grew 5 percent during 2009 while the economy contracted 2 percent. After the crisis, the growth rate of expenditures slowed in response to tighter fiscal conditions in most countries. These dynamics raise the question of whether small children will continue to benefit as much from public budget allocations as they did in the past decade. They also put the spotlight on efficiency issues: if room for increasing public expenditure levels is severely constrained, spending well becomes a policy priority.

Program Costs

Program costs are critical because they determine the extent to which coverage of public programs can be expanded as governments in the region increase their budgets on early childhood development.

Program costs are also important to determine the overall resource costs that, together with benefits, determine which types of programs are expected to have the greatest return to investment.

Following the areas analyzed in the book, three major programs are considered. The first is home visits. In this program, trained staff visit mothers of young children in their homes to demonstrate enriching activities through play sessions that include homemade toys, songs, and games. The second program is full-time daycare, which presumably provides children with safe and healthy environments and parents with the freedom to pursue other productive activities. Finally, children attending preschools participate in part-time educational activities to enhance their development and improve school readiness. Table 6.3 summarizes the goals and services of these three types of programs.

The analysis considers two main questions. First, what are the costs related to improving program quality? Second, what are the costs associated with providing home visits daycare and preschool services at different levels of quality? Answering these questions can inform policy decisions on how to improve the quality of existing programs and the options to improve program quality when expanding access to services. To explore the robustness of the results across different Latin American and Caribbean contexts, program costs are derived for three very different countries: Chile, Colombia, and Guatemala.

To simulate costs for different programs, levels of quality, and countries, a model was developed that approximates the annual per child costs for each initiative based on quality parameters (such as educational attainment of caregivers, and the ratio of children to provider) and local wages and prices. Critical parameter values

Table 6.3   Major Early Childhood Programs

	Home visits	Daycare	Preschool
Goal	Improve parenting practices	Child care and development	Child development
Services provided	Demonstrations at the homes with parent and child	Full-time child care	Part-time educational activities

Source: Author's elaboration.

were defined to approximate costs to those of prototype basic- and enhanced-quality programs that already exist in the region.

The model incorporates two distinct dimensions of program quality that were discussed in Chapters 4 and 5. First, structural quality refers to the type of resources that tend to remain stable across time, such as physical facilities, average schooling attainment of caregivers, and the ratio of children per adult. Second, process quality refers to the frequency and nature of interactions between caregivers and children, among children, and between caregivers and families, all of which in principle can be changed relatively quickly.

The model estimates costs for three groups of inputs: human resources; infrastructure; and nutrition, equipment, and materials. Investments in these inputs can be expected to directly improve measures of structural quality. This upgrading process may entail decreasing child-adult ratios, raising the required educational attainment of teachers, increasing the size of physical infrastructure, and improving the nutritional services provided. Chapter 4, for example, described the case of a quality-upgrading experience in Colombia where some children who were previously attending home-based daycare (largely in the homes of community mothers) were transferred to formal daycare centers. In this instance, large investments in structural inputs, such as buildings and sanitation, were made (Bernal and others 2014b).

The model also estimates costs for a fourth input: expenses in specific training and supervision. Investments in this category of inputs focus directly on improving process quality measures by promoting better interaction between caregivers and children. An example of this type of initiative is a program that provided three-day training and a structured curriculum to community health workers in Pakistan to develop stimulating activities for parents of young children to use at their homes (Yousafzai and others 2014). Coaching programs that involve an initial training followed by observation sessions and feedback to caregivers can be effective in improving child-provider interactions. A review of the US literature documented that in 14 out of 16 evaluations, coaching programs generated improvements in the quality of teacher-child interactions (Aikens and Akers 2011). Box 6.2 presents the values assumed for key structural and process quality parameters in the costing model.

Box 6.2   Cost Parameters

A three-step process was used to approximate model parameters across programs and quality levels. First, studies on the characteristics and costs associated with early childhood programs were reviewed (e.g., Bernal 2013; Faverio, Rivera, and Cortázar 2013). Second, data on the variation of quality parameters across early childhood programs in Latin America and the Caribbean surveyed by Araujo, López Boo, and Puyana (2013), such as children per caregiver ratio, were used to approximate the characteristics of basic- and enhanced-quality programs in the region. Third, early childhood experts were consulted for final decisions. The values assumed for key parameters are presented in Table B6.1.

Table B6.1   Cost Parameters for Early Childhood Programs Analyzed

	Home visits		Day care		Preschool	
	Basic	Enhanced	Basic	Enhanced	Basic	Enhanced
Panel a. Structural quality						
Human resources						
Children per caregiver	40	15	12	12	18	12
Caregivers' years of education	9	11	9	16	14	16
Payment relative to market compensation (%)	100	110	50	110	100	110
Infrastructure						
Dedicated classroom space (m²)	N	N	N	2	1.5	2
Nutrition						
Morning snack	N	N	Y	Y	Y	Y
Lunch, afternoon snack	N	N	Y	Y	N	N
Panel b. Process quality						
Training and supervision						
Initial training (weeks)	2	4	2	4	2	4
Caregivers per supervisor	20	10	20	10	20	10

Notes: N = no; Y = yes. Payment relative to market compensation corresponds to the ratio between wages paid to providers and the average market wage for individuals with the same educational attainment.
Source: Author's elaboration.

The basic-quality home visits program involved a monthly home visit complemented with two group visits at community centers. The enhanced-quality option involved weekly home visits. Basic-quality daycare involved a home-based model, while a center-based model was assumed for the enhanced-quality option. Finally, both the basic- and enhanced-quality options for preschool involved the provision of educational services in centers.

Letting Numbers Speak for Themselves

Table 6.4 presents costs per child of four programs—each with four combinations of basic and enhanced structural and process quality— for Chile, Colombia, and Guatemala. Comparisons of the different options suggest several important points about program costs that can better inform choices among early childhood policy options.

Take, for example, the case of preschools. Higher structural quality preschools have fewer children per teacher and more classroom space per child; teachers have more schooling and higher compensation,

Table 6.4 Estimated Annual Program Costs per Child in Alternative Programs ($ pear Child)

Process quality Structural quality	Basic Basic	Enhanced Basic	Basic Enhanced	Enhanced Enhanced
a. Chile				
Home visits	242	276	738	871
Daycare	681	758	2610	2717
Preschool	977	1028	1723	1815
b. Colombia				
Home visits	187	213	595	714
Daycare	575	642	2260	2354
Preschool	817	861	1492	1572
c. Guatemala				
Home visits	116	136	442	515
Daycare	409	450	1597	1654
Preschool	630	658	1055	1103

Source: Author's calculations.

given their years of education. A higher process quality preschool involves more training and more intensive supervision. Differences in costs across quality levels can be analyzed by comparing figures across columns. In Colombia, for example, program costs for the enhanced structural quality option are about 80 percent greater than for the basic structural quality option. In contrast, program costs for the enhanced process quality option are only about 5 percent greater than the basic process quality option.

The results in Table 6.4 are robust across countries and programs: moving from the basic to the enhanced quality option requires substantially larger investments for the inputs related to structural quality (e.g., infrastructure) compared to those related to process quality (e.g., training). The case of daycare is clear: the enhanced structural quality option costs about 300 percent more than the basic structural quality option, whereas enhancing process quality requires only about a 10 percent cost increase. Improving structural quality for home visits requires a cost increase of more than 200 percent, compared with a 15 percent increase for process quality improvement.

Comparisons across programs indicate that home visits are the least expensive option, basically because there are no infrastructure or nutritional costs. For the basic structural quality programs, daycare is less expensive than preschool. Though preschools provide services to children for only 4.5 hours compared to 8 hours in daycare programs, the latter are less expensive because they are home-based (hence, they entail lower infrastructure costs) and providers have lower educational attainment, and thus lower compensation. For the enhanced structural quality option, daycare is more costly compared to preschool because the daycare centers have similar quality parameters in a range of dimensions (such as teachers with 16 years of schooling), but provide care for longer hours.

Finally, comparisons across panels reveal that costs for Chile are about 20 percent higher than for Colombia, whereas costs in Guatemala are about 30 percent lower. These cost differences basically reflect varying wage and price levels, but are less than the differences in per capita income across countries. Thus, the program costs relative to per capita income are highest in Guatemala and lowest in Chile.

Which Early Childhood Programs Should Be Expanded?

Early childhood programs differ in costs and government resources are limited. Therefore, governments should implement those programs that allow them to reap greater benefits given costs. This reasoning lends itself to the use of cost-benefit analysis. Akin to investment decisions made in the private sector, governments should invest in those programs with the highest returns.

To apply this methodology the benefits and costs of programs must be monetized. This is not a trivial task as it requires assigning a price for every resource used and monetizing all present and future costs and benefits. The advantage of making some of these (sometimes heroic) assumptions is that this methodology produces a clear ranking of projects. The shortcoming is that the ranking is sensitive to omitting costs or benefits, or valuing them incorrectly.

Of course, efficiency is not the only metric by which governments may want to allocate resources to programs. In fact, redistribution is a key policy concern for government policy, and the crowding-out effect of private expenditure as a consequence of public policy is a key concern in this area. This section provides an illustrative analysis of the potential benefit-cost ratios for home visits, daycare, and preschool programs for children in Chile, Colombia, and Guatemala.

Benefits

There are two main potential benefits of early childhood programs. First, they can enhance the development of children and generate increases in lifetime productivity. These programs enhance productivity primarily by developing child cognitive and other skills—which in turn augment academic achievement and schooling attainment in later childhood and adolescence—which leads to increases in productivity and income in adulthood (Table 6.5). Second, certain programs provide custodial care for parents. In other words, parents can leave their children someplace where they will be safe and healthy for a certain number of hours while parents spend their time in other activities. This service benefits families by reducing expenses and saving time. These services are especially

Table 6.5   Impact of Better Early Childhood Development through Subsequent Lifecycle Stages

Stage	Key outcomes
Preschool	Cognitive skills Socioemotional skills
Childhood	Cognitive skills Socioemotional skills Academic achievement Schooling attainment
Adolescence	Cognitive skills Socioemotional skills Academic achievement Schooling attainment
Adulthood	Income Productivity

Source: Author's elaboration.

relevant for daycare programs that typically provide full-time care and, hence, facilitate mothers' participation in the labor market. To a lesser extent, they are also relevant for preschools that typically provide only part-time care.

Access to early childhood programs can have other long-term benefits for children as they influence their decisions as an adult to engage in crime, civic duty, and family formation. These benefits to society are difficult to quantify but are nonetheless important. For example, the cost-benefit analysis of a high-quality preschool intervention in the United States computed a present discounted benefit for society in terms of reduced criminal activities of about $6 for each dollar spent in the program (Belfield and others 2006). Given the lack of data necessary to monetize these benefits in the case of Latin America and the Caribbean countries, we do not include them in the quantitative analysis. Hence, the benefit-cost ratios of the analyzed programs may be even larger than the ratios presented here.

Notice that adult productivity gains due to early childhood programs are likely to occur in both market and nonmarket activities. The empirical challenges in estimating the monetary value of gains in nonmarket productivities are substantial and virtually unsurmountable. Therefore, the estimates in this chapter assume that changes in adult productivity due to early childhood programs are the same in market and nonmarket activities. Ideally, estimates of the productivity impacts of early childhood programs would be made by following children in Latin America and the Caribbean with different exposures to programs when they are 0–5 years of age through their adult lives, decades later. Data do not exist to estimate the direct impact of such programs on adult productivity for most Latin American and Caribbean early childhood programs. Instead, the estimates in this chapter are based on the links in the sequence of lifecycle stages in Table 6.5, and the assumption that adult labor market earnings reflect adult productivity.

The first link pertains to the impact of early childhood programs on cognitive skills. Tables 6.6 and 6.7 summarize the limited systematic evidence on this link from Latin America and the Caribbean for home visits (Table 6.6) and daycare and preschool (Table 6.7).[4] Effects on child cognitive skills are expressed in standard deviations.[5]

Evaluations of home visits account for the majority of the studies in Tables 6.6 and 6.7. Most of these home visit evaluations, however, are for small-scale experiments carried out in Jamaica, which makes it difficult to generalize these results to large-scale programs and other contexts. The average impact of home visits on children's cognitive skills is 0.63 of a standard deviation in cognitive skills, with a range from 0.19 to 1.26. These are large impacts and indicate considerable promise for such programs. However, these estimates raise at least two questions. First, why is the variation so great for Jamaica? Probably, program quality varies substantially even within similar contexts in a country with a relatively small population. Second, would these estimates largely from small experiments and primarily from one country hold up if the programs were scaled up in other countries? The answer would appear to be yes, based on three estimates for studies beyond Jamaica, including two on a larger scale. All three estimates are relatively close to the average (0.19 for Colombia, 0.55 for Ecuador, and 0.72 for Brazil).

As discussed in Chapters 4 and 5, evidence on the impact of daycare and preschool programs in Latin America and the Caribbean is very limited. The estimates for Bolivian and Colombian daycare

Table 6.6   Impact of Home Visits on Cognitive Skills

Evaluation	Total visits	Duration (months)	Visits per month	Country	N	Cognitive skills effects (SD)
Grantham-McGregor, Schofield, and Harris (1983)	129	36	3.6	Jamaica	39	1.26
Powell and Grantham-McGregor (1989)— Visits weekly	103	24	4.3	Jamaica	58	1.15
Grantham-McGregor and others (1991)	103	24	4.3	Jamaica	123	0.86
Rosero and Oosterbeek (2011)	90	21	4.3	Ecuador	1,473	0.55
Attanasio and others (2014)	77	18	4.3	Colombia	1,263	0.19
Powell and Grantham-McGregor (1989)— Visits biweekly	52	24	2.2	Jamaica	94	0.34
Powell and Grantham-McGregor (1989)— Visits monthly	24	24	1.0	Jamaica	90	0.20
Eickmann and others (2003)	10	5	2.0	Brazil	156	0.72
Gardner and others (2003)	9	2	4.3	Jamaica	140	0.38
Average	*66*	*20*	*3.4*	—	*382*	*0.63*

Notes: N = number of observations. Cognitive skills effects are presented in standard deviations (SD).
Source: Author's elaboration.

programs indicate a positive impact of about 0.20 standard deviation in cognitive skills scores, but the estimates for Ecuador are about the same magnitude and opposite in sign. The estimate for Ecuador does not seem to be the result of any design flaws in the study or other potential problems with the methodology. Overall, on average, these three Latin American and Caribbean daycare programs have an impact of 0.06 standard deviations on cognitive skills. For preschool, only one study has presented solid evidence on the impact on children's cognitive skills. In this case, attending preschool in

Table 6.7   Impact of Daycare and Preschool on Cognitive Skills and Academic Achievement

Evaluation	Children per provider	Country	N	Effect size (SD)
a. Effects of full-time daycare on child cognitive skills				
Behrman, Cheng, and Todd (2004)	5	Bolivia	1,489	0.19
Bernal and others (2009)	12	Colombia	1,263	0.20
Rosero and Oosterbeek (2011)	9	Ecuador	769	−0.21
Average	*9*	*n.a.*	*1,174*	*0.06*
b. Effects of part-time preschool on academic achievement				
Berlinski, Galiani, and Gertler (2009)	n.d.	Argentina	121,811	0.24
Average	*n.d.*	*n.a.*	*121,811*	*0.24*

Notes: n.d. = no data; n.a. = not applicable; N = number of observations. Effects are presented in standard deviations (SD) and were measured at the end of exposure for daycare programs (ages 3–5) and in third grade for preschool (age 8).

Source: Author's elaboration.

Argentina had a positive impact of 0.24 standard deviations on third grade academic achievement.

Home visits and daycare programs vary dramatically in their effects on child cognitive skills.[6] Figure 6.4 ranks the evaluations in this regard. The figure highlights the stark differences in impact between the two types of programs. While the home visit interventions produced effects between 0.2 and 1.2 standard deviations, the effects for daycare programs range between −0.2 and 0.2. The home visit programs produced average effects on cognitive skills about 10 times larger than daycare programs (0.63 versus 0.06).

In considering these values, it is important to keep two things in mind. First, these numbers only reflect the benefits of the programs that were evaluated, and not the universe of programs. For example, daycare of higher quality would likely result in greater impacts on child development and parenting programs of lower quality would result in lesser impacts.

Second, the evaluations of daycare and preschool programs measure the effects on child development when children attend these programs instead of receiving the care arranged by their parents in the absence of government intervention. The care in the absence of

Figure 6.4   Effects on Cognitive Skills of Home Visits versus Daycare Programs

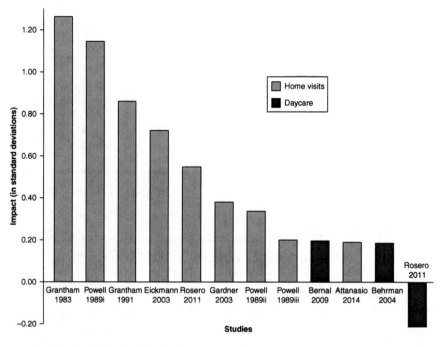

Notes: Powell i refers to the weekly program. Powell ii refers to the biweekly program. Powell iii refers to the monthly program.

Source: Author's calculations.

government intervention could include a nonpaid caregiver such as the mother, the grandmother, or any other relative. Alternatively, such care could include a paid caregiver such as a babysitter or a private daycare. That is, these evaluations do not measure the effect of attending daycare per se against a specific alternative such as mother care. Instead, the evaluations document how child development would be affected by attending publicly funded daycare instead of the childcare arrangement that otherwise would be used.

The next step in estimating adult productivity benefits is to link the impact of various Latin American and Caribbean early childhood programs on childhood cognitive skills to outcomes such as schooling achievement and attainment, and adult earnings, assumed to be related to productivity (see Table 6.8). There are few

Table 6.8   Impact of Three Early Childhood Experimental Evaluations
That Followed Children into Early Adulthood

	Perry Preschool Project	Carolina Abecedarian	Jamaica stimulation study	Average
Cognitive skills	0.89	0.93	0.86	0.89
Achievement	0.33	n.d.	n.d.	0.33
Grades of schooling attainment	0.90	1.15	0.61	0.89
Earnings (% change)	0.28	0.61	n.d.	0.45
Employment (% change)	0.20	0.42	0.18	0.27
Earnings for those employed (% change)	0.06	0.14	0.30	0.17

Note: n.d. = no data.

Source: Author's elaboration.

studies that permit direct estimates of such linkages, and only one
for Latin America and the Caribbean. Table 6.8 summarizes some
longer-term linkages at least into young adulthood drawing from
a Jamaican study on home visits and two studies from the United
States. The Jamaican program provided psychosocial stimulation
to growth-stunted children living in poverty. The two studies from
the United States were the Perry Preschool Study and the Carolina
Abecedarian program. In the former, low-socioeconomic-status
children attended a preschool and their families received a weekly
home visit. The Carolina Abecedarian program was a more intensive program, providing eight-hour care for children from birth to
age 5, a stimulating curriculum, and nutritional and health services.
All these programs positively impacted a number of important
dimensions of child development; in some cases, these persisted over
a number of years as the children aged.

Beyond the potential effects of early childhood programs on children's human capital development, daycare (and to a lesser extent
preschool programs) also provides custodial care to families. Ideally,
these benefits would be monetized using information on how much
families value this service, that is, how much families are willing to
pay for custodial care. However, plausible estimates of families' willingness to pay for this service are typically unavailable for the countries considered. Still, it is important to factor this service into the

cost-benefit calculation to ensure a fair comparison across early child-hood programs. Based on conceptual considerations, it was assumed that families' valuation of the custodial care benefit was 75 percent of the cost of the service provided for preschool and daycare.[7] The ranking of the three analyzed programs in terms of their benefit-cost ratios is robust to choosing alternative plausible valuations.

Of course, the benefits to society of providing childcare might not be circumscribed to the individual willingness to pay for the service. For example, daycare programs that facilitate an increase in female labor supply could have a strong public policy rationale for several reasons. First, they can be seen as an instrument to pro-mote female labor force participation (which is low in many Latin American and Caribbean countries; see Box 6.3) and gender equal-ity. Second, womens' decisions to enter the labor force could be distorted if their wages do not reflect their market productivity. In fact, the evidence suggests that this may be the case as wage gaps across genders in the region remain unexplained even after controlling for numerous characteristics (Atal, Ñopo, and Winder 2009). Third, increases in female labor supply could generate other difficult-to-quantify benefits, including reductions in family vio-lence, spending changes due to differences in consumption prefer-ences across genders, and an overall boost in women's self-esteem and social standing in society.

Box 6.3   Women in the Labor Market

The decision to participate in the labor market is affected by family characteristics. Particularly among women, the presence of children and related childcare activities are a major determinant of labor supply. The issue has long been well understood by scholars and policymakers who have argued that childcare-related policies could be a useful tool to increase the participation of women in the labor market. While the focus of this book is on child well-being, it is useful to see if some of the policies considered have at least the potential to impact female labor supply in the labor market. Data from 18 household surveys in Latin America and the Caribbean provide the basis for some descriptive evidence. The focus is on 25- to 55-year-old women with at least one child 0–5 years of age.

Figure B6.1   Labor Force Participation: Latin America and All Available Countries (1992–2012)

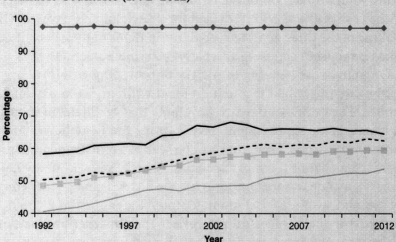

Source: Household and labor surveys collected by national statistical offices.

Figure B6.1 presents the participation rate of men and women over time.[8] Three main results are immediately evident:

1. While the male participation rate has been very stable, female participation of prime age women with young children has been increasing over time.
2. This increase over time of female participation has been leveling off since the early 2000s.
3. The current gender differential in participation is significant in all countries in the region, ranging between 30 and 50 percentage points.

Figure B6.2 presents the participation rate of women with young children according to three education categories. Two main results emerge:

1. Participation rates are increasing for women in all schooling levels for all countries in the region.
2. In all countries where there is a clear time trend, the trend is common to all three education categories.

Figure B6.2 Female Labor Force Participation by Education Category, Average for Latin America (1992–2012)

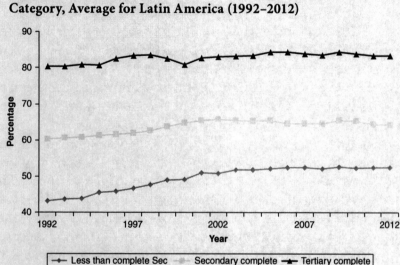

Note: Sample = prime-age individuals with children 0–5 years old.

Source: Household and labor surveys collected by national statistical offices.

In sum, there is substantial room to increase female labor participation since women's participation is between 30 and 50 percentage points lower than men's. This is particularly true for women with lower levels of education.

Costs

The resource costs of an early childhood program are not equivalent to the program costs that directly affect governmental budgets for several reasons. To start with, if these programs cause children to attend additional grades of schooling, as suggested in Table 6.8, then there are public outlays for this schooling. Moreover, if children stay longer in schools, we could expect reduced earnings due to a delay in their entrance to the labor market. Finally, if governments must raise revenue to finance early childhood programs, then raising revenue causes distortions that entail real costs. The resource cost estimates incorporate all these elements.

Benefit-Cost Ratios

The benefit-cost ratios are simply the ratio of the benefits to the resource costs, all in present discounted terms. If the benefits exceed the costs, this ratio exceeds 1 and the program therefore merits serious consideration. Table 6.9 presents benefit-cost ratios for home visits, daycare, and preschool for Chile, Colombia, and Guatemala. These estimates use a 3 percent discount rate, as is common for many social sector programs.

The patterns in these estimated benefit-cost ratios are similar across the three different countries. This suggests they may also hold for other countries in Latin America and the Caribbean. The highest benefit-cost ratios are for preschool, with benefits about four times the resource costs. The second highest benefit-cost ratios are for home visits, with benefits about three times the resource costs. These two types of early childhood programs look promising, with benefits expected to significantly exceed costs. In contrast, the benefit-cost ratios for daycare are much lower, around 1. For the latter, however, benefits do not account for any market imperfections that could generate low demand or supply of daycare services that public subsidies could help tackle.

These estimated benefit-cost ratios for home visits and daycare are based on the average effects of the multiple studies in Tables 6.5 and 6.6 (but there is only one study in Table 6.6 for preschool). The estimates may be sensitive to the impact of one particular and possibly idiosyncratic study. For home visits, this is not the case. The benefit-cost ratios change slightly if any of the underlying studies are dropped. For daycare, however, the benefit-cost ratios are sensitive to which studies are included. They increase to over 2 if the

Table 6.9   Benefit-Cost Ratios for Home Visits, Daycare, and Preschool with a Discount Rate of 3%

	Home visits	Daycare	Preschool
Chile	3.5	1.5	4.3
Colombia	2.6	1.1	3.4
Guatemala	3.6	1.2	5.1

Source: Author's calculations.

Ecuadorian study is dropped. But they drop to 0.5 if the Ecuadorian study is included and one of the other studies is dropped. The implication is that the estimated benefit-cost ratios may be sensitive to the context considered.

Three important caveats should be noted. First, most of the evaluations that were used to estimate the effect of programs on child cognitive skills or academic achievement refer to interventions that targeted poor populations. Similarly, the three long-term studies that were used to predict the effect of increases in early childhood development on productivity and wages focused on low-socioeconomic populations. Hence, this analysis provides strong support for expanding services focused on poor populations. It is not clear, however, whether the predicted benefits would materialize if programs do not actively target services to such populations.

Second, the benefit-cost ratios in Table 6.9 are informative of expected effects of programs similar to those reviewed here. For example, the typical home visit programs provided weekly home visits to participant families and had a strong training and supervision component. Consequently, home visit programs that share these features can be considered highly promising. But less intense programs (in terms of frequency of visits or overall quality) may not generate the documented high benefit-cost ratios.

Third, the number of available evaluations is small, and many do not refer to at-scale programs. It is, therefore, important to be cautious in generalizing from these results. Ideally, a government would gradually build up the knowledge base on the impacts of parenting, daycare, and preschool programs, and use these estimates to revise the cost-benefit calculations mentioned earlier, and make decisions about the allocation of resources.

Public Intervention without Stepping on Private Toes

Beyond the rationale for governmental intervention in early childhood development, it is also important to consider whether public expansion of a service can displace (crowd out) private supply. In an extreme case of complete crowding out, the opening of a public preschool of a certain size induces the closure of a private facility with similar enrollment and hence the number of children receiving the services remains constant. In this case—assuming that resource costs and qualities are constant across the private and public preschools—no increases in future productivity are expected because the type of services received by children does not change. Thus, the governmental intervention simply transfers resources from taxpayers to families with children enrolled in the public facility.

To produce actual increases in service coverage, it is necessary to limit the extent to which expanding public services crowd out private service providers. The evidence from studies of preschool expansions in Argentina and Brazil suggests little crowding out in these contexts (Berlinski, Galiani, and Gertler 2009; Bastos and Straume 2013). On the other hand, crowding out can be substantial with other services, in particular daycare (Paes de Barros and others [2011] present evidence for Brazil). Policymakers can employ different strategies to reduce crowding-out effects. To start with, the government can target expansions geographically to areas with low penetration of private providers. For example, typically high-quality private suppliers have a limited presence in less populated areas; hence the risk of displacing private supply with public supply is lower. More generally, crowding out will be lower in areas with fewer private suppliers compared to areas where they are more common.

Moreover, just because the use of governmental resources to support early childhood investments may be warranted does not mean that governments should necessarily operate early childhood services. Instead, governments can provide subsidies directly to suppliers or indirectly to consumers regardless of the ownership—public or private—of the service provider. In fact, the evaluation by Rosero and Oosterbeek (2011) described earlier analyzes the effects on child development of attending daycares run by NGOs and funded by the government in Ecuador. Similarly, the government of Mexico runs a large-scale program that provides funding to private daycares attended by young children (Estancias Infantiles) to support working mothers.

Furthermore, the government can introduce eligibility requirements to give priority to consumers with low underlying demand for private services. This mainly would entail implementing means-tested requirements for program beneficiaries. Finally, the government can actively promote the expansion of early childhood services to low-income households (with low expected demand for private services). This would involve spending resources on community outreach activities and requiring existing conditional cash transfer programs to target enrollment in services in low-income groups.

How important are crowding-out aspects for the three major early childhood programs analyzed? They are particularly relevant for the provision of daycare services. Families in which both parents work full time, have high earnings, and do not have support from family members will demand daycare services even in the absence of public provision. Hence, the free public provision of the service will induce them to switch from private to public providers (especially if the public services offered are similar in quality to those provided by private suppliers). In the case of preschool, most enrollment is currently public or private but publicly subsidized (like in Chile), and providing high-quality free public services may produce small crowding-out effects. Finally, since private and public use of home visits is low, crowding-out effects are expected to be minimal when expanding home visit programs.

The Price Tag

Armed with an analysis to guide policy decisions on expanding early childhood services and assuring service quality, the question becomes, how much will potential expansions cost? This issue is particularly important given expected constraints in public budgets for Latin American and Caribbean countries in the coming years (Powell 2014). The answer depends on a country's population in the target age ranges, rural/urban composition (because of higher expected costs in rural areas), type of programs and their quality, and the program costs per child. To illustrate, consider two possible scenarios (Table 6.10).

Expansion option A: Expand coverage of home visits (1- to 2-year-olds) and preschool programs (3- to 5-year-olds) with enhanced

Table 6.10   Expansion Options: Simulated Additional Program Costs (Percentage of GDP)

Program types	Chile		Colombia		Guatemala	
	A	B	A	B	A	B
Home visits	0.01	0.02	0.01	0.03	0.02	0.08
Daycare	0.00	0.15	0.00	0.31	0.00	0.79
Preschool	0.03	0.05	0.06	0.11	0.16	0.27
Total	*0.03*	*0.21*	*0.07*	*0.45*	*0.18*	*1.14*

Source: Author's calculations.

process quality and basic structural quality by 10 percentage points. This scenario requires additional program costs as a share of GDP ranging from 0.03 percent in Chile to 0.07 percent in Colombia to 0.18 percent in Guatemala.

Expansion option B: Expand coverage for home visits, daycare, and preschool with enhanced structural and process quality by 10 percentage points. This scenario requires a fiscal effort that is about six–seven times higher than option A.

These simulations illustrate some important points. First, because of differences in program costs, the composition of programs matters a lot. Implementing programs of enhanced structural quality increases costs substantially. The additional governmental budgetary commitments are much more feasible when focused on home visits and preschool and low investment in structural quality. Expanding home visits and preschool programs significantly while ensuring adequate investments in process quality will not demand large fiscal outlays.

Second, even though the costs per program beneficiary are lower for countries like Guatemala, the program costs for a given expansion are higher as a proportion of GDP because the percentage of the population in the targeted age ranges and in rural areas is higher, and program costs per beneficiary relative to per capita income are also higher. Moreover, if poverty is taken as a measure for targeting, implementing these programs in the poorest countries is far more onerous. Taking a poverty rate of $2.5 a day, 3 percent of children in Chile are poor while 58 percent of those in Guatemala are poor. Therefore, expanding home-visits of enhanced-structural quality for the poor in Chile will cost 0.0015 percent of GDP in Chile but 0.12 percent of GDP in Guatemala. Hence, different countries should be expected to choose distinct quality and coverage options based on their economic and budgetary restrictions.

The Bottom Line

Latin American and Caribbean countries face two major policy challenges. First, average per capita productivity has inched up slowly in the past five decades (Powell 2014). Second, inequality levels in the region, though recently falling, are still among the highest in the world (World Bank 2013). Hence, policy options that can tackle both challenges should receive considerable public attention. Investing in early childhood development is one of these options. Early childhood programs tend to produce high returns given their costs, and can be targeted at underserved populations to boost not only productivity but also equity. However, simply increasing investments is not enough. The expected returns of greater investments will depend largely on the characteristics of the programs expanded. Hence, policymakers should carefully weigh early childhood policy options to maximize the returns on the expected investments.

This chapter reviews critically the existing evidence on benefits and costs of options to provide some quantitative guidance for policy decisions. In terms of program expansion, the analysis suggests that preschool and home visits generate larger returns per dollar spent than daycare. The sizeable expansion of preschool services that countries have undertaken in recent decades can be expected to help build human capital in the future. Thus, the current allocation of about half of the early childhood public budget to preschool education seems warranted, given the limited available evidence. On the other hand, an opportunity lies ahead. Public spending in home visits is low in the region, leaving much room to expand these programs in the coming years. However, pilot projects should precede major expansions.

Governments that seek to improve child development and facilitate the incorporation of women into the labor market may face a difficult trade-off. On the one hand, in the region, parenting and preschools have had the greatest impact on child development; however, these programs are unlikely to impact female labor supply significantly. On the other hand, daycare programs can make it easier for women to work; however, unless they are of high quality, daycare programs will not benefit children. To minimize this trade-off, it is critical that governments in the region look for realistic options to increase the quality of daycare at a reasonable cost. One option is to combine daycare with a parenting intervention delivered at the daycare center, as is typical of high-quality daycare programs for disadvantaged families in developed countries. The combination of both services could create important costs savings. Another option is to invest in improving process quality in daycare centers, as discussed in Chapter 4.

The analysis of this chapter (and the book in general) makes evident that in the region decisions are made with a limited knowledge base circumscribed to few programs and contexts. Assuming that Latin America and the Caribbean increase investments in early childhood by 0.5 percent of GDP, new spending in this area should reach about $30 billion per year. The costs of mistakes, therefore, can be very large. These costs can be lessened by devoting a small percentage of this increased spending to carefully design pilot studies and to monitoring and evaluating new programs. Generating solid evidence on actual impacts can go a long way to ensuring that investments in early childhood development contribute to sustained improvements in standards of living and lower inequality and poverty in the region.

7

Drawing Up an Institutional Architecture

Much of the research on early childhood development focuses on evaluating the impact of interventions and developing best practices. However, interventions are not implemented by fiat; they take place in a cultural, socioeconomic, and institutional context that affects both whether best practices are implemented and how effective they will be. Ultimately, the institutional arrangements a country puts in place to implement public policy have important implications for the quality, equity, and sustainability of early childhood services.

The institutional architecture behind the implementation of public policy in early childhood development is unique in the public sector and critical to its success for several reasons. First, services should be delivered in a synergistic manner over a relatively short period of the life cycle. Second, responsibility for interventions is spread across a variety of departments including education, health, and social protection; in many countries, these services are further spread across federal, provincial, and local levels of government. Coordination across levels and among departments is a major challenge. Finally, in addition to public institutions, private and not-for-profit providers play important roles in delivering services and require further coordination and regulation. All these challenges magnify both the importance of the institutional architecture and the difficulties of policy implementation.

This chapter analyzes the institutional arrangements that affect the implementation of public policy in early childhood. It is based on a thorough study of a number of country cases in the region, which offer examples of the spectrum of institutional approaches to public policy toward young children in Latin America and the

Caribbean: Brazil, Chile, Colombia, Guatemala, and Trinidad and Tobago.[1] These country cases reflect the main challenges that the region faces in building a strong institutional architecture to support program delivery.

The Lay of the Land

The way in which a country regards its obligation to young children is embedded in its sociocultural history, which defines not only what services should be delivered, but also how and to whom they are delivered. How policymakers across much of Latin America and the Caribbean think about early childhood development has undergone three recent shifts.

First, policymakers are recognizing the importance of focusing on children during their early years. This heightened awareness has translated into service expansion either by increasing services to more children within the same age group, extending services to younger children, and/or diversifying the kinds of services delivered. While the institutional mechanisms chosen for such expansion vary from country to country, policymakers agree that services still need to be expanded and improved.

Second, there is a growing consensus that early childhood services are a universal human right and should be guaranteed by government intervention either directly through public provision or indirectly by financing and regulating private providers. Some countries, like Brazil, prioritize direct public provision as the policy option to ensure this right. Other countries, like Trinidad and Tobago, have also voiced a commitment to young children, but to date the public sector has provided limited services.

Third, a conceptual shift in the delivery of services in the early years is under way. Countries are moving away from a model of fragmented service providers (such as health, education, or social protection) toward an integrated approach that considers the comprehensive development of each child. The extent of this change, however, varies considerably across countries. In many countries in the region, such as Brazil, Chile, Colombia, and Trinidad and Tobago, early childhood development is increasingly viewed as a multidimensional phenomenon. However, in other countries, such as Guatemala, the focus on young children is still primarily directed toward health and nutrition.

Despite these increased commitments and important conceptual shifts, a large gap persists between discourse and implementation. The development of a strong institutional architecture is required to ensure quality, equitable, and comprehensive policies for young children in the region.

Four Pillars for a Strong System

This chapter focuses on four critical pillars that support the implementation of public policy in early childhood: governance, finance, quality assurance, and human capacity (Kagan and others forthcoming). Box 7.1 describes this framework and other approaches to study this issue. The strength of these pillars varies across countries and reflects the challenges the region faces in building a strong foundation for their institutional architecture.

Box 7.1 Approaches for Analyzing the Institutional Architecture of Early Childhood Service Provision

Increasing awareness of the importance of early childhood development has led to a corresponding increase in scholarly interest in the institutional architecture of systems to oversee these programs. Scholars have suggested a number of different approaches to understanding their architecture (Sugarman 1991; Bruner 1996; Kagan and Cohen 1996; Kagan and Kauerz 2012). The broadest framework, Bruner (2004), suggests that a system for young children must address health and nutrition, family support systems, early care and education services, and services for children with special needs or early intervention systems. Kagan and Cohen (1996) defines a system as having programs or direct services and an infrastructure to support these services; the infrastructure consists of governance; finance; quality, standards, and transitions; assessment, data, and accountability; human capacity development; family and community engagement; and linkages with external influencers. Vargas-Barón (2013) defines eight elements of an early childhood development system, including equity and rights; multisectorality, integration, and coordination; governance; legislation, standards, regulations, and agreements; quality improvement; accountability; investment; and policy advocacy and social communications. Coffman and Parker (2010) suggest that systems building must take the following elements into consideration: context, components (services and programs), and connections; infrastructure (governance and administrative supports); and scale. In their framework paper—one in the series of Systems Approach for Better Education Results (SABER)—Neuman and Devercelli (2013) suggest that systems implementation includes the establishment of a supportive environment, the wide-scale implementation of services, and the monitoring and assurance of quality. Finally, building on systems theory, Britto and others (2014) and Yoshikawa and others (2014) have examined elements of systems in four low- and middle-income countries with a focus on planning, implementation, coordination, and financing mechanisms.

This chapter adopts the framework developed by Kagan and Cohen (1996), which posits that an early childhood development system is composed of both individual programs and an infrastructure that supports those programs. Based on the methodology described in Kagan and others (forthcoming), this chapter focuses on four elements of the infrastructure that are critical to the delivery of quality, equitable, and sustainable services: governance, finance, quality assurance, and human capacity (the framework also includes family and community engagement and linkages with external influencers, which this analysis forgoes). These elements of the early childhood development infrastructure act as a booster or a limitation to the implementation of individual programs and services. Good governance, for example, ensures that services are coordinated across sectors so programs do not overlap or work at cross-purposes. Proper financing mechanisms ensure sufficient resources initially and secure funding for the life of the program. Quality assurance requires national measures and standards to supplement program-specific standards. The availability and pertinence of data in the country may limit evaluation options in individual programs. Finally, programs require well-trained human resources. While human resource development may be included as an individual program feature, the actual availability of a pool of well-trained potential personnel depends on elements that transcend the individual program, including the general mechanisms to attract qualified individuals to work in early childhood development, salary structures for the sector, and the quality of pre-service training of workers.

Governance: Who Does What, and How?

Along with the move toward a more comprehensive understanding of early childhood development, some countries in the region have been developing integrated governance mechanisms among the various sectors and institutions responsible for programs and policies. The idea behind this shift is to organize services around the comprehensive development and needs of each child and his/her family, rather than that of service providers. Both horizontal coordination (among sectors such as health, nutrition, sanitation, education, labor, and social protection) and vertical coordination (across national, subnational, and local levels of government) are important for implementing integrated services.

One solution to assure horizontal and vertical coordination has been the development of *boundary spanning entities* (BSEs)—institutions with an explicit mandate to coordinate efforts among the myriad of relevant institutions. The push for the use of BSEs has been strongest in Chile and Colombia with Chile Crece Contigo (ChCC) and De Cero a Siempre (DCAS), respectively (see Box 7.2 for more on ChCC).

Box 7.2   Chile Crece Contigo: Comprehensive Early Childhood Policies

In 2006, President Michelle Bachelet appointed a Presidential Advisory Council for the Reform of Policies for Children, with the mandate to design a comprehensive child protection system. Following the council's recommendation, on October 2006, President Bachelet launched Chile Crece Contigo (ChCC), and in 2009, a law formalized its existence. ChCC established an intersectoral system of social protection in charge of the comprehensive development of young children (from gestation until age 4).

What makes ChCC innovative is that it articulates, organizes, and integrates the services provided by the health, education, welfare, and protection services based on the needs of young children and their families. A child's first contact with the system occurs in utero, during her mother's first prenatal control. Part of the success of the system relates to the very large coverage and utilization of the public health network throughout the country. It is in the clinic that each family is assessed not only on its health, but also on a number of areas of socioeconomic vulnerability. Through this evaluation, families can be referred to specific services provided in their municipalities by other sectors (anything from a poverty alleviation program to a childcare service, home visits, housing improvements, or screenings for developmental delays). The intersectoral structure of ChCC highlights the multidimensionality of child development and the importance of making multiple supports and interventions available simultaneously.

ChCC articulates services that are of universal coverage and others that are designed to reach the most vulnerable. An example of a universal service is education programs aimed at reaching all families in the country with information on child stimulation and development, delivered through mass media and the Internet. An example of a targeted service is access to poverty alleviation programs, a subsidized childcare slot, or specialized assistance for children with disabilities.

Chile has opted to manage horizontal intersectoral coordination by superimposing institutional arrangements over existing institutions in charge of managing service provision. Organizationally, ChCC resides in the Ministry of Social Development and coordinates service provision across government agencies. Management of service provision remains the responsibility of line ministries, such as health and education. ChCC is implemented through contracting mechanisms between the Ministry of Social Development and the line ministries that manage and regulate service provision. Contracts stipulate which services are to be provided and how they will be monitored.

To vertically coordinate national, regional, and municipal service providers, ChCC has developed specific structures at each level of government. At the national level, a central unit coordinates actions across the national-level ministries. At the regional level, coordination is the responsibility of the regional representative of the Ministry of Social Development, who acts as the regional coordinator of ChCC and convenes the regional representatives of the line ministries. At the municipal level, a local level coordinator and municipal networks of local providers manage intersectoral coordination.

Recognizing that in decentralized countries the success of the BSE depends on the actions taken at the local level, ChCC has developed mechanisms to strengthen implementation capacity at this level. ChCC earmarks specific funds for municipalities to manage local coordination, uses a data system to track policy implementation at the local level, and provides training to municipal officials in intersectoral management and the use of this data system.

The institutional choices made by ChCC are just one way in which a more consolidated approach to governance can be organized. Others exist. Colombia's DCAS has some institutional features similar to ChCC, but others that respond specifically to the Colombian context. In the case of DCAS, the central coordinating agency is not part of any particular line ministry, but rather of the president's office, signaling a strong political mandate for coordination. On the other hand, DCAS does not have a direct operational structure. Consequently, it has no staff at the regional and local levels, and coordination relies on the varying degrees of effort and commitment of line ministry and local government representatives—resulting in important implementation challenges.

While BSEs are an attractive tool for coordinating policy and services, conflict is intrinsic to them. BSEs attempt to realign deeply rooted practices and ideas in line ministries. Employees and managers in line ministries are not yet held accountable for coordinating with other sectors; as a result, they have little incentive to cooperate with coordination efforts. Instead, line ministry employees often see cross-sectoral coordination as an add-on to already heavy workloads. Furthermore, BSE staff requires specific knowledge and skills to implement coordination goals successfully. In the case of Chile, professional development efforts have been undertaken to change practices and ideas in line with the new approach, but there is still room for improvement.

Chile and Colombia share many of the same challenges. For coordination mechanisms to be successful, they must change existing practices, assure adequate human and financial resources, and develop new incentive structures that promote coordination and better human resources. A comprehensive move to an integrated system requires extensive time and effort. These efforts must also include coordination and regulation of nongovernmental actors (see Box 7.3 on the role of nongovernmental actors).

Box 7.3   Partnering for Children

Government agencies and officials are not alone in pushing for an increased focus on young children's issues in the policy agenda; nongovernmental actors have played a major role in bringing children and their families to the forefront. These so-called external influencers include individuals from civil society, grassroots organizations, academics, the business sector, and international organizations, all of whom have strong voices in matters relating to the protection and the development of young children. External influencers not only promote and support policies for young children, but they can also work to create consensus regarding other aspects of the policy process in areas such as accountability, monitoring and evaluation, or standards.

The degree of influence of nongovernmental actors and the channels though which they exercise this influence vary from country to country. There are two main types of partnership arrangements between the public sector and external influencers. In the first type, external influencers partner with governmental initiatives for young children, as early childhood development is positioned on the social and governmental agenda. They not only promote and support policies for young children and their families, but can also work to create consensus regarding other aspects of the policy process in areas such as accountability, monitoring, evaluation, or standards. A second type of partnership occurs when external influencers provide support to directly implement social policies and programs and provide services.

When the appropriate coordination between governmental initiatives and the external influencer exist, these partnerships are beneficial. However, that is not always the case. The case of Guatemala deserves special mention: a myriad of private entities, nongovernmental organizations, and international organizations pour resources into the country to support efforts in education and health—but there is an important need to better channel and coordinate donor efforts so that the intended objectives are met. Beyond the challenges of donor coordination, Guatemala seems to require a deeper dialogue among all the key actors (government and external influencers) on the priorities and vision for early childhood development policies and programs.

Despite the many challenges faced by Chile, Colombia, and others, recognizing the importance of coordination is a positive step, and as more countries move in this direction, the number of inventive solutions to the problems faced by all should increase.

Finance: Money—and Its Distribution—Matters

Public funding for services for young children in the region has increased (see Chapter 6). In Brazil, for example, spending (including health, education, and social protection) on early childhood grew by 7 percent annually between 2004 and 2012 (Tavares de Araujo and Cavalcanti de Almeida 2014), well above the corresponding 4.25 percent rate of GDP growth. Despite the expansion in budget allocations, spending on the early years is still insufficient to fund not only an adequate supply of high-quality services, but also to sustain the institutional elements that assure quality, equity, and sustainability.

Some countries rely on sporadic sources of funding including private sources, redirected budget surpluses, and royalties related to natural resource exports, which make the provision of services unpredictable. This, of course, hampers the development of long-term initiatives as funding is tied to government priorities within and across political cycles. Even in countries that have developed more sustainable funding mechanisms, early childhood is still a second-tier area. For example, in Brazil, while the constitution sets expenditure floors for both health and education, it makes no specific provision for expenditures on early childhood.

Even when funding is sufficient and sustained, it needs to be strategically allocated to support the timely implementation of quality services. Generally, funding is based on implementing specific programs within sectoral lines, and not necessarily tied to indicators of service quality. This tends to introduce intersectoral competition for funding, redundancies in programs, and a suboptimal resource allocation.

The equitable allocation of funding across local governments is a source of concern, particularly in countries where funding (and service provision) is decentralized. In those cases, local funding for services comprises a national/federal share and a local share. Wealthier local governments can supplement federal funding with their own resources, reinforcing regional inequality. However, some countries are attempting to compensate for these inequities in funding by developing redistribution mechanisms. In Brazil, for example, FUNDEB (Fundo de Manutenção e Desenvolvimento da Educação Básica e de Valorização dos Profissionais da Educação) provides additional resources to localities that are unable to guarantee a minimum level of expenditure per child per year. The redistribution formula weighs factors such as the population attending daycare, preschools, and elementary schools, as well as the percentage of urban and rural students (see Box 7.4 for more on the challenges of decentralization in Colombia).

Box 7.4   The Challenges of Decentralization in Colombia

In Colombia, young children's differential access to services is a critical issue that produces unintentional inequities that may persist throughout their lives. There are multiple reasons for service inequities, with family income and location being foremost among them.

Geographic location is a considerable source of inequalities. Young children from wealthier, more urban areas have greater access to services than poorer, more rural children. Service inequities also exist by age. For example, 4-year-old children attending an early education center-based modality receive 70 percent of their nutritional requirements, but when these same children go to kindergarten at age 5, they are lucky to receive any nutritional support through the school nutrition program, as nutrition is not universally provided to all youngsters in the school system. Moreover, there are the differences in schedules between early education services, which are full time, and formal schooling, which are part-time. These might be causing problems in the transitions to formal schooling by making parents delay entry into kindergarten.

An unintentional element that can potentially exacerbate inequality relates to the decentralized administrative structure of the country. Children born or living in richer regions of the country who use public services could be receiving better quality services than those living in less well-off areas. For example, Bogota, Medellin, Barranquilla, and Cali consider early childhood services so essential that they supplement central government funds with local resources to provide services for youngsters. In addition, these cities exert some control over quality by, for example, in Bogotá, mandating private operators to be registered and establishing quality criteria that facilities have to meet in order to operate.

Economic and geographic status is not the only source of inequity; structural inhibitors exist as well. In Colombia, inequities seem to be unintentionally reinforced by a commitment to the decentralization of decision-making and service delivery, without a strong compensatory mechanism in place. In adhering to the need for customization of services, the management tool created to support the comprehensive provision of services (Ruta Integral de Atenciones, or RIA) is expected to be customized to respond to varying contexts. The construction of customized RIAs in each municipality has proven to be a highly complex task, in part, because the levels of commitment to early childhood development and the technical capacity of local authorities vary heavily across municipalities and departments.

Such heterogeneous implementation mirrors and perhaps reproduces the social and economic disparities within diverse subnational governments. Children's limited and uneven access to services is a practical reality that compromises youngsters' optimal development. It also contradicts the good intentions of promoting the rights of all children and supporting their full development. The reality is that children's experiences in early childhood services are heavily conditioned on their family income and their area of residence, among other factors.

Quality Assurance and Accountability: Setting Up a Virtuous Circle

Quality assurance can be thought of as a (virtuous) circular process. It begins with a statement of the required characteristics of services and the outcomes they are expected to produce. Then, it moves to the mechanisms in place to measure whether such outcomes are achieved, and if not, why. Finally, the circle closes with mechanisms that allow for changes to be made based on the assessment of these outcomes. While there has been progress in introducing quality assurance processes, in most cases they are still limited in their design and implementation.

Outcome and Service Standards

Quality assurance processes begin by determining the required characteristics and expected outcomes of services. The growing consensus is that this can be achieved by developing and implementing child and services standards. Child standards specify the age-specific and measurable outcomes that services are trying to achieve. In early childhood development, these are often referred to as early learning and development standards. Service standards, on the other hand, relate to the nature of the services children should receive. They specify parameters of health, safety, and space; they may also refer to the dosage and duration of the services needed to be part of an effective protocol.[2]

Countries in Latin America and the Caribbean tend to assign limited attention to child outcome standards. Particularly in relation to learning, there is a hesitation to specify what young children should know and be able to do. This reflects, in part, the fear that specifying outcomes might lead to unfair and premature labeling or tracking of young children. Despite the scarcity of precise standards for children's outcomes, some child development curricula specify very general outcomes for children. In several cases, however, the curricula are considered guidelines; their usage, while recommended, is not required.

In contrast to the paucity of child outcome standards, service standards are much more abundant. It is common to have program standards for the major educational stages, as well as standards for most health and social protection programs. The mere existence of standards, however, is not an effective barometer of success; the content and quality of the standards must be examined. Often, they focus on what can be easily counted, rather than on process variables that may have a greater impact on outcomes. In the education sector, this tendency results in an abundance of standards that address structural variables or variables that are easy to regulate, such as group size, child-to-adult ratios, and teacher pre-service training requirements. Attention to process variables, such as teacher-child interactions, is absent, even though they are most directly linked to child outcomes. In the health sector, service standards focus mainly on the number of services delivered or on administrative and/or contractual data, rather than on service quality.

It is common for several sets of standards to coexist for similar types of services. This occurs for a number of reasons. First, standards tend to be developed at the program level, rather than at the system level. A typical example involves the services provided by JUNJI (Junta Nacional de Jardines Infantiles) and INTEGRA (Fundación Nacional para el Desarrollo Integral del Menor) in Chile. Both are public providers of daycare services for the same age group. However, each institution has its own set of standards, which results in differences in service provision. Second, standards at the local and central levels of government, and across local governments, are rarely aligned. This can result in regional inequities in the quality of services provided. In Colombia, for example, standards can be altered to meet the needs of the local context. However, this can exacerbate regional inequality, depending on the quality of standards that are developed and implemented in each locality. Third, in many countries, standards do not consistently apply to both public and private sector providers, thus exacerbating differences in the services provided.

The appropriate service characteristics and pedagogical approaches, as well as the expected child outcomes, vary depending on the age of the child, and as young children transition from home to daycare and from daycare to schools. To ensure continuity of experience, outcome and service standards need to be aligned across services catering to different age groups. This can be achieved by having structured transitions. With the exception of Trinidad and Tobago, most countries have neglected transitions. Trinidad and Tobago has developed a curriculum guide that promotes smooth transitions for young children across service modalities. For example, it stresses the importance of transferring records and addressing the continuity of children's pedagogical experiences. There is limited data available, however, to verify the implementation of transition efforts or their success.

Data and Monitoring

Data production and monitoring systems—a crucial component of quality assurance processes—allow public officials, researchers, evaluators, and others to measure whether the expected service characteristics and child outcomes are actually being achieved. While policymakers acknowledge the importance of data to inform policy decisions, the actual availability and use of data and monitoring systems for quality improvement are still limited.

Data and monitoring systems face challenges in four main areas: practical (a focus on inputs over outputs); conceptual (using data systems as repositories rather than as tools for quality enhancement); attitudinal (a hesitation to obtain developmental information at the child level); and technical (the lack of adequate instruments or human capacity).

Among practical challenges, data systems in most countries amass information on programmatic inputs (such as cases attended in clinics, children in school, and beneficiaries of a specific program) and tend to use such information for accountability purposes against output standards (such as number of children per classroom and amount spent on materials). Much less attention is devoted to collecting indicators of results, outcomes, or impacts (such as developmental indicators at the child level). This limits the use of available data for accountability that goes beyond outputs. For example, the health sector clearly needs to evolve beyond data sets focused exclusively on numbers of people served. Countries see the importance of transitioning toward nominal data systems, where the unit of analysis is the individual, so that individuals and the interventions they receive can be tracked throughout and/or within a given sector, or ultimately merged across sectors.

The lack of results and impact measurements also springs from a lack of consensus on the need for measuring quality, as well as on how best to measure it. Data systems act largely as repositories for information about service delivery, rather than as vehicles for quality enhancement and policy development.

Attitudinally, the assessment of young children is a source of much debate and angst in many countries of the region. From a public policy perspective, however, this information is a necessary condition to develop more effective programs and interventions that can best optimize children's development.

Finally, there are a number of technical challenges. First, an important issue is the appropriateness of the instruments and diagnostic tools to carry out assessments in early childhood. Municipal-level initiatives to collect child development data have been completed in Rio de Janeiro, and data on provider-level quality for center-based care services have been collected in Florianopolis, Brazil. Critics of many current assessments base their skepticism on differences—mostly cultural—that, they argue, make it difficult to generalize expectations regarding what young children should know or be able to do at a given age. Despite the difficulties involved, however, countries in the region urgently need to agree on a set of instruments for measuring early child development that can be collected on representative samples of individuals, as is done in the household surveys, and others that can be collected for the population at large.

Second, data are not always up-to-date or well aggregated. For example, whether due to fiscal limitations or governmental choices, or both, Guatemala relies on census data that are more than a decade old. That current data do not exist is troublesome as it is the only available information to determine the siting of programs and the allocation of resources. Data aggregation is also challenging. In Trinidad and Tobago, for example, fairly recent data are collected and even reported, but much of the data is aggregated for children from birth to 19 years of age. Given this aggregation frame, it is difficult to filter out relevant data to improve programs or for other key decisions that affect age-related services for younger children.

Third, shortcomings in institutional and human capacities contribute to all of the challenges involved in generating, managing, and using information systems. In some countries (and in less-developed regions within all countries), technological gaps and connectivity problems still impose constraints on the construction of modern data systems. Technical and institutional capacity varies greatly not only between countries, but also across different sectors and institutions within each country.

Conceiving quality from a systemic perspective requires thinking beyond programmatic data collection efforts toward more systemic collection and utilization of data. Data collection efforts do not necessarily need to be integrated into one central database; they can still be housed in separate sectors. What makes them systemic is that the different data sets are conceived as part of an integrated system, with the data being available to, and easily merged with, data from other ministries. This type of organization requires strong central planning.

In some countries, such as Chile, BSEs have consolidated data systems that foster data integration. Other countries, such as Brazil, have also moved toward data integration even in the absence of a formal BSE. An example is the Cadastro Unico in the Brazilian conditional cash transfer program, Bolsa Familia. Information on health, education, and social protection is collected for different purposes, but mainly to check on the degree to which the beneficiaries meet the requirements, and then to take action at the municipal and individual levels. In the case of the Cadastro Unico, the information is not only shared horizontally between ministries, but also vertically between the federal government and the municipalities, which receive budget resources based on meeting specific performance indicators.

Closing the Accountability Circle

The circle of accountability and quality assurance is closed when countries introduce mechanisms that allow for changes to be made when standards are not met. The development of these mechanisms is still weak in most countries. Accountability processes can promote change in policies and programs in at least three ways: by establishing regulatory mechanisms that enforce consequences for noncompliance with standards; by publicizing information so that social actors can participate in an informed manner in decision-making; and by promoting direct involvement of families at the center/service level.

Mechanisms that trigger consequences for noncompliance with standards are still at the very early stages. As mentioned, countries are trying to produce data on policies and programs, but these data still focus on outputs rather than on outcomes. Thus, mechanisms that introduce consequences tend to focus on noncompliance with program standards, rather than on the quality of service provision or the outcomes achieved by children. For example, in the case of Chile, the Ministry of Social Development has recently been tasked with evaluating social programs to determine whether funding for specific programs should be continued. In the case of early childhood programs, such decisions are limited by the availability of data on quality and child outcomes.

Accountability processes can also be informed by community members who formally and informally influence decisions regarding service provision. The councils at the municipal/community level in Brazil are an example. Councils function as a public accountability mechanism by monitoring the work of government. For community members to make informed decisions, data on early childhood development need to be publicly available. Only a few national and subnational governments, including in Brazil, make data publicly accessible. These commendable data-sharing efforts can make information available to citizens, expand public accountability processes, and enhance family and community engagement in planning services for children.

Finally, engaging families in their children's programs at the point of service provision may also act as an accountability mechanism; families can and informally do observe programs and can consequently affect change at that level. Family engagement also allows for more informed decision-making regarding priorities and local needs; furthermore, it can help build consensus about child development and needed services. In general, however, family members are most often seen as providers of resources or labor (including caregiving, food preparation, or improvements of physical infrastructure), rather than as a possible force for quality improvement.

Human Capacity: The Weakest Link

High-quality programs rely on highly qualified staff. In order for services to be staffed with high-quality personnel, the system needs to ensure that enough professionals have the right competencies to perform their functions and that incentive structures attract and maintain top professionals.[3] Human capacity is one of the weakest elements of the institutional infrastructure in the region. This gap stems mainly from two factors: overreliance on the use of community members and families as the workforce for some services; and poorly designed personnel requirements and policies that do not effectively produce and maintain a high-quality professional workforce.

Some countries rely on the labor of families or community members to provide services (including caregiving, food preparation, or improvements in physical infrastructure). In Colombia, for example, a large share of daycare provision has historically relied on community mothers with little training, as discussed in Chapter 4. They receive a modest government transfer to provide childcare services to small groups of neighborhood children in their own homes. This strategy increases the number of staff available, while also increasing employment opportunities for low-income families. Nevertheless, this approach has many limitations. It relies completely on unqualified staff with little supervision and few mentoring and training opportunities. Moreover, the system does not provide incentives, such as remuneration or career advancement, to build and maintain quality human resources. In recent years, Colombia's government has taken an important step toward formalizing the employment conditions of community mothers. This initiative is likely to reduce turnover and attract more qualified individuals. In addition, efforts have been made to train community mothers in key competencies for their jobs through the country's main adult training services.

Where programs require professional credentials to work with young children, personnel policies are not well-designed to effectively produce a high-quality professional workforce. For instance, early childhood educators tend to be treated as a lower-tier of workers within the education profession. This occurs for a variety of reasons: low entry requirements, inadequate compensation schemes, and poor in-service professional development.

Entry requirements for the profession are lower than for other types of educators. In countries where early childhood is understood as a field of specialization, pre-service or initial teacher education programs for early childhood educators tend to attract less-qualified students compared to primary or secondary educator programs. Teaching in most pre-service training programs is considered to be of low quality and academic requirements for completion are less stringent than in teacher training programs for primary or secondary school educators.

Early childhood educators often face inadequate and inequitable compensation schemes. They tend to have lower remuneration and less attractive career paths than primary and secondary school teachers. Of course, this makes the early childhood field less attractive to qualified individuals. To make matters worse, in decentralized countries such as Brazil and Colombia there are significant regional differences in salaries for public sector workers, where wealthier municipalities can offer more competitive salaries. This generates a shortage of qualified early childhood educators in less affluent areas, which is where the returns to their skills are likely to be highest.

Finally, opportunities for staff training tend not to be systematic. This happens both at the pre-service and the in-service level. There is little regulation of pre-service training providers, which results in varying quality levels among institutions. In-service training initiatives, in turn, tend to be scattered, with limited continuity and little alignment to the identified needs of staff. Some countries are trying to provide training more systematically, to ensure that all early childhood educators acquire a core set of competencies. In the case of pre-service education, Trinidad and Tobago is focusing on the consistency of training across providers, with aligned pre-service training programs for teachers of children aged 3–5 across a network of eight universities, described in detail in Box 7.5. In the case of in-service initiatives, the federal Ministry of Education in Brazil has developed the National Network for Continuing Teacher Education (Rede Nacional de Formação Continuada de Professores) to support the professional development of teachers. The ministry is currently developing curriculum guidelines for educators to be implemented through the network.

Box 7.5   Teacher Training in the Tropics

A necessary condition for expanding coverage of high-quality early childhood services is the availability of qualified human resources who can serve young children and their families in all types of services: nutritional, health, education, protection, and other. However, the region faces a personnel shortage to meet the growing demands generated by expansions of coverage; moreover, existing staff must be upgraded with the right competences and qualifications. The experience of Trinidad and Tobago is worth highlighting in the area of training for early childhood education teachers and may provide valuable lessons beyond the scope of the education sector.

Trinidad and Tobago has carried out important efforts to strengthen both its in-service training system as well as its pre-service training initiatives. In the area of in-service professional development, the country recently approved the Standards of Practice for the Teaching Profession in the Caribbean Community, which, importantly, includes an in-service professional development path for early childhood education teachers that is expected to transform how professional development is perceived, implemented, and actualized. Aligned with these standards, the country recently approved a new in-service Professional Development Model, which is composed of four career stages, with distinct teacher expectations described at each stage. In order to progress from one career stage to the next, teachers must acquire knowledge-in-practice and demonstrate their ability to meet the relevant performance standards. Modern views of professional development characterize professional learning as a long-term process that extends from university to in-service training in the workplace. Additionally, the model values informal training (e.g., workplace interactions) that facilitate learning and that inspire teachers to alter or reinforce their teaching and educational practices.

With the goal of improving the pre-service training model for early childhood education teachers, in 2012, the Trinidad and Tobago Ministry of Education, in collaboration with the main teacher-training institutes in the country, worked to align the pre-service training curriculum for teachers who educate children between 3 and 5 years of age across eight universities. These eight institutions now offer the program, which will become a mandatory requirement for teachers interested in a permanent position as early childhood educators.

Although Trinidad and Tobago has taken important steps to professionalize early childhood teachers, challenges are likely to arise as this model is implemented. One major hurdle is that, as of now, early childhood teachers are not recognized as regular teachers under the law, and hence they are not eligible to receive the same benefits as other teachers (including participating actively in teachers' unions, for example).

Putting the Pieces Together: Policy Recommendations

The emphasis on development in early childhood is growing in many countries in Latin America and the Caribbean. New laws and policies, framework documents, and regulatory or guidance materials have been produced. Political leaders have expressed commitment to the sector, generating public will and enthusiasm. National, subnational, and local governments are implementing innovative programs, often significantly increasing the number of direct services available to children and families. The philanthropic and business communities are partnering with governments to enhance services. And yet, enormous challenges remain to ensure that quality services reach those children who need them the most. Four main recommendations emerge from this chapter.

First, a focus on programs is necessary, but not sufficient: The region requires a systemic orientation that values both programs and the institutional architecture that supports them. High-quality, equitably distributed, and sustainable services cannot be achieved merely from a programmatic perspective.

This book does not advocate any one form of governance structure. It does, however, advocate putting in place the functions typically carried out by a consolidated structure: notably, comprehensive planning, establishing quality standards, monitoring functions, developing appropriate data systems, coordinating services across sectors and levels of government, and developing public information regarding child development.

One possible and promising approach to achieve coordination is using BSEs. To coordinate efforts successfully, BSEs must meet a set of institutional, fiscal, and political conditions. Institutionally successful BSEs have three key characteristics: authority over programs and policies—rather than simply deliberative or convening roles; built-in horizontal and vertical cooperation mechanisms; and a strong monitoring and evaluation component. Fiscally successful BSEs need a sufficiently large and stable budget to allow for long-term planning; they also need budget authority to allocate funds flexibly according to strategic needs. Politically, BSEs must enjoy enough support to induce cooperation across the sectors they seek to coordinate;

conversely, BSEs must be perceived as politically neutral—rather than associated with a specific sector or administration—to ensure longevity. In countries where there is no BSE, other efforts, notably through data and accountability mechanisms, can serve as coordination vehicles.

Second, the system should reduce disparities, not enhance them: Services for the poor do not have to be poor services. However, often the allocation of funding, technical capacity, human resources, and program standards contribute to reinforce disparities rather than reduce them.

This problem is more obvious in decentralized systems but is not exclusive to them. Disparities cannot be solved with a single policy instrument. For example, it is not enough to provide more funding in less affluent localities if there are no incentives at the local level for the money to be spent efficiently. Thus, compensatory funding is necessary but it should be accompanied by other policies that foster the provision of quality services.

Third, accountability mechanisms need to be in place: Policies and programs for young children in the region lack a robust system of accountability. To date, quality monitoring mechanisms have largely focused on outputs (rather than on child outcomes or impacts). A key policy action is to produce reliable and centralized information on child development outcomes that can be shared among providers. This is needed to ensure that every child receives the attention that she requires. Urgent steps must be taken to decide what child development measure should be collected and to start following (at the least) the most disadvantaged children. Understanding their development path will provide valuable cues for deciding how public policy can best serve them.

Fourth, human resource investments should precede expansions of coverage: Quality outcomes are contingent upon quality personnel, but countries in the region still face serious challenges to attract and keep qualified personnel to deliver services to young children.

In many cases, this is driven by a fragmented view of the labor market that does not recognize that providers of early childhood services are competing for quality personnel with many other areas of the public sector and the economy.

Countries must develop a systematic and competitive approach to recruit, train, retain, and motivate workers that provide services to children. Investments in human resources are the foundation on which any expansion in coverage and improvement in services need to be built.

The potential returns to public investment in early childhood are being compromised by the absence of a systemic understanding of the policy challenges in providing quality services to young children. As important as picking the right programs is the development of an institutional architecture to support them.

8

The Task at Hand:
Anything but Child's Play

Children are the adults of the future. How they are raised will determine their well-being and the future of the countries they live in. Policies for young children should be at the core of a country's development agenda—no less than policies to develop infrastructure or to strengthen institutions.

Spending on effective programs for young children is not charity. It is an investment that, if done well, will have very high returns. It is both efficient and can reduce the intergenerational transmission of poverty and inequality. And it is an investment that, if not made, will lower the returns to the substantial investments being made in education for school-aged children throughout the region. However, if the services provided (or funded) by governments in Latin America and the Caribbean are to benefit young children, they need to be of a substantially higher quality than those that are currently in place.

How Early Childhood Matters

Development in early childhood casts a long shadow. Long-term panels show that the benefits of early investments can be seen all the way into adulthood. In one study from Jamaica, children who benefited from a parenting intervention in the first two years of their life earned wages in adulthood that were 25 percent higher than comparable children who had not participated. Children who had received the parenting intervention were also less likely to be engaged in criminal activities in early adulthood. Credible evidence from a number of sources reveals that children with deficits in nutrition, cognition, language, motor, and socioemotional development early on are less likely to learn in school; are more likely to engage in risky behaviors that result in early pregnancy, school dropout, and violence in adolescence; and are less likely to become productive adults.

Because the acquisition of skills is a cumulative process, investments early on increase the returns to all investments made later in the life cycle. The benefit-cost ratios to programs in child nutrition, early stimulation, or school quality can be very high. The early years in the life of a child are also special in another way. Later in the life cycle, there is often a trade-off between equity and efficiency in investments—the highest returns to investments occur when these are made in people who already have a high level of skills. There is no such trade-off in early childhood. Investments in young children have the highest returns when they target children who are most at risk. Effective programs for at-risk children are both efficient and equity-enhancing.

How Is the Region Doing in Early Childhood Development?

Latin America and the Caribbean has made remarkable progress in improving child health and nutrition. Over the course of the past 50 years, most countries in the region have reduced infant mortality by three-quarters or more. In both 1990 and 2010 roughly 10 million children were born in Latin America and the Caribbean. Of these 10 million children, 428,000 died before their first birthday in 1990, but only 149,000 in 2010. Chronic malnutrition has also fallen in many countries. By and large, improvements in mortality and malnutrition have been particularly notable among the poor.

The picture is less positive with regard to other dimensions of early childhood development. Young children in poor households lag seriously behind their counterparts in better-off households. The gap between the rich and the poor is apparent early on, and grows as children become older, at least until the age when they begin formal schooling. It is particularly large in two dimensions of development that are most strongly associated with early school performance: language and cognition.

Once children begin school, many of them learn very little. Their poor progress is a result of the deficits they have upon entering school, and the low quality of the education they receive. Children in the region generally perform poorly on tests of early learning. On a recent test of math among third graders in 14 countries in Latin America, 75 percent of children in the Dominican Republic, the country with the overall lowest scores, could not solve simple addition or multiplication problems. Even in Chile, the highest performer in the region, 10 percent of children could not solve these problems. In every country where data are available, children in poor households perform substantially worse than those in better-off households.

Policymakers in the region (rightly) worry a great deal about the poor test scores of 15-year-olds on the international PISA exam, in particular relative to high-performing countries like China, Korea, and Singapore. They understand that the low levels of skills of Latin American teenagers have important implications for their productivity as adults, and for a country's growth potential. However, the seeds for this are sown early on and are apparent in the poor developmental and learning outcomes of many children in the region at very young ages.

The Case for Government Intervention

Poverty among young children in the region has declined sharply in the past decade. But growth alone will not take care of the deficits in critical dimensions of development observed among many children in Latin America and the Caribbean. What, then, is an appropriate role for government policy in the early years? Broadly speaking, there are two justifications for government intervention: failures in decision-making at the household level, and failures in various markets that deliver services to young children.

Most parents want the best for their children. They want them to be happy, healthy, and smart. They want them to be successful in school, and productive citizens thereafter. If the returns to investments are in fact so high, why are families not making them? A number of circumstances can lead parents to make decisions about children that are not optimal from a social point of view. If parents are poor, and are credit-constrained, they may not be able to invest enough in their children. If they have high discount rates, they will prioritize spending on goods and services that yield benefits now (like consumer goods) over spending that will yield large benefits only in the future (like tutoring for a child in kindergarten). Parents may also be unaware of the benefits of certain actions (e.g., providing a warm, nurturing environment for their children) or may be incapable of carrying them out (e.g., parents who are poor readers will have difficulty reading to their children). Many of these are not problems unique to poor countries—they occur in developed countries, too. But all of them provide a powerful rationale for government intervention to help shape the choices made by parents and other caregivers of young children.

Markets that deliver services for young children do not always work well. This is particularly apparent in the market for daycare services. Daycare is what economists call an "experience good." Experience goods are characterized by large information asymmetries between providers and consumers. It is difficult for parents to tell high-quality from low-quality daycare. They will notice whether their baby's diaper is clean at pick-up time, but this may say very little about what occurred over the course of the day. Under these circumstances, governments can provide information about the quality of daycare services (e.g., by licensing providers), or they can directly provide daycare services themselves.

In the case of early education, it is widely accepted in most countries in the region that the government will directly provide schooling, or subsidize provision by the private sector (as in Chile), or some combination of private, religious, and not-for-profit schools (as in Jamaica).

In fact, governments in the region have acted to increase the provision of services for young children. The proportion of children who are in daycare (mostly publicly provided daycare) has increased dramatically in the past decade—by a factor of two in Brazil and Chile, and by a factor of six in Ecuador. The proportion of 5-year-old children who are enrolled in kindergarten has increased by 40 percentage points in Mexico in the past decade, and by 60 percentage points in Honduras. But the quality of these services is generally very poor, and this raises serious questions as to whether children are in fact benefitting from these services. In this case, more may be less.

How to Invest in Early Childhood

Overall, in comparison with developed countries, and in comparison with the expenditures made later in the life cycle, countries in Latin America and the Caribbean spend very little on the early years. In the region, for every dollar that is spent on a child 5 and under, more than $3 are spent on a child between the ages of 6 and 11.

At first glance, these figures would suggest that countries in the region simply need to spend more on young children. To some extent, this is correct—governments spend too little on early childhood. However, more spending will do little to solve the problem of poor development in early childhood if resources are not spent well. In particular, what is critical is the *quality* of services (parenting programs, daycare, early schooling) provided to young children. By and large, however, the quality of the services that many young children in Latin America and the Caribbean receive is dismal. In fact, some of the services are of such low quality that they may harm—rather than help—the children who use them.

What is quality? At home, in daycare centers, and in early school, quality refers to a large extent to the interactions of children with those who surround them. Research in neurology shows that the interactions young children have with each other and with adults shape a child's brain in ways that have lifelong implications. When adults are sensitive and responsive to children's cues and needs, children begin to develop. When they provide early stimulation and focused instruction, children learn.

Because improving quality is, in large measure, about changing the nature of the interactions of children with their parents, caregivers, and teachers, spending on physical infrastructure does not by itself help. Parenting programs do not require infrastructure, but they do require well-trained, carefully supervised home visitors who can establish a relationship of trust with families and deliver a given curriculum with high fidelity. Building state-of-the-art daycare centers does nothing for child development if children are not actively engaged, encouraged, and stimulated. Reducing class sizes or giving teachers or children laptops will not improve learning outcomes if it does not change the day-to-day experiences children have in the classroom.

Increasing access is straightforward, but improving quality is not. Improving quality is painstaking work—more difficult than building roads or bridges, and much less glamorous than inaugurating new daycare centers. It requires moving slowly with the expansion of services, especially because access to daycare and preschool has already increased dramatically in the past decade in many countries in the region.

If they want to raise quality, policymakers need to take the long view. There is still much to be learned. Research from Ecuador shows that kindergarten teachers—often kindergarten teachers in the same school, teaching comparable children—vary dramatically in their effectiveness. But how are these teachers best rewarded, and what can be done to improve the performance of other, less-effective teachers? Research from the United States shows that innovative programs of in-service training, combined with coaching and mentoring, have potential. But little is known about how best to adapt programs like these to the very different circumstances of countries in Latin America and the Caribbean.

Improving quality does require more resources, but what is most lacking is capable staff—home visitors, daycare staff, teachers, coaches, supervisors—who can ensure that the services that are delivered actually benefit children. And raising the quality of services provided to young children in the region demands a virtuous cycle of experimentation, careful evaluation, and redesign.

The Challenge of Institutions

Programs for young children—parenting programs, programs to promote breastfeeding, daycare programs, cash transfers that seek to benefit children, preschool and early primary school—are delivered by a large number of actors. These actors are in different ministries in a country—education, health, social protection, the family, among others—and, in some countries, different levels of government—national, state, and municipal. In some countries, too, the private sector plays an important role, in particular in delivering daycare services. The fact that no single actor "owns" the issue of early childhood may be one of the reasons behind the low level of expenditures in the sector.

A coherent policy for development in the early years is more than a collection of programs—even if these programs are, by themselves, effective. To coordinate these efforts, an institutional architecture must support them. A consolidated governance structure should clearly define roles, planning, quality standards, monitoring, data systems, and coordination across sectors and levels. Accountability is key. Adequate and sustainable funding is needed. In addition, the institutional architecture must place great emphasis on monitoring and rigorous evaluation. Countries have to develop the capacity to experiment, learn from evaluations, and adapt methods and modes of delivery. Most of all, there needs to be a clear policy to develop human capacity to provide high-quality services.

Many countries in the region have made some progress creating a coherent institutional architecture to formulate, implement, coordinate, monitor, and evaluate interventions for young children. But, despite this progress, there is much to be done. Bureaucratic silos and service duplication are still frequent. Services are built around the agencies that provide them, not around those who matter most—young children.

Policymakers in Latin America and the Caribbean face a huge economic and moral challenge. They need to identify how best to invest in what is surely their most precious resource: their children. While the road is long, concrete steps can be taken. Gradually expanding the coverage of parenting services for at-risk children is promising. Experimenting with how best to use conditional cash transfers to effect behavioral change should be a priority. Providing high-quality daycare services to poor children in peri-urban areas may help. Upgrading teachers' skills (through personalized, hands-on in-service training and coaching) and rewarding the performance of outstanding teachers is likely to improve learning outcomes. Countries will have to find the right mix of these and other policies based on their own individual circumstances. There is no single recipe.

The road ahead is not easy. Improving quality is much more difficult than increasing access to services. Ensuring that every child in the region can develop to her full potential will require a sustained effort. But, for reasons of both equity and long-run productivity, it is an effort the region can ill afford not to make.

Notes

1   Raising Children: The Case for Government Intervention

1. The Convention on the Rights of the Child (CRC) is based upon the following four principles: (i) The convention applies to all children without discrimination of any type (Article 2); (ii) the primary consideration in all actions concerning children is the best interest of the child (Article 3); (iii) every child has an inherent right to life, survival, and development (Article 6); and (iv) children have a right for their views to be respected in accordance to their age and maturity (Article 12).

2. The standards are based on the WHO Multicentre Growth Reference Study Group (2006), and represent the best description of physiological growth of children from birth to 5 years of age from around the world with widely different ethnic backgrounds and cultural settings. The study, conducted from 1997 to 2003, collected growth data from approximately 8,500 children from Brazil, Ghana, India, Norway, Oman, and the United States. The sample consists of children whose health needs are met, and thus describes how children should grow.

3. The average of the median for boys and girls is presented.

4. "Length" is the distance from the bottom of the feet to the top of the head measured during the first two years of life, and a standing measure of height after that. "Head circumference" is the measurement of a child's head around the largest part.

5. However, catch-up growth is observed before 2 (Luo and Karlberg 2000) and after 2 (Crookston and others 2013; Lundeen and others 2014; Prentice and others 2013) years of age.

6. Motor skills are usually divided in two categories: gross and fine. Gross motor skills are associated with the ability to perform strenuous contractions of large muscles and usually entail movements that involve the whole body. Fine motor skills are associated with the ability to control smaller parts of the body or to perform minimal muscle contraction of larger body muscles.

7. Executive function is often classified as a subcategory of cognitive skills, although it encompasses the cognitive and socioemotional domains. The more cognitive executive function processes have been called "cool" processes (remembering arbitrary rules). "Hot" executive function processes

describe the more emotional aspects of executive function—those involving inhibition or delaying gratification (Hongwanishkul and others 2005).

8. Children who are not able to discern the thoughts and feelings of others are more likely to behave aggressively and experience peer rejection (Denham and others 2003), and children with both "internalizing" behavior problems characterized by depressed, withdrawn behavior, and "externalizing" behavior problems, characterized by aggressive, angry behavior are more likely to have difficulty in school (Rimm-Kaufman, Pianta, and Cox 2000).

9. The fetal origins hypothesis posits that "conditions, most likely nutritional, 'program' the fetus for the development of chronic diseases in adulthood" (Rasmussen 2001, p. 74); for a recent review, see Almond and Currie (2011).

10. See Chapter 3 for more details of this randomized experiment in Jamaica.

11. Although imprecisely estimated, smaller class sizes do not seem to have a significant effect on earnings at age 27.

12. There is no doubt that events and circumstances at the community level are important to shape children's experiences. However, in this book, we focus on the role of interactions between children and those caring for them at home, the daycare center, and in schools and therefore communities is not a central issue of this book.

13. "In development science, the term 'sensitive period' is generally preferred to 'critical period' because it implies less rigidity in the nature and timing of formative early experiences" (Shonkoff and Phillips 2000, p. 195).

14. Unfortunately, in this specific application, better information did not lead to the changes in behavior required to reduce obesity rates in the long run.

15. As an incomplete contract in the presence of asymmetric information, child-care services are defined as an *experience good*. Although the economic transaction between parents and childcare providers is very straightforward (paying for childcare services), the resulting relationship between buyers (parents) and sellers (childcare providers) is rather complex. First, the contract between parents and the provider is a highly incomplete one because it is impossible to specify how the provider should act in every possible circumstance. Second, parents cannot observe what happens in the center while they are away, and children can communicate only partially information about what goes on there (thus, there is asymmetric information). Third, providers may overinvest in aspects of quality that are easy to see by parents, such as infrastructure, and underinvest in process quality (that parents do not see and/or do not know how much it matters for child outcomes).

16. The direct provision of a standardized childcare service by the public sector may substantially reduce the information gap between providers and government, but it is not clear if it makes the parents more informed. If the childcare services provided directly by the public sector are all very homogeneous, then parents may actually have less incentive to acquire information about quality. Moreover, if the level of quality varies little among providers, then

demand may be unmet because the variety of services offered is too limited. However, if parents demand a very low level of quality (either because they are not altruistic enough, or do not understand the technology of human capital formation, or are financially constrained), then direct public provision may be a quick way to boost childcare quality.

17. Few can afford private school, and school assignment is mainly determined by residency. A notable exception is Chile, which has a highly developed voucher system.

2   A Report Card on Early Childhood Development

1. There is a very large literature on this in the fields of medicine, child development, and economics. The literature for developing countries is summarized in Walker and others (2007). Some important references from the economics literature, mainly from the United States and other developed countries, include Almond, Chay, and Lee (2005); Behrman and Rosenzweig (2004); Black, Devereux, and Salvanes (2007); Currie and Hyson (1999); and Currie and Moretti (2007). See also Hack, Klein, and Taylor (1995).

2. Note that these may be underestimates of the effect of special care because of selection on survival: mortality is lower at just below the 1,500 gram cutoff, and it is likely that the "additional" children who survive are on average weaker and may have lower learning ability than other children.

3. GDP growth rates are generally poor predictors of reductions in infant mortality (Deaton 2013; Vollmer and others 2014). On the other hand, economic crises can result in spikes in the infant mortality rate. See Bhalotra (2010) on India; Baird, Friedman, and Schady (2011) on a large sample of developing countries; and Paxson and Schady (2005) on Peru.

4. Historically, the most successful countries have reduced the infant mortality rate by almost half every decade over a 30- to 40-year period. Large declines have occurred in countries where infant mortality was high (between 1960 and 2012 Turkey reduced its infant mortality rate from 171 to 12 per 1,000 children born), as well as in countries where it was low (between 1990 and 2010 Portugal reduced its infant mortality rate from 12 to 3 per 1,000 children born); in countries that were relatively rich (Singapore reduced its infant mortality rate from 22 to 3 per 1,000 between 1970 and 2000), as well as in those that were very poor (Bangladesh reduced its infant mortality rate from 100 to 33 per 1,000 between 1990 and 2012). Long-term changes in the infant mortality rates in Brazil, Chile, El Salvador, Honduras, and Peru are all of a magnitude comparable to those observed in those countries outside Latin America and the Caribbean that have been most successful in reducing infant mortality.

5. This is also the case for Colombia, Ecuador, and Trinidad and Tobago.

6. This is also the case for Paraguay.

7. This is also the case for Bolivia, Guatemala, Mexico, Peru, Uruguay, and Venezuela.

8. This is also the case for the Dominican Republic.

9. The methodology used for the calculations in this chapter follows Baird, Friedman, and Schady (2011), Bhalotra (2010), and Paxson and Schady (2005).

10. In keeping with this, the declines in infant mortality in Peru have been much larger in the poorer, more isolated highlands, where there are heavy concentrations of indigenous people, than in the better-off, coastal areas, where the proportion of indigenous people is small.

11. In Peru, as in many other countries, the infant mortality rate of boys is consistently higher than that of girls. Medical research attributes this girl advantage to sex differences in genetic makeup, with boys being biologically weaker than girls in utero and at early ages. In countries where there is preferential treatment of boys in society, the infant mortality rate of boys may be lower than that of girls, as is the case in China and India; however, this is not the case in any country in Latin America and the Caribbean.

12. These are decompositions in the spirit of Oaxaca and Blinder (see Paxson and Schady [2005] for an earlier application to decomposing the changes in the infant mortality rate in Peru).

13. The reductions in infant mortality in Peru since the early 1980s were also broken down into declines in neonatal mortality (defined as death within the first 28 days of life) and postneonatal mortality (defined as death after day 28 but before the first year of life). This distinction is instructive because neonatal mortality is driven to a large extent by complications around birth (e.g., prematurity, low birth weight, congenital malformations); medical technology, such as neonatal intensive care units for low birth weight babies, has a substantial effect on neonatal mortality. On the other hand, postneonatal mortality is to a much larger extent a result of infections (e.g., pneumonia, intestinal infections); access to clean water and adequate sanitation, vaccination rates, nutrition, and easy access to basic health care are all important determinants of postneonatal mortality. The decline in the infant mortality rate in Peru has been driven by declines of neonatal mortality and postneonatal mortality of almost exactly the same magnitude.

14. See Deaton (2013), Fogel (1994, 2004), Fogel and Costa (1997), Floud and others (2011), and Victora and others (2008), among many others. Particularly compelling evidence from the region on the effects of poor nutrition in early childhood on a variety of outcomes in adulthood is based on the INCAP study in Guatemala (see Hoddinott and others 2008, 2013; Maluccio and others 2009, among many references).

15. To ensure that differences in the age and gender distribution of children do not have a substantive effect on these comparisons across countries and over time, for every survey, the sample was limited to children between the ages of 48 and 59 months. The height of boys and girls in each month of age was then

calculated separately. The final average is calculated as the equally weighted average of these 24 separate averages.

16. Because height in childhood is highly correlated with height attained in adulthood (Stein and others 2010), one would expect that adults born in the late 2000s will eventually be substantially taller than those born in the late 1990s in Honduras, Nicaragua, and Peru.

17. Important references include Deaton (2013); Fogel (1994, 2004); Floud and others (2011); Victora and others (2008), among many others.

18. These comparisons are made for women ages 20–49, when women have attained their final stature, but before they have begun to become shorter in old age.

19. This is done with the use of widely accepted "growth tables" provided by the World Health Organization (WHO). These tables are based on the distribution of weight and height of a reference population of well-nourished children. The most recent growth curves produced by the WHO, known as the WHO Multicentre Growth Reference Study, are based on data collected on a sample of approximately 8,500 children in Brazil, Ghana, India, Norway, Oman, and the United States. See de Onis and others (2004).

20. Chronic malnutrition is a cumulative measure. A number of authors have argued that stunting is the best omnibus measure of nutritional status—see, for example, the paper by Horton and Hoddinott (2014), produced as part of the Copenhagen Consensus.

21. The exact number of births was 9.95 million in 1990, 10.15 million in 2000, and 9.87 million in 2010.

22. Increases in overweight and obesity among school-aged children appear to be a much more severe problem for somewhat older children. Rivera and others (2014) estimate that between 20 and 25 percent of all children and adolescents (ages 0–18 years) in Latin America are overweight or obese.

23. In fact, this calculation underestimates the progress that the region has made in reducing infant mortality because, although the total number of births in the region has remained relatively constant at 10 million, a higher proportion of births in later years took place in relatively high-mortality countries than was the case in earlier years. For example, the total number of births in Chile, a low-mortality country, was approximately 295,000 in 1990, but only 225,000 in 2010. On the other hand, the total number of births in Guatemala, a higher-mortality country, was 315,000 in 1990, but 451,000 in 2010. Calculations of the evolution of the number of deaths for the region as a whole ignore these shifts in the proportion of births across countries. Another reason these calculations probably understate the progress that has been made is that a larger proportion of babies with prenatal problems or very low birth weight are now born alive than was the case before (and are therefore taken into account in the calculations of infant mortality). These babies have a higher probability of death in their first year than other babies.

24. The exact number is 49.6 million in 1990, 50.2 million in 2000, and 49.8 million in 2010.

25. This problem is not unique to the region. In an influential article, Grantham-McGregor and others (2007) estimated that there are 200 million children 5 and under in developing countries that do not reach their potential level of cognitive development. However, because there are no comparable data on cognitive development, the authors use poverty and stunting to approximate the number of children with cognitive delays in every developing country.

26. This stands in stark contrast with measures of child health and nutrition where it is generally accepted that comparing the stature of children in any country (or in any subgroup within a country, like the indigenous) with children of a similar age in a well-nourished population is appropriate and is a useful measure of the nutritional status of children.

27. Some of these instruments (like the Bayley Scale of Infant Development) need to be applied by trained psychologists in a controlled environment, while others (like the Denver Developmental Screening Test or the Ages and Stages Questionnaire [ASQ]) can reasonably be applied in a child's home by enumerators who have been adequately trained, but do not need to be psychologists.

28. These are averages for all four countries. Specifically, they are the differences in the average score for children in the poorest quintile in each country, relative to the average score for children in the wealthiest quintile in each country.

29. The sample of children in each country in Schady and others (2015) was drawn in a different way but, as the authors show, in rural areas, the distribution of wealth roughly approximates the distribution of wealth in nationally representative household surveys in every country.

30. This is noteworthy because the Ecuadorean sample includes only children below the 50th percentile of the distribution of wealth—presumably, differences in child development between the wealthiest and poorest children in the country as a whole would be larger.

3   Family First

1. Although the association between breastfeeding and positive child growth and development is well established, identifying a causal effect of breastfeeding on child outcomes is substantially more complicated because of the possibility that there are omitted variables (or "confounders"). For example, babies who do not adapt to immediate breastfeeding include a disproportionate number of babies who are born prematurely, have low birth weight, or have other such conditions. These conditions are negatively associated with good child outcomes, and so breastfeeding may in large part be proxying for other variables. Of course, the same caveat holds for many other parental behaviors that are positively correlated with child development.

2. A number of studies have also focused on declining breastfeeding rates in Mexico, from about 29 percent in the late 1980s to 21 percent in the 2006, and to 14 percent in 2012—one of the lowest rates in the region (Pérez-Escamilla and others 2012; Colchero and others 2015).

3. A similar picture emerges in data collected in the poorest areas of the Mesoamerican region (El Salvador, Guatemala, Honduras, the Chiapas region of Mexico, Nicaragua, and Panama) (IHME 2014). With the exception of El Salvador, fewer than half of children in these poor areas have minimum levels of dietary diversity (defined as receiving food from four or more food groups in the last day), with particularly low proportions in Guatemala, Panama, and Chiapas. On the other hand, a recent study on Peru suggests that the elasticity of expenditures on animal source food products is higher for lower quintile households, and these households have increased their consumption relatively more during the period of recent Peruvian growth than better-off households (Humphries and others 2014).

4. Important references include Aboud and others (2013); Boivin and others (2013); Hamadani and others (2010); and Tofail and others (2012).

5. Although there appear to be differences across countries, these results could be quite sensitive to the population covered by the surveys, and in differences in how enumerators were trained to observe the interactions between parents and children.

6. Questions about corporal punishment are not fully comparable across surveys, and so care should be taken in making comparisons across countries.

7. The American Academy of Pediatrics (1998, 2012) opposes all forms of corporal punishment for children (also Shelov and Altman 2009), and UNICEF, among others, urges governments worldwide to ban "all forms of violence against children within the family" (UN 2006).

8. The seminal early work on this is Hart and Risley (1995), who compared the vocabulary development of three groups of children in the United States: children whose parents are "professionals," children in "working class" families, and children of families on welfare. Based on in-depth, structured observations, they found that children from all three groups of families started to speak around the same time. However, children in professional families heard more words per hour: on average, children in "professional" families heard an average of 2,153 words per hour, while children in welfare-recipient families heard an average of 616 words per hour. As a result, by age 4, a child from a welfare-recipient family would have heard 32 million words less than a child of a "professional" family. By age 3, the observed cumulative vocabulary for children in the "professional" families was about 1,100 words, while the vocabulary of children in welfare-recipient families was just above 500 words.

9. While this seems intuitive, it need not be the case. The association between poverty and child development, or between poverty and various parental behaviors that affect development, may not have a causal interpretation.

Rather, it could be driven by a variety of omitted characteristics of parents (e.g., education levels or parental intelligence). For this reason, one cannot simply assume that, if households that are poor today were to have more income in the future, the development of children in these households would improve. This is a hypothesis that needs to be tested.

10. The evaluation actually assigned communities to one of four groups. A control group; a treatment group 1 that received the "basic" cash transfer equivalent to 15 percent of median consumption; a treatment group 2 that received a transfer of the same magnitude as households in group 1 but were also offered a scholarship that allowed one of the household members to choose among a number of vocational training courses offered at the municipal headquarters; and a treatment group 3, that received the same transfer as households in group 1, but were also given a lump-sum payment to start a small nonagricultural activity. This lump-sum payment was equivalent to 11 percent of the consumption of the mean recipient household. Macours, Schady, and Vakis (2012) first compare households that received any of the three treatments with the control group, and then focus on comparisons between treatment groups 1 and 3. These are the values reported in this chapter.

11. In Ecuador, the BDH program had a positive effect on child development only for the poorest households, while in Nicaragua no such differences are apparent. Nicaragua is a substantially poorer country than Ecuador. As a result, the beneficiaries of the Atención a Crisis program were also substantially poorer than those of the BDH program. In practice, 82 percent of households in the evaluation sample in Nicaragua had income below $1 per capita per day; in Ecuador, 34 percent of households in the evaluation sample had income below $1 per capita per day, and 93 percent below $2 per capita per day. The finding that impacts appear to be larger when recipients are poorer makes sense because for these households a given cash transfer represents a bigger proportional increase in household income.

12. The most relevant findings are those that focus on young children (below the age of 11). Løken, Mogstad, and Wiswall (2012) analyze the oil boom in Norway, which affected some communities more than others. They find that the positive income shock from oil resources increased school attainment, in particular in the lower parts of the income distribution. Milligan and Stabile (2011) focus on differences across provinces and over time in the generosity of the National Child Benefit in Canada. They find that income has a positive effect on math and vocabulary scores of boys only, in particular for children of parents with low education levels. Duncan, Morris, and Rodrigues (2011) use cross-site variation in the design and implementation of a variety of antipoverty programs in the United States. They find that, on average, a $1,000 increase in family income when children are between 2 and 5 years of age results in a 0.05 standard deviation increase in child learning outcomes. See also Duncan, Magnuson, and Votruba-Drzal (2014) for a thoughtful discussion.

13. Moreover, rates of exclusive breastfeeding of children 6 months of age or younger in Brazil (39 percent), continue to be almost 30 percentage points below those found in Peru (67 percent), and Chile (82 percent), although they are substantially higher than those in Mexico (14 percent).

14. For example, in Peru, in 2012, almost 1.2 million children received milk or other foodstuffs from the municipal Vaso de Leche program, and an even larger number received food from the Programa Nacional de Apoyo Alimentario (PRONAA). (In 2013, PRONAA was abolished and replaced by Qali Warma, a program that provides school meals to children in preschool and elementary school.) Jointly, these programs had a budget of 0.2 percent of GDP. In Uruguay, the Programa Alimentario Nacional has a budget equivalent to 0.12 percent of GDP.

15. Evidence from the region can be found in Cunha (2014) for Mexico; and in Hidrobo and others (2014) for Ecuador.

16. See discussions in Alive and Thrive (2014); Gilmore and McAuliffe (2013); Lassi and others (2013); and Pérez-Escamilla and others (2012).

17. Half of the children in the intervention group, and half of those in the control group received a nutritional supplement, which consisted of one kilogram of formula per week. Although children who received the supplement initially outperformed those who did not, with effect sizes comparable to those found for the early stimulation intervention, the effects of the supplement were no longer apparent after late childhood. As a result, researchers have generally worked with two groups only: one in which half the children are a pure control group, and half received the nutritional supplement only (jointly referred to as the "control" group); and one in which half the children received the stimulation intervention only, and the other half received the stimulation and the nutritional supplement (jointly referred to as the "treatment" group). This is the approach that was followed in the discussion in this chapter.

18. Half the children in both the treatment and control groups in Colombia received a nutritional intervention (in this case, micronutrient supplements), but this had no effect on child nutritional status or other measures of child development.

19. Relatively little is known about the FODI intervention itself (e.g., about the qualifications of the home visitors, the curriculum of the intervention, whether it was implemented with fidelity, or about the number of visits that each family received in practice), and the program has since been discontinued. The estimated effect sizes are surprisingly large, especially when compared to the Colombian intervention. It is important to corroborate these findings from evaluations of at-scale programs elsewhere in the region.

20. References include Arnold and others (1994); Huebner (2000); Jordan, Snow, and Porche (2000); Lonigan and Whitehurst (1998); Whitehurst and others (1988).

21. References include Allington and others (2010); Pagan and Sénéchal (2014); and White and Kim (2008).

22. See the discussion in Aboud and Yousafzai (2015); Baker-Henningham and López Boo (2010); and Howard and Brooks-Gunn (2009).

23. It is widely believed that income that is controlled by women is more likely to be spent on children than income that is controlled by men (Lundberg, Pollack, and Wales 1997; Ward-Batts 2008), although some recent evidence has cast doubt on this hypothesis (Benhassine and others forthcoming; Undurraga and others 2014).

24. References include Benhassine and others (forthcoming); Kooreman (2000); Thaler (1999).

25. See Behrman and others (2009); Hoddinott and others (2008); Maluccio and others (2009).

26. Three randomized evaluations of at-scale interventions in Peru (the Cuna Más program), Brazil (Cresça com Seu Filho), and Mexico (the PEI-CONAFE program) are under way. The results from these evaluations will be very important for policy purposes.

4   Daycare Services: It's All about Quality

1. Some of the household surveys from the region do not distinguish between preschool and daycare. See Mateo and Rodríguez-Chamussy (2015) for a discussion of these methodological difficulties.

2. In Colombia, the urban sample is representative of all but approximately the richest 10 percent of the population, while the rural sample is representative of the full distribution of households in only four geographic subregions (see Schady and others 2015, Table 1). For this reason, the data cannot be merged to calculate a national average.

3. Infants are children between 0 and 11 months old; toddlers are between 12 and 35 months; and preschoolers are between 36 and 59 months.

4. The data for Colombia covers urban areas only, and data for the early 2000s are not available. Guatemala is excluded from the figure because of the very low coverage.

5. The middle category, mothers who are primary school graduates, is omitted from these calculations.

6. . These findings are consistent with those reported in Evans and Kosec (2012) for Brazil, which show that, among households that use daycare (crèches) for children aged 0–3, 81 percent of households in the highest income quintile use private rather than public providers, compared to only 15 percent in the lowest income quintile.

7. In Chile, approximately one-quarter (22 percent) of children who attend private daycare attend a center that receives a public subsidy.

8. ITERS-R is a revised version of the ITERS; ECERS-R is a revised version of the ECERS; and FCCERS-R is a revised version of the FDCRS. The chapter

refers to the scales as ITERS, ECERS, and the FCCERS, without making the distinction between the earlier and revised versions of the scales.

9. Important references include Baker, Gruber, and Milligan (2008); Berry and others (2014); Currie (2001); Deming (2009); Garces, Thomas, and Currie (2002); Gupta and Simonsen (2010); Loeb and others (2007); Ludwig and Phillips (2008).

10. The Bolivian program, PIDI, is no longer in existence, while the Colombian program, Hogares Comunitarios, is still in existence and currently covers about 1.2 million children in 80,000 centers (Bernal and Camacho 2012).

11. FODI has since been replaced by the CIBV program described earlier in the chapter.

12. The follow-up survey was carried out between 6 and 18 months after children were moved from the Hogares Comunitarios to the new centers. It is possible that the absence of effects is partly a result of the short time horizon and the difficulty of transitioning from one modality to the other.

13. The evaluations of PIDI and the Hogares Comunitarios rely on comparisons between children who had spent more or less time in the program to identify impact. If these children and their families differ in unmeasured ways, the results could be biased. In Ecuador, the FODI program was evaluated with a regression discontinuity design, which can provide credible estimates of impact, but only for centers around the threshold that determined eligibility for funding. The training program for community mothers in Colombia was evaluated with propensity score matching, which leaves open the possibility of biases from omitted variables. Finally, the evaluation of the transition from community to institutional care in Colombia relied on random assignment, but there was substantial noncompliance.

14. A number of evaluations suggest that daycare has increased female labor force participation rates in the region. The most convincing study, by Paes de Barros and others (2011), exploits the fact that access to crèches in the city of Rio de Janeiro was allocated on the basis of public lotteries. The authors show that access to public daycare increased mothers' employment by 10 percentage points (from 36 to 46 percent). Other studies from the region also suggest that access to daycare increases female employment. For example, access to daycare provided by FODI in Ecuador appears to have roughly tripled the probability that a mother works, from a baseline rate of about 20 percent (Rosero and Oosterbeek 2011).

15. Most studies find that increases in mandated paid leave decreases unemployment and increases long-run employment of women (Ruhm 1998; Baker and Milligan 2008).

16. Levy and Schady (2013) show that, in many countries, a substantial proportion of workers are not salaried or are salaried but hired illegally. These workers do not contribute to social security, and a mandated period of parental leave would not be enforceable. The number of "informal" workers varies a great deal by country, from 81 percent in Peru, to 63 percent in Mexico, to

44 percent in Brazil, and to 17 percent in Chile. In all countries, low-income workers are overrepresented among the informal. See also Bosch, Melguizo, and Pagés (2013).

17. If benefits were funded from wage taxes, the bulk of the cost is likely to be passed on to workers in the form of lower wages, unless there are barriers like a minimum wage. This could result in more or less formal employment, depending on the value that is attached to these benefits. An alternative would be to fund benefits out of general tax revenues, in which case they would represent a transfer from informal to formal workers, and would be an incentive to formal work. However, because the poor are overrepresented among informal workers, this would imply a regressive transfer from poor to rich. Another issue arises because it would be necessary to legislate how much time a worker would have had to be in formal employment prior to being eligible for mandated leave to avoid strategic switching from informal to formal employment to take advantage of these benefits.

5 Early Schooling: Teachers Make the Difference

1. We use the words "enrollment" and "attendance" interchangeably. Some household surveys ask respondents about enrollment, others about attendance.
2. Countries in the region use different terms for the first years of formal schooling. For the purposes of this chapter, "primary school" is defined as starting with the grade that children are expected to begin at age 6 ("first grade"); and "pre-primary" is defined as kindergarten (for children age 5), and pre-K (for children age 4 or younger).
3. However, and importantly, there was no difference in completed schooling between those who attended one year of pre-primary education (kindergarten) and those who attended two years (pre-K and kindergarten) (Berlinski, Galiani, and Manacorda 2008).
4. Note that the values in Figure 5.1 are not comparable to the UNESCO (2015) estimates for gross pre-primary school enrollment, for a variety of reasons. First, the age ranges are frequently different. This is because UNESCO calculates pre-primary enrollment rates based on the "theoretical entrance age" in a given country. This varies from country to country. For example, in Argentina, Honduras, and Jamaica, pre-primary enrollment rates correspond to children aged 3–5; in Chile, Costa Rica, and Mexico, to children aged 4–5; in Brazil, to children aged 4–6; and in Guatemala, to children aged 5–6. By contrast, the calculations reported in this chapter always correspond to the proportion of children age 5 years who attend school. Second, the data sources vary. The UNESCO values are calculated by taking the total population of different ages in a country (using the most recent population census, and the population projections based on it) and the number of children enrolled in school (using administrative data). By contrast, the calculations

used in this chapter are based on household survey data. It is unclear which source of data is more accurate.

5. Comparisons of language scores are more complicated because of differences across countries in the proportion of children who are not native Spanish speakers.

6. The test developers for SERCE and TERCE also report the proportions of children who score at levels 1 (lowest) through 4 (highest) in each country. In the Dominican Republic, 75 percent of all children in TERCE had scores that placed them in the lowest level. These students could not solve simple addition or multiplication problems using natural numbers, or recognize the organization of the decimal-positional numeral system. Even in Chile and Costa Rica, the two best-performing countries in Latin America, 10 and 16 percent of children, respectively, placed in the lowest level of TERCE.

7. See Kane and Staiger (2002a) for an early application; Chetty and others (2011) for an application to the estimation of teacher effects in kindergarten in Tennessee; and Araujo and others (2014) for an application to the estimation of kindergarten teacher effects in Ecuador.

8. Wealth aggregates were constructed using only those household characteristics and assets that were asked in a comparable way in both the sample of children who took the tests and nationally representative household surveys for each country—the 2012 Encuesta Nacional de Empleo, Desempleo, Subempleo (ENEMDU) in Ecuador, the 2010 Encuesta Nacional de Ingresos y Gastos de los Hogares (ENIGH) in Mexico, and the 2010 Encuesta Nacional de Hogares (ENAHO) in Peru. This allows for comparisons to be made between the distribution of wealth of children who took the test and the distribution of wealth of households with children in the same age range in the nationally representative survey. This, in turn, makes it possible to assign children who were tested to quintiles of the national distribution of wealth (as in Schady and others 2015).

9. These gradients are similar to those found in the United States, where 5-year-olds in the lowest income quartile have math scores that are 0.8 standard deviations below those in the highest quartile (Cunha and Heckman 2007).

10. In contrast, gradients in behavioral problems were modest: teacher reports indicate that children in the lowest asset group were 0.18 standard deviations more likely to have internalizing problems (which include being withdrawn or lacking self-esteem) in pre-K than those in the highest asset group, but 0.30 less likely to have externalizing problems (which include aggression and defiant behavior).

11. This section draws heavily on a background paper for the report written by Yyannu Cruz-Aguayo, Tomas Guanziroli, Bridget Hamre, Sadie Hasbrouck, Marcia E. Kraft-Sayre, Jennifer LoCasale-Crouch, Carolina Melo, Robert Pianta, and Sara C. Schodt.

12. Many examples from developing countries show that improving one or another dimension of structural quality does not improve child learning outcomes (or does so only modestly). In a particularly discouraging example, Duflo, Dupas, and Kremer (2011) analyze a program that halved student-to-teacher ratios in Kenya, from a baseline level of about 80 children per teacher. They conclude that the program did not improve learning outcomes—apparently, because it did not change teaching practices, did not lead to more individualized attention of teachers to students, and therefore did not change children's daily classroom experiences. In a recent study from the region, laptop computers were distributed to children in third through sixth grade in Lima, Peru, as a way of improving their learning outcomes. This pilot, which was related to a larger initiative by the Peruvian government to purchase and distribute 860,000 laptops to students, was evaluated in a randomized fashion. The results show that children randomly assigned to receive laptops report using computers more frequently than those in the control group. However, there were no differences between children who received the laptops and those who did not in terms of their test scores on language and mathematics, or on their cognitive skills, as measured by the Raven's Progressive Matrices Test (Beuermann and others 2015).

13. The Stallings, which was originally developed for research on school quality in the United States in the 1970s (Stallings 1977; Stallings and Mohlman 1988), takes ten separate "snapshots" at regular intervals over the course of a class period. Each "snapshot" takes 15 seconds. During those 15 seconds, the observer scans the room and registers four key aspects of classroom dynamics: Whether the teacher is engaged in instruction, classroom management, or is "off-task"; if the time is being used for instruction, which pedagogical practices are being used (e.g., reading aloud, or question and answer); if the time is being used for instruction, what learning materials are being used; and how many students are visibly engaged in the activity led by the teacher, rather than being off-task or not paying attention (Bruns and Luque 2015, especially 99–105).

14. Important references include Blair (2002); Burchinal, Lee, and Ramey (1989); Campbell and Ramey (1995); Greenberg, Domitrovich, and Bumbarger (2001); Hamre and Pianta (2007); Howes and Hamilton (1993); Kisker and others (1991); Kontos and Wilcox-Herzog (1997); and Phillips and others (2000).

15. Perry, Donohue, and Weinstein (2007) found that across 14 first-grade classrooms, higher emotional support at the beginning of the year was associated with more positive peer behavior and less problem behaviors as the year progressed. Similarly, in an examination of 36 first-grade classrooms serving 178 6- and 7-year-old students, emotionally supportive classrooms demonstrated decreased peer aggression over the course of the year (Merritt and others 2012). Emotional climate appears to influence academic outcomes, as well. In a sample of 1,364 third-grade students, the classroom's emotional

support was related to a child's reading and mathematics scores at the end of the year (Rudasill, Gallagher, and White 2010).

16. For example, data from 172 first graders across 36 classrooms in a rural area of the United States demonstrated that classroom organization was significantly predictive of literacy gains (Ponitz and others 2009).

17. References include Burchinal and others (2008, 2010); Hamre and Pianta (2005); Mashburn and others (2008). For example, examining 1,129 low-income students enrolled in 671 pre-kindergarten classrooms in the United States, Burchinal and others (2010) found a significant association between instructional support and academic skills; classrooms demonstrating higher instructional support had students who scored higher on measures of language, reading, and math than those enrolled in classrooms with low-quality instructional support. Similarly, Mashburn and others (2008) used data from the United States and found that the instructional support of a classroom was related to all five academic outcomes measured (receptive language, expressive language, letter naming, rhyming, and applied math problems).

18. References include Denny, Hallam, and Homer (2012); Hamre and others (2013); La Paro, Pianta, and Stuhlman (2004); LoCasale-Crouch and others (2007); Pianta and others (2007).

19. However, the data provided by the SNAPSHOT is somewhat more detailed than that collected in the Stallings. It systematically observes the type of academic setting (e.g., whether it is whole group, small group, individual time, free choice/centers, routines) and academic activity (e.g., whether students were read to, students read aloud, letter/sounds learning, writing, math, science, social studies, aesthetics, physical activity, foreign language, or no activity) in which students are engaged. The fact that the data collected in the SNAPSHOT are more detailed than those collected in the Stallings is an advantage, but it also means that the qualifications and training that the observers need to have is higher in the SNAPSHOT. This is a disadvantage, as it limits the possibility of applying the instrument at scale.

20. This pattern—scores on Emotional Support and Classroom Organization that are higher than those on Instructional Support—is similar in the United States, but the scores on Instructional Support in Brazil, Chile, and Ecuador were consistently lower than in the United States, by one CLASS point or more, on average.

21. This is consistent with another study of Chilean classrooms. Strasser, Lissi, and Silva (2009) examined 12 kindergarten classrooms in Chile for approximately three hours each, detailing how teachers engaged students. Fifty-three percent of classroom time was spent on noninstructional activities.

22. Another way of putting the magnitude of the effects in context is by comparing them with the socioeconomic gradients in kindergarten test scores. On average, the difference in test scores between children of mothers who are primary school dropouts and those who are secondary school graduates is

about 0.8 standard deviations, so being assigned to an outstanding, rather an average, teacher for a single year has an impact that is equivalent to one-fifth of the difference in accumulated learning between children of high- and low-education mothers.

23. Being assigned to a teacher who has a one-standard deviation higher IQ results in 0.04 standard deviations more learning.

24. Important references include Brennan and others (2008); Domitrovich and others (2009); Fox and others (2011); Hamre and others (2012); Pianta and others (2008).

25. Important references include Fryer (2013); Rouse and others (2013); Springer and others (2010); Vigdor (2008), among many others.

26. Research from the United States indicates that teachers' aptitude has declined markedly since the 1960s, primarily as a result of the compression of teacher wages (rather than overall low wages) (Hoxby and Leigh 2004).

27. The scores from the previous grade serve as a measure of the baseline learning outcomes for the current grade.

28. For example, teachers could be rewarded on the basis of a locally appropriate version of the Teaching through Interactions (TTI) framework. This avoids many of the concerns related to high-stakes testing (cheating, teaching to the test, focusing primarily on a particular group of students). However, classroom observations are likely to be at least as noisy a measure of teacher performance as teacher value added. Araujo and others (2014) show that, in Ecuador, CLASS scores for the same teacher vary a great deal from one day to another, and even more from one year to the next. Because they have more than one cohort of children taught by the same teacher, Araujo and others can test whether teacher value added and teacher CLASS scores with one cohort of students (cohort 1) are good predictors of learning outcomes with a *different* group of students (cohort 2). When only one of the two measures (teacher value added with cohort 1, CLASS scores when teaching cohort 1) is used as a predictor, both are significantly associated with learning outcomes for cohort 2. However, the CLASS is not significant and has no predictive power once value added with cohort 1 is controlled for. In other words, teacher value added with one cohort of children is much more robustly associated with child learning outcomes with another group of children than is the CLASS, a measure of teacher behaviors.

29. Many countries, including Brazil and Chile, have laws on the books that permit the dismissal of low-performing teachers in the first years of their careers, before they are awarded tenure. In practice, these provisions are rarely used.

30. Specifically, this involves taking the 10 percent of kindergarten teachers with the lowest value added, replacing them with a teacher whose value added is equivalent to that of the average kindergarten teacher in her school (with the average excluding the low-performing teacher), and reestimating the total distribution of test scores with these changes. Note that the estimated

increase in learning is therefore for the entire distribution of kindergarten children, not just those who received the better teacher (for whom, of course, the benefits are much larger).

6   More Bang for the Buck: Investing in
Early Childhood Development

1. This section draws heavily on a background study that collected and standardized child-specific budget data in Latin America and the Caribbean. See Alcázar and Sánchez (2014) and Box 6.1 for details.
2. The corresponding figure for the United States, a country with a particularly strong age bias in public expenditures, is 2.4 overall, with the ratio rising to 7:1 if only the federal budget is considered (Isaacs 2009).
3. Levy and Schady (2013, p. 202) show that, in 2011, the budget for the largest cash transfer programs in Latin America was substantially larger than the numbers in Table 6.2. In percentage points of GDP the budget for the programs was 0.49 in Argentina, 0.41 in Brazil, 0.71 in Ecuador, 0.46 in Mexico, and 0.48 in Uruguay. However, these are the values for the entire budget of a given cash transfer program, while the values in Table 6.2 correspond to the budget of a given program that is assigned to children between 0 and 5 years of age.
4. To be included in Tables 6.6 and 6.7, the studies had to report standardized effects on child cognitive skills or academic achievement, present information about cost parameters, and apply a solid empirical strategy.
5. Throughout the chapter, all effects on child cognitive skills are presented in standard deviations. This is the conventional way of measuring impacts on cognitive skills. In a sample of children 3–6 years old in Colombia, test differences in a measure of cognitive skills between children belonging to families in the top quartile in wealth versus those in the bottom quartile were about 0.6 in rural areas and 1.2 in urban areas (Schady and others 2015).
6. The only included evaluation of preschools measured effects on test scores in math and language in third grade. In contrast, effects on cognitive skills for daycare and home visits programs were measured before entering primary school.
7. Why 75 percent? First, families that sign up their child to a free public daycare are expected to be willing to pay higher than 0 (this is why they take up the service). Second, families will be unwilling to pay more than the market price for this service. The market price of the service can be approximated by the cost of public provision (as markets are quite competitive due to low barriers to entry). Consequently, one would expect that families should not be willing to pay more than 100 percent of the cost of providing the service. Thus, it means that the average willingness to pay for families taking up the service is expected to lie between 0 and 100 percent of the cost of providing the service. A valuation of 75 percent is assumed because many families will

be willing to pay close to the full market price (i.e., 100 percent) because they are already sending their children to a private daycare. Still, the ordering of the three analyzed programs in terms of their benefit-cost ratios is robust to choosing any valuation between 0 and 100 percent.

8. Participation rate is defined as the proportion of women who either work or are actively searching for a job. For additional details on the sample selection and variable definitions and for additional country-by-country evidence, see Busso and Fonseca (forthcoming).

7   Drawing Up an Institutional Architecture

1. The information on which this chapter is based comes from case studies conducted in 2014 in Brazil, Chile, Colombia, Guatemala, and Trinidad and Tobago. The cases were selected so as to maximize variability regarding (i) the characteristics of the institutional approaches to public policy in early childhood, and (ii) country context characteristics that may affect institutional choices such as level of decentralization, geographic dispersion, and GDP, among others. Data collection included a thorough document review (including major laws and regulations, program documents, and program monitoring and evaluation reports) and in-depth interviews with current and former ministry heads, program managers, political parties' representatives, elected officials, leaders of key nongovernment organizations (NGOs), private philanthropy representatives, and academics. The analysis focused on identifying the main characteristics of the institutional infrastructure that supports program delivery along four main areas: governance, finance, quality and accountability, and human capacity.

2. A third kind of standards relates to the standards for professional certification that specify what teachers, doctors, nurses, and social workers need to know and be able to do to deliver services effectively. These are discussed in the section on human capacity.

3. Human resources that staff early childhood services come from a range of professional backgrounds including medicine, education, and psychology. The data collection that accompanied this study focused on early childhood educators; for that reason, the remainder of this section will frame the discussion around this group. However, many of the findings are generalizable to the other professions that staff ECD programs.

References

Aboud, F. E., D. R. Singla, M. I. Nahil, and I. Borisova. 2013. "Effectiveness of a Parenting Program in Bangladesh to Address Early Childhood Health, Growth and Development." *Social Science and Medicine* 97(November): 250–58.

Aboud, F. E., and A. K. Yousafzai. 2015. "Global Health and Development in Early Childhood." *Annual Review of Psychology* 66(January): 433–57.

Afifi, T. O., N. P. Mota, P. Dasiewicz, H. L. MacMillan, and J. Sareen. 2012. "Physical Punishment and Mental Disorders: Results from a Nationally Representative U.S. Sample." *Pediatrics* 130(2) August: 184–92.

Aikens, N., and L. Akers. 2011. "Background Review of Existing Literature on Coaching." Final report. Mathematica Policy Research, Washington, DC.

Ainsworth, M. D. S. 1969. "Object Relations, Dependency, and Attachment: A Theoretical Review of the Infant-Mother Relationship." *Child Development* 40(4) December: 969–1025.

Akresh, R., S. Bhalotra, M. Leone, and U. O. Osili. 2012. "War and Stature: Growing Up during the Nigerian Civil War." *American Economic Review* 102(3) May: 273–77.

Alcázar, L., and A. Sánchez. 2014. "El gasto público en la infancia y niñez en América Latina: ¿cuánto y cuán efectivo?" Inter-American Development Bank, Washington, DC. Unpublished.

Alive and Thrive. 2014. "Getting Strategic with Interpersonal Communication: Improving Feeding Practices in Bangladesh." E-magazine. Alive and Thrive, Washington, DC. Available at http://aliveandthrive.org/wp-content/uploads/2014/11/Getting-strategic -with-IPC-Bangladesh-June-2014.pdf. Accessed June 2015.

Allington, R. L., A. McGill-Franzen, G. Camilli, L. Williams, J. Graff, J. Zeig, C. Zmach, and R. Nowak. 2010. "Addressing Summer Reading Setback among Economically Disadvantaged Elementary Students." *Reading Psychology* 31(5): 411–27.

Almond, D. 2006. "Is the 1918 Influenza Pandemic Over? Long-Term Effects of *In Utero* Influenza Exposure in the Post-1940 U.S. Population." *Journal of Political Economy* 114(4) August: 672–712.

Almond, D., K. Y. Chay, and D. S. Lee. 2005. "The Costs of Low Birth Weight." *Quarterly Journal of Economics* 120(3): 1031–83.

Almond, D., and J. Currie. 2011. "Killing Me Softly: The Fetal Origins Hypothesis." *Journal of Economic Perspectives* 25(3) Summer: 153–72.

American Academy of Pediatrics. 1998. "Guidance for Effective Discipline." *Pediatrics* 101(4) April: 723–28.

———. 2005. "Quality Early Education and Child Care from Birth to Kindergarten." Policy statement. *Pediatrics* 115(1) January: 187–91.

———. 2012. "Spanking Linked to Mental Illness." Press release, July 2. Available at http://www.aap.org/en-us/about-the-aap/aap-press-room/Pages/Spanking-Linked -to-Mental-Illness.aspx. Accessed April 2015.

Anderson, V. 1998. "Assessing Executive Functions in Children: Biological, Psychological, and Developmental Considerations." *Neuropsychological Rehabilitation* 8(3): 319–49.

Araujo, M. C., P. Carneiro, Y. Cruz-Aguayo, and N. Schady. 2014. "A Helping Hand? Teacher Quality and Learning Outcomes in Kindergarten." Inter-American Development Bank, Washington, DC. Unpublished.

Araujo, M. C., and F. López Boo. 2015. "Los servicios de cuidado infantil en América Latina y el Caribe." *El Trimestre Económico* 82(326) April–June: 249–75.

Araujo, M. C., F. López Boo, R. Novella, S. Schodt, and R. Tomé. 2015. "La calidad de los Centros Infantiles del Buen Vivir en Ecuador." Inter-American Development Bank, Washington, DC. Unpublished.

Araujo, M. C., F. López Boo, and J. M. Puyana. 2013. *Overview of Early Childhood Development Services in Latin America and the Caribbean.* Washington, DC: Inter-American Development Bank.

Ariès, P. 1962. *Centuries of Childhood: A Social History of Family Life.* New York: Vintage Books.

Arnold, D. H., C. J. Lonigan, G. J. Whitehurst, and J. N. Epstein. 1994. "Accelerating Language Development through Picture Book Reading: Replication and Extension to a Videotape Training Format." *Journal of Educational Psychology* 86(2) June: 235–43.

Atal, J. P., H. Ñopo, and N. Winder. 2009. "New Century, Old Disparities: Gender and Ethnic Wage Gaps in Latin America." Working Paper No. IDB-WP-109. Inter-American Development Bank, Washington, DC.

Attanasio, O., E. Battistin, E. Fitzsimons, A. Mesnard, and M. Vera-Hernández. 2005. "How Effective Are Conditional Cash Transfers? Evidence from Colombia." Briefing Note No. 54. Institute for Fiscal Studies, London.

Attanasio, O., S. Cattan, E. Fitzsimons, C. Meghir, and M. Rubio-Codina. 2015. "Estimating the Production Function for Human Capital: Results from a Randomized Control Trial in Colombia." NBER Working Paper No. 20965. National Bureau of Economic Research, Cambridge, MA.

Attanasio, O. P., C. Fernández, E. Fitzsimons, S. M. Grantham-McGregor, C. Meghir, and M. Rubio-Codina. 2014. "Using the Infrastructure of a Conditional Cash Transfer Program to Deliver a Scalable Integrated Early Child Development Program in Colombia: Cluster Randomized Controlled Trial." *BMJ* 349: g6126.

Avellar, S., D. Paulsell, E. Sama-Miller, P. Del Grosso, L. Akers, and R. Kleinman. 2014. "Home Visiting Evidence of Effectiveness Review: Executive Summary." OPRE Report No. 2014–59. Office of Planning, Research and Evaluation, Administration for Children and Families, U.S. Department of Health and Human Services, Washington, DC.

Baird, S., J. Friedman, and N. Schady. 2011. "Aggregate Income Shocks and Infant Mortality in the Developing World." *Review of Economics and Statistics* 93(3) August: 847–56.

Baker, M., J. Gruber, and K. Milligan. 2008. "Universal Child Care, Maternal Labor Supply, and Family Well-Being." *Journal of Political Economy* 116(4) August: 709–45.

Baker, M., and K. Milligan. 2008. "How Does Job-Protected Maternity Leave Affect Mothers' Employment?" *Journal of Labor Economics* 26(4) October: 655–91.

———. 2010. "Evidence from Maternity Leave Expansions of the Impact of Maternal Care on Early Child Development." *Journal of Human Resources* 45(1) Winter: 1–32.

Baker-Henningham, H., and F. López Boo. 2010. "Early Childhood Stimulation Interventions in Developing Countries: A Comprehensive Literature Review." IZA Discussion Paper No. 5282. Institute for the Study of Labor, Bonn, Germany.

Barnett, W. S., J. T. Hustedt, K. B. Robin, and K. L. Schulman. 2004. "The State of Preschool: 2004 State Preschool Yearbook." Report. National Institute for Early Education Research (NIEER), Rutgers University, Newark, NJ. Available at http://nieer.org/sites/nieer/files/2004yearbook.pdf. Accessed June 2015.

Barnett, W. S., and L. N. Masse. 2007. "Comparative Benefit-Cost Analysis of the Abecedarian Program and Its Policy Implications." *Economics of Education Review* 26(1) February: 113–25.

Barnett, W. S., K. B. Robin, J. T. Hustedt, and K. L. Schulman. 2003. "The State of Preschool: 2003 State Preschool Yearbook." Report. National Institute for Early Education Research (NIEER), Rutgers University, Newark, NJ. Available at http://nieer.org/sites/nieer/files/2003yearbook.pdf. Accessed June 2015.

Bastos, P., and O. R. Straume. 2013. "Preschool Education in Brazil: Does Public Supply Crowd out Private Enrollment?" Working Paper No. IDB-WP-463. Inter-American Development Bank, Washington, DC.

Baumrind, D. 2001. "Does Causally Relevant Research Support a Blanket Injunction against Disciplinary Spanking by Parents?" Paper presented at the American Psychological Association's 109th Annual Convention, August 24, San Francisco, CA.

Becker, G. S. 1981. *A Treatise on the Family.* Cambridge, MA: Harvard University Press.

———. 1993. *Human Capital: A Theoretical and Empirical Analysis, with Special Reference to Education.* Third edition. Chicago, IL: University of Chicago Press.

Bedregal, P., and M. Pardo. 2004. "Desarrollo infantil temprano y derechos del niño." Serie reflexiones: Infancia y adolescencia No. 1. UNICEF, Santiago, Chile.

Behrman, J. R., M. C. Calderón, S. H. Preston, J. Hoddinott, R. Martorell, and A. D. Stein. 2009. "Nutritional Supplementation in Girls Influences the Growth of Their Children: Prospective Study in Guatemala." *American Journal of Clinical Nutrition* 90(5) November: 1372–79.

Behrman, J. R., Y. Cheng, and P. E. Todd. 2004. "Evaluating Preschool Programs When Length of Exposure to the Program Varies: A Nonparametric Approach." *Review of Economics and Statistics* 86(1) February: 108–32.

Behrman, J. R., and J. Hoddinott. 2005. "Programme Evaluation with Unobserved Heterogeneity and Selective Implementation: The Mexican PROGRESA Impact on Child Nutrition." *Oxford Bulletin of Economics and Statistics* 67(4) August: 547–69.

Behrman, J. R., S. W. Parker, P. E. Todd, and K. I. Wolpin. 2015. "Aligning Learning Incentives of Students and Teachers: Results from a Social Experiment in Mexican High Schools." *Journal of Political Economy* 123(2): 325–64.

Behrman, J. R., and M. R. Rosenzweig. 2004. "Returns to Birth Weight." *Review of Economics and Statistics* 86(2) May: 586–601.

Belfield, C. R., M. Nores, S. Barnett, and L. Schweinhart. 2006. "The High/Scope Perry Preschool Program: Cost-Benefit Analysis Using Data from the Age-40 Follow-up." *Journal of Human Resources* 41(1) Winter: 162–90.

Benhassine, N., F. Devoto, E. Duflo, P. Dupas, and V. Pouliquen. 2015. "Turning a Shove into a Nudge? A 'Labeled Cash Transfer' for Education." *American Economic Journal: Economic Policy* 7(3) August: 86–125.

Berlin, L. J., J. M. Ispa, M. A. Fine, P. S. Malone, J. Brooks-Gunn, C. Brady-Smith, C. Ayoub, and Y. Bai. 2009. "Correlates and Consequences of Spanking and Verbal Punishment for Low-Income White, African-American, and Mexican-American Toddlers." *Child Development* 80(5) September–October: 1403–20.

Berlinski, S., S. Galiani, and P. Gertler. 2009. "The Effect of Pre-Primary Education on Primary School Performance." *Journal of Public Economics* 93(1–2) February: 219–34.

Berlinski, S., S. Galiani, and M. Manacorda. 2008. "Giving Children a Better Start: Preschool Attendance and School-Age Profiles." *Journal of Public Economics* 92(5–6) June: 1416–40.

Bernal, R. 2013. "Costos de la política de atención a la primera infancia en Colombia." Inter-American Development Bank, Washington, DC. Unpublished.

———. 2014. *Diagnóstico y recomendaciones para la atención de calidad a la primera infancia en Colombia.* Cuadernos de Fedesarrollo Series. Bogotá: Fedesarrollo.

———. Forthcoming. "The Impact of a Vocational Education Program for Childcare Providers on Children's Well-Being." *Economics of Education Review.* doi:10.1016/j.econedurev.2015.07.003

Bernal, R., O. Attanasio, X. Peña, and M. Vera-Hernández. 2014a. "The Effects of the Transition from Home-Based Childcare to Center-Based Childcare in Colombia." Universidad de los Andes, Bogotá, and Institute for Fiscal Studies, London. Unpublished.

———. 2014b. "Haciendo la transición hacia atención en centros: evaluación del impacto de los centros de desarrollo infantil." Policy Note No. 18. Universidad de los Andes, Bogotá.

Bernal, R., and A. Camacho. 2012. "La política de primera infancia en el contexto de la equidad y movilidad social en Colombia." CEDE Working Paper No. 33. Centro de Estudios sobre Desarrollo Económico, Universidad de los Andes, Bogotá.

Bernal, R., and C. Fernández. 2013. "Subsidized Childcare and Child Development in Colombia: Effects of Hogares Comunitarios de Bienestar as a Function of Timing and Length of Exposure." *Social Science and Medicine* 97(2013) November: 241–49.

Bernal, R., C. Fernández, C. E. Flórez, A. Gaviria, P. R. Ocampo, B. Samper, and F. Sánchez. 2009. "Evaluación de impacto del Programa Hogares Comunitarios de Bienestar del ICBF." CEDE Working Paper No. 16. Centro de Estudios sobre Desarrollo Económico, Universidad de los Andes, Bogotá.

Bernal, R., and M. P. Keane. 2011. "Child Care Choices and Children's Cognitive Achievement: The Case of Single Mothers." *Journal of Labor Economics* 29(3) July: 459–512.

Berry, D., C. Blair, A. Ursache, M. Willoughby, P. Garrett-Peters, L. Vernon-Feagans, M. Bratsch-Hines, W. R. Mills-Koonce, D. A. Granger, and Family Life Project Key Investigators. 2014. "Child Care and Cortisol across Early Childhood: Context Matters." *Developmental Psychology* 50(2) February: 514–25.

Beuermann, D. W., J. Cristiá, S. Cueto, O. Malamud, and Y. Cruz-Aguayo. 2015. "One Laptop per Child at Home: Short-Term Impacts from a Randomized Experiment in Peru." *American Economic Journal: Applied Economics* 7(2) April: 53–80.

Bhalotra, S. 2010. "Fatal Fluctuations? Cyclicality in Infant Mortality in India." *Journal of Development Economics* 93(1) September: 7–19.

Bhandari, N., R. Bahl, S. Mazumdar, J. Martines, R. E. Black, M. K. Bhan, and the Infant Feeding Study Group. 2003. "Effect of Community-Based Promotion of Exclusive Breastfeeding on Diarrhoeal Illness and Growth: A Cluster Randomised Controlled Trial." *Lancet* 361(9367) April: 1418–23.

Bharadwaj, P., J. Eberhard, and C. Neilson. 2014. "Health at Birth, Parental Investments and Academic Outcomes." University of California, San Diego, CA. Unpublished.

Bharadwaj, P., K. V. Løken, and C. Neilson. 2013. "Early Life Health Interventions and Academic Achievement." *American Economic Review* 103(5) August: 1862–91.

Black, S. E., P. J. Devereux, and K. G. Salvanes. 2007. "From the Cradle to the Labor Market? The Effect of Birth Weight on Adult Outcomes." *Quarterly Journal of Economics* 122(1): 409–39.

Blair, C. 2002. "School Readiness: Integrating Cognition and Emotion in a Neurobiological Conceptualization of Children's Functioning at School Entry." *American Psychologist* 57(2) February: 111–27.

Blau, D., and J. Currie. 2006. "Pre-School, Day Care, and After-School Care: Who's Minding the Kids?" In E. Hanushek and F. Welch, eds., *Handbook of the Economics of Education*. Volume 2. Amsterdam: North-Holland.

———. 2008. "Efficient Provision of High-Quality Early Childhood Education: Does the Private Sector or Public Sector Do It Best?" *CESifo DICE Report* 6(2): 15–20.

Bloom, L. 1998. "Language Acquisition in Its Developmental Context." In D. Kuhn and R. S. Siegler, eds., *Handbook of Child Psychology: Volume 2: Cognition, Perception, and Language*. Fifth edition. New York: John Wiley and Sons.

Boivin, M. J., P. Bangirana, N. Nakasujja, C. F. Page, C. Shohet, D. Givon, J. K. Bass, R. O. Opoka, and P. S. Klein. 2013. "A Year-Long Caregiver Training Program to Improve Neurocognition in Preschool Ugandan HIV-Exposed Children." *Journal of Developmental and Behavioral Pediatrics* 34(4) May: 269–78.

Bosch, M., Á. Melguizo, and C. Pagés. 2013. *Better Pensions, Better Jobs: Towards Universal Coverage in Latin America and the Caribbean*. Washington, DC: Inter-American Development Bank.

Bowlby, J. 1958. "The Nature of the Child's Tie to His Mother." *International Journal of Psycho-Analysis* 39(5) September–October: 350–73.

Bradbury, B., M. Corak, J. Waldfogel, and E. Washbrook. 2012. "Inequality in Early Childhood Outcomes." In J. Ermisch, M. Jäntti, and T. M. Smeeding, eds., *From Parents to Children: The Intergenerational Transmission of Advantage*. New York: Russell Sage Foundation.

Bradley, R. H. 1993. "Children's Home Environments, Health, Behavior, and Intervention Efforts: A Review Using the HOME Inventory as a Marker Measure." *Genetic, Social, and General Psychology Monographs* 119(4) November: 437–90.

Bradley, R. H., and B. M. Caldwell. 1977. "Home Observation for Measurement of the Environment: A Validation Study of Screening Efficiency." *American Journal of Mental Deficiency* 81(5) March: 417–20.

Brennan, E. M., J. R. Bradley, M. D. Allen, and D. F. Perry. 2008. "The Evidence Base for Mental Health Consultation in Early Childhood Settings: Research Synthesis Addressing Staff and Program Outcomes." *Early Education and Development* 19(6) December: 982–1022.

Britto, P. R., H. Yoshikawa, J. van Ravens, L. A. Ponguta, M. Reyes, S. Oh, R. Dimaya, A. M. Nieto, and R. Seder. 2014. "Strengthening Systems for Integrated Early Childhood Development Services: A Cross-National Analysis of Governance." *Annals of the New York Academy of Sciences* 1308(January): 245–55.

Brophy, J., and T. L. Good. 1986. "Teacher Behavior and Student Achievement." In M. C. Wittrock, ed., *Handbook of Research on Teaching*. Third edition. New York: Macmillan.

Bruner, C. 1996. "Where's the Beef? Getting Bold about What 'Comprehensive' Means." In R. Stone, ed., *Core Issues in Comprehensive Community-Building Initiatives.* Chicago, IL: Chapin Hall Center for Children, University of Chicago.

Bruner, C. (with M. Stover Wright, B. Gebhard, and S. Hibbard). 2004. "Building an Early Learning System: The ABCs of Planning and Governance Structures." Monograph. State Early Childhood Policy Technical Assistance Network (SECPTAN), Des Moines, IA. Available at http://www.finebynine.org/uploaded/file/SECPTAN_Build_PROOF .pdf. Accessed April 2015.

Bruns, B., and J. Luque. 2015. *Great Teachers: How to Raise Student Learning in Latin America and the Caribbean.* Washington, DC: World Bank.

Burchinal, M., C. Howes, R. Pianta, D. Bryant, D. Early, R. Clifford, and O. Barbarin. 2008. "Predicting Child Outcomes at the End of Kindergarten from the Quality of Pre-Kindergarten Teacher–Child Interactions and Instruction." *Applied Developmental Science* 12(3): 140–53.

Burchinal, M., M. Lee, and C. Ramey. 1989. "Type of Day-Care and Preschool Intellectual Development in Disadvantaged Children." *Child Development* 60(1) February: 128–37.

Burchinal, M., N. Vandergrift, R. Pianta, and A. Mashburn. 2010. "Threshold Analysis of Association between Child Care Quality and Child Outcomes for Low-Income Children in Pre-Kindergarten Programs." *Early Childhood Research Quarterly* 25(2): 166–76.

Busso, M., and D. Romero Fonseca. Forthcoming. "Facts and Determinants of Female Labor Supply in Latin America." In L. Gasparini and M. Marchioni, eds., *Bridging Gender Gaps? The Rise and Deceleration of Female Labor Force Participation in Latin America.*

Caldwell, B. M. 1967. "Descriptive Evaluations of Child Development and of Developmental Settings." *Pediatrics* 40(1) July: 46–54.

Caldwell, B. M., and R. H. Bradley. 1984. *Administration Manual: Home Observation for Measurement of the Environment (HOME).* Revised edition. Little Rock, AR: University of Arkansas.

Campbell, F., G. Conti, J. J. Heckman, S. H. Moon, R. Pinto, E. Pungello, and Y. Pan. 2014. "Early Childhood Investments Substantially Boost Adult Health." *Science* 343(6178) March: 1478–85.

Campbell, F. A., E. P. Pungello, S. Miller-Johnson, M. Burchinal, and C. T. Ramey. 2001. "The Development of Cognitive and Academic Abilities: Growth Curves from an Early Childhood Educational Experiment." *Developmental Psychology* 37(2) March: 231–42.

Campbell, F. A., and C. T. Ramey. 1995. "Cognitive and School Outcomes for High-Risk African-American Students at Middle Adolescence: Positive Effects of Early Intervention." *American Educational Research Journal* 32(4) Winter: 743–72.

Campbell, F. A., C. T. Ramey, E. Pungello, J. Sparling, and S. Miller-Johnson. 2002. "Early Childhood Education: Young Adult Outcomes from the Abecedarian Project." *Applied Developmental Science* 6(1): 42–57.

Carlson, S. M. 2005. "Developmentally Sensitive Measures of Executive Function in Preschool Children." *Developmental Neuropsychology* 28(2): 595–616.

Carneiro, P., and J. J. Heckman. 2003. "Human Capital Policy." In J. J. Heckman and A. B. Krueger, eds., *Inequality in America: What Role for Human Capital Policies?* Cambridge, MA: MIT Press.

Carneiro, P., K. V. Løken, and K. G. Salvanes. 2015. "A Flying Start? Maternity Leave Benefits and Long-Run Outcomes of Children." *Journal of Political Economy* 123(2) April: 365–412.

Case, A., and C. Paxson. 2008. "Stature and Status: Height, Ability, and Labor Market Outcomes." *Journal of Political Economy* 116(3): 499–532.

Casey, B. M., D. D. McIntire, and K. J. Leveno. 2001. "The Continuing Value of the Apgar Score for the Assessment of Newborn Infants." *New England Journal of Medicine* 344(7) February: 467–71.

Chang, S. M., S. M. Grantham-McGregor, C. A. Powell, M. Vera-Hernández, F. López Boo, H. Baker-Henningham, and S. P. Walker. 2015a. "Delivering Parenting Interventions through Health Services in the Caribbean: Impact, Acceptability and Costs." Inter-American Development Bank, Washington, DC. Unpublished.

———. 2015b. "Integrating a Parenting Intervention with Routine Primary Health Care: A Cluster Randomized Trial." *Pediatrics* 136(2) August: 272–80.

Chetty, R., J. N. Friedman, N. Hilger, E. Saez, D. W. Schanzenbach, and D. Yagan. 2011. "How Does Your Kindergarten Classroom Affect Your Earnings? Evidence from Project STAR." *Quarterly Journal of Economics* 126(4) November: 1593–660.

Chetty, R., J. N. Friedman, and J. E. Rockoff. 2014. "Measuring the Impacts of Teachers I: Evaluating Bias in Teacher Value-Added Estimates." *American Economic Review* 104(9) September: 2593–632.

Clarke, J. 2004. "Histories of Childhood." In D. Wyse, ed., *Childhood Studies: An Introduction.* Malden, MA: Wiley-Blackwell.

Clements, D. H., and J. Sarama. 2011. "Early Childhood Mathematics Intervention." *Science* 333(6045) August: 968–70.

Coffman, J., and S. Parker. 2010. "Early Childhood Systems Building from a Community Perspective." Issue brief. Colorado Trust, Denver, CO. Available at http://mchb.hrsa .gov/programs/earlychildhood/comprehensivesystems/resources/2010meeting /issuebrief.pdf. Accessed May 2015.

Cohen, J. 1969. *Statistical Power Analysis for the Behavioral Sciences.* New York: Academic Press.

Colchero, M. A., D. Contreras-Loya, H. López-Gatell, and T. González de Cosío. 2015. "The Costs of Inadequate Breastfeeding of Infants in Mexico." *American Journal of Clinical Nutrition* 101(3) March: 579–86.

Crookston, B. T., W. Schott, S. Cueto, K. A. Dearden, P. Engle, A. Georgiadis, E. A. Lundeen, M. E. Penny, A. D. Stein, and J. R. Behrman. 2013. "Postinfancy Growth, Schooling, and Cognitive Achievement: Young Lives." *American Journal of Clinical Nutrition* 98(6) December: 1555–63.

Cruz-Aguayo, Y., J. LoCasale-Crouch, S. Schodt, T. Guanziroli, M. Kraft-Sayre, C. Melo, S. Hasbrouck, B. Hamre, and R. Pianta. 2015. "Early Schooling Classroom Experiences in Latin America: Focusing on What Matters for Children's Learning and Development." Inter-American Development Bank, Washington, DC. Unpublished.

Cunha, F., and J. Heckman. 2007. "The Technology of Skill Formation." *American Economic Review* 97(2) May: 31–47.

Cunha, J. M. 2014. "Testing Paternalism: Cash versus In-Kind Transfers." *American Economic Journal: Applied Economics* 6(2) April: 195–230.

Currie, J. 2001. "Early Childhood Education Programs." *Journal of Economic Perspectives* 15(2) Spring: 213–38.

Currie, J., and R. Hyson. 1999. "Is the Impact of Health Shocks Cushioned by Socioeconomic Status? The Case of Low Birth Weight." *American Economic Review* 89(2) May: 245–50.

Currie, J., and E. Moretti. 2007. "Biology as Destiny? Short- and Long-Run Determinants of Intergenerational Transmission of Birth Weight." *Journal of Labor Economics* 25(2) April: 231–63.

Currie, J., and D. Thomas. 2001. "Early Test Scores, School Quality and SES: Long-Run Effects on Wage and Employment Outcomes." In S. W. Polachek, ed., *Worker Wellbeing in a Changing Labor Market*. Research in Labor Economics series (Volume 20). Bingley, UK: Emerald Group Publishing.

Daelmans, B., K. Dewey, and M. Arimond. 2009. "New and Updated Indicators for Assessing Infant and Young Child Feeding." *Food and Nutrition Bulletin* 30(2 Supplement) June: S256–62.

de Onis, M., C. Garza, C. G. Victora, A. W. Onyango, E. A. Frongillo, and J. Martines. 2004. "The WHO Multicentre Growth Reference Study: Planning, Study Design, and Methodology." *Food and Nutrition Bulletin* 25(1) supplement 1: S15–S26.

Deaton, A. 2013. *The Great Escape: Health, Wealth, and the Origins of Inequality.* Princeton, NJ: Princeton University Press.

Deming, D. 2009. "Early Childhood Intervention and Life-Cycle Skill Development: Evidence from Head Start." *American Economic Journal: Applied Economics* 1(3) July: 111–34.

Denham, S. A., H. H. Bassett, and K. Zinsser. 2012. "Early Childhood Teachers as Socializers of Young Children's Emotional Competence." *Early Childhood Education Journal* 40(3) June: 137–43.

Denham, S. A., K. A. Blair, E. DeMulder, J. Levitas, K. Sawyer, S. Auerbach-Major, and P. Queenan. 2003. "Preschool Emotional Competence: Pathway to Social Competence?" *Child Development* 74(1) January–February: 238–56.

Denny, J. H., R. Hallam, and K. Homer. 2012. "A Multi-Instrument Examination of Preschool Classroom Quality and the Relationship between Program, Classroom, and Teacher Characteristics." *Early Education and Development* 23(5): 678–96.

Der, G., G. D. Batty, and I. J. Deary. 2008. "Results from the PROBIT Breastfeeding Trial May Have Been Overinterpreted." *Archives of General Psychiatry* 65(12) December: 1456–57.

Dewey, K. G., and S. Adu-Afarwuah. 2008. "Systematic Review of the Efficacy and Effectiveness of Complementary Feeding Interventions in Developing Countries." *Maternal and Child Nutrition* 4(Supplement s1) April: 24–85.

Dickinson, D. K., J. A. Griffith, R. M. Golinkoff, and K. Hirsh-Pasek. 2012. "How Reading Books Fosters Language Development around the World." *Child Development Research* 2012: 1–15. doi:10.1155/2012/602807.

Domitrovich, C. E., S. D. Gest, S. Gill, K. L. Bierman, J. A. Welsh, and D. Jones. 2009. "Fostering High-Quality Teaching with an Enriched Curriculum and Professional Development Support: The Head Start REDI Program." *American Educational Research Journal* 46(2) June: 567–97.

Downer, J. T., L. M. Booren, O. K. Lima, A. E. Luckner, and R. C. Pianta. 2010. "The Individualized Classroom Assessment Scoring System (inCLASS): Preliminary Reliability and Validity of a System for Observing Preschoolers' Competence in Classroom Interactions." *Early Childhood Research Quarterly* 25(1): 1–16.

Duflo, E., P. Dupas, and M. Kremer. 2011. "Peer Effects, Teacher Incentives, and the Impact of Tracking: Evidence from a Randomized Evaluation in Kenya." *American Economic Review* 101(5) August: 1739–74.

Duncan, G. J. 2011. "The Importance of Kindergarten-Entry Academic Skills." In E. Zigler, W. S. Gilliam, and W. S. Barnett, eds., *The Pre-K Debates: Current Controversies and Issues*. Baltimore, MD: Brookes Publishing Co.

Duncan, G. J., C. J. Dowsett, A. Claessens, K. Magnuson, A. C. Huston, P. Klebanov, L. S. Pagani, L. Feinstein, M. Engel, J. Brooks-Gunn, H. Sexton, K. Duckworth, and C. Japel. 2007. "School Readiness and Later Achievement." *Developmental Psychology* 43(6) November: 1428–46.

Duncan, G. J., and K. Magnuson. 2011. "The Nature and Impact of Early Achievement Skills, Attention Skills, and Behavior Problems." In G. J. Duncan and R. J. Murnane, eds., *Whither Opportunity? Rising Inequality, Schools, and Children's Life Chances*. New York: Russell Sage Foundation.

Duncan, G. J., K. Magnuson, and E. Votruba-Drzal. 2014. "Boosting Family Income to Promote Child Development." *The Future of Children* 24(1) Spring: 99–120.

Duncan, G. J., P. A. Morris, and C. Rodrigues. 2011. "Does Money Really Matter? Estimating Impacts of Family Income on Young Children's Achievement with Data from Random-Assignment Experiments." *Developmental Psychology* 47(5) September: 1263–79.

Dustmann, C., and U. Schönberg. 2012. "Expansions in Maternity Leave Coverage and Children's Long-Term Outcomes." *American Economic Journal: Applied Economics* 4(3) July: 190–224.

Early, D., O. Barbarin, D. Bryant, M. Burchinal, F. Chang, R. Clifford, G. Crawford, W. Weaver, C. Howes, S. Ritchie, M. Kraft-Sayre, R. Pianta, and W. S. Barnett. 2005. "Pre-Kindergarten in Eleven States: NCEDL's Multi-State Study of Pre-Kindergarten and Study of State-Wide Early Education Programs (SWEEP)." Preliminary report. National Center for Early Development and Learning (NCEDL), Frank Porter Graham Child Development Institute, Chapel Hill, NC.

Eccles, J. S., and R. W. Roeser. 2005. "School and Community Influences on Human Development." In M. H. Bornstein and M. E. Lamb, eds., *Developmental Science: An Advanced Textbook*. Fifth edition. New York: Psychology Press.

Eickmann, S. H., A. C. Lima, M. Q. Guerra, M. C. Lima, P. I. Lira, S. R. Huttly, and A. Ashworth. 2003. "Improved Cognitive and Motor Development in a Community-Based Intervention of Psychosocial Stimulation in Northeast Brazil." *Developmental Medicine and Child Neurology* 45(8) August: 536–41.

Evans, D. K., and K. Kosec. 2012. *Early Child Education: Making Programs Work for Brazil's Most Important Generation*. Washington, DC: World Bank.

Faverio, F., L. Rivera, and A. Cortázar. 2013. "¿Cuánto cuesta proveer educación parvularia de calidad en Chile?" Policy Paper No. 21. Instituto de Políticas Públicas, Facultad de Economía y Empresa, Universidad Diego Portales, Santiago.

Fernald, L., and M. Hidrobo. 2011. "Effect of Ecuador's Cash Transfer Program (*Bono de Desarrollo Humano*) on Child Development in Infants and Toddlers: A Randomized Effectiveness Trial." *Social Science and Medicine* 72(9) May: 1437–46.

Fernald, L. C., P. Kariger, P. Engle, and A. Raikes. 2009. *Examining Early Child Development in Low-Income Countries: A Toolkit for the Assessment of Children in the First Five Years of Life*. Washington, DC: World Bank.

Fiszbein, A., and N. Schady (with F. Ferreira, M. Grosh, N. Keleher, P. Olinto, and E. Skoufias). 2009. *Conditional Cash Transfers: Reducing Present and Future Poverty.* Washington, DC: World Bank.

Floud, R., R. W. Fogel, B. Harris, and S. C. Hong. 2011. *The Changing Body: Health, Nutrition, and Human Development in the Western World since 1700.* New York: Cambridge University Press.

Fogel, R. W. 1994. "Economic Growth, Population Theory, and Physiology: The Bearing of Long-Term Processes on the Making of Economic Policy." *American Economic Review* 84(3) June: 369–95.

———. 2004. *The Escape from Hunger and Premature Death, 1700–2100: Europe, America, and the Third World.* Cambridge, UK: Cambridge University Press.

Fogel, R. W., and D. L. Costa. 1997. "A Theory of Technophysio Evolution, with Some Implications for Forecasting Population, Health Care Costs, and Pension Costs." *Demography* 34(1) February: 49–66.

Fox, L., M. L. Hemmeter, P. Snyder, D. Pérez Binder, and S. Clarke. 2011. "Coaching Early Childhood Special Educators to Implement a Comprehensive Model for Promoting Young Children's Social Competence." *Topics in Early Childhood Special Education* 31(3) November: 178–92.

Fox, S. E., P. Levitt, and C. A. Nelson. 2010. "How the Timing and Quality of Early Experiences Influence the Development of Brain Architecture." *Child Development* 81(1) January–February: 28–40.

Fryer, R. G. 2013. "Teacher Incentives and Student Achievement: Evidence from New York City Public Schools." *Journal of Labor Economics* 31(2) April: 373–407.

Garces, E., D. Thomas, and J. Currie. 2002. "Longer-Term Effects of Head Start." *American Economic Review* 92(4) September: 999–1012.

Gardner, J. M., S. P. Walker, C. A. Powell, and S. Grantham-McGregor. 2003. "A Randomized Controlled Trial of a Home-Visiting Intervention on Cognition and Behavior in Term Low Birth Weight Infants." *Journal of Pediatrics* 143(5) November: 634–39.

Gershoff, E. T. 2002. "Corporal Punishment by Parents and Associated Child Behaviors and Experiences: A Meta-Analytic and Theoretical Review." *Psychological Bulletin* 128(4) July: 539–79.

Gertler, P. 2004. "Do Conditional Cash Transfers Improve Child Health? Evidence from PROGRESA's Control Randomized Experiment." *American Economic Review* 94(2) May: 336–41.

Gertler, P., J. Heckman, R. Pinto, A. Zanolini, C. Vermeersch, S. Walker, S. M. Chang, and S. Grantham-McGregor. 2014. "Labor Market Returns to an Early Childhood Stimulation Intervention in Jamaica." *Science* 344(6187) May: 998–1001.

Gilmore, B., and E. McAuliffe. 2013. "Effectiveness of Community Health Workers Delivering Preventive Interventions for Maternal and Child Health in Low- and Middle-Income Countries: A Systematic Review." *BMC Public Health* 13(2013): 847.

Grantham-McGregor, S. M., Y. B. Cheung, S. Cueto, P. Glewwe, L. Richter, B. Strupp, and the International Child Development Steering Group. 2007. "Developmental Potential in the First Five Years for Children in Developing Countries." *Lancet* 369(9555) January: 60–70.

Grantham-McGregor, S. M., L. Fernald, R. Kagawa, and S. Walker. 2014. "Effects of Integrated Child Development and Nutrition Interventions on Child Development and Nutritional Status." *Annals of the New York Academy of Sciences* 1308 (January): 11–32.

Grantham-McGregor, S. M., P. I. Lira, A. Ashworth, S. S. Morris, and A. M. Assunção. 1998. "The Development of Low Birth Weight Term Infants and the Effects of the Environment in Northeast Brazil." *Journal of Pediatrics* 132(4) April: 661–66.

Grantham-McGregor, S. M., C. A. Powell, S. P. Walker, and J. H. Himes. 1991. "Nutritional Supplementation, Psychosocial Stimulation, and Mental Development of Stunted Children: The Jamaican Study." *Lancet* 338(8758) July: 1–5.

Grantham-McGregor, S. M., W. Schofield, and L. Harris. 1983. "Effect of Psychosocial Stimulation on Mental Development of Severely Malnourished Children: An Interim Report." *Pediatrics* 72(2) August: 239–43.

Greenberg, M. T., C. Domitrovich, and B. Bumbarger. 2001. "The Prevention of Mental Disorders in School-Aged Children: Current State of the Field." *Prevention and Treatment* 4(1) March: 1–59.

Greenough, W. T., J. E. Black, and C. S. Wallace. 1987. "Experience and Brain Development." *Child Development* 58(3) June: 539–59.

Gupta, N. D., and M. Simonsen. 2010. "Non-Cognitive Child Outcomes and Universal High Quality Child Care." *Journal of Public Economics* 94(1–2): 30–43.

Hack, M., N. K. Klein, and H. G. Taylor. 1995. "Long-Term Developmental Outcomes of Low Birth Weight Infants." *The Future of Children* 5(1) Spring: 176–96.

Haider, R., A. Ashworth, I. Kabir, and S. R. Huttly. 2000. "Effect of Community-Based Peer Counsellors on Exclusive Breastfeeding Practices in Dhaka, Bangladesh: A Randomised Controlled Trial." *Lancet* 356(9242) November: 1643–47.

Hamadani, J. D., S. M. Grantham-McGregor, F. Tofail, B. Nermell, B. Fängström, S. N. Huda, S. Yesmin, M. Rahman, M. Vera-Hernández, S. E. Arifeen, and M. Vahter. 2010. "Pre- and Postnatal Arsenic Exposure and Child Development at 18 Months of Age: A Cohort Study in Rural Bangladesh." *International Journal of Epidemiology* 39(5): 1206–16.

Hamre, B. K., B. Hatfield, R. C. Pianta, and F. Jamil. 2014. "Evidence for General and Domain-Specific Elements of Teacher–Child Interactions: Associations with Preschool Children's Development." *Child Development* 85(3) May–June: 1257–74.

Hamre, B. K., K. M. La Paro, J. LoCasale-Crouch, and R. C. Pianta. 2006. "Children's Experiences in Kindergarten and Stability from the Preschool Year." Unpublished.

Hamre, B. K., K. M. La Paro, R. C. Pianta, and J. LoCasale-Crouch. 2014. *Classroom Assessment Scoring System (CLASS) Manual: Infant.* Baltimore, MD: Brookes Publishing Co.

Hamre, B. K., and R. C. Pianta. 2005. "Can Instructional and Emotional Support in the First-Grade Classroom Make a Difference for Children at Risk of School Failure?" *Child Development* 76(5) September–October: 949–67.

———. 2007. "Learning Opportunities in Preschool and Early Elementary Classrooms." In R. C. Pianta, M. J. Cox, and K. L. Snow, eds., *School Readiness and the Transition to Kindergarten in the Era of Accountability.* Baltimore, MD: Brookes Publishing Co.

Hamre, B. K., R. C. Pianta, M. Burchinal, S. Field, J. LoCasale-Crouch, J. T. Downer, C. Howes, K. La Paro, and C. Scott-Little. 2012. "A Course on Effective Teacher-Child Interactions: Effects on Teacher Beliefs, Knowledge, and Observed Practice." *American Educational Research Journal* 49(1) February: 88–123.

Hamre, B. K., R. C. Pianta, J. T. Downer, J. DeCoster, A. J. Mashburn, S. M. Jones, J. L. Brown, E. Cappella, M. Atkins, S. E. Rivers, M. A. Brackett, and A. Hamagami. 2013. "Teaching through Interactions: Testing a Developmental Framework of Teacher Effectiveness in over 4,000 Classrooms." *Elementary School Journal* 113(4) June: 461–87.

Hanushek, E. A. 1971. "Teacher Characteristics and Gains in Student Achievement: Estimation Using Micro Data." *American Economic Review* 61(2) May: 280–88.

———. 2003. "The Failure of Input-Based Schooling Policies." *Economic Journal* 113(485) February: F64–F98.

———. 2009. "Teacher Deselection." In D. Goldhaber and J. Hannaway, eds., *Creating a New Teaching Profession.* Washington, DC: Urban Institute Press.

———. 2011. "The Economic Value of Higher Teacher Quality." *Economics of Education Review* 30(3) June: 466–79.

Hanushek, E. A., and S. G. Rivkin. 2012. "The Distribution of Teacher Quality and Implications for Policy." *Annual Review of Economics* 4(1) September: 131–57.

Hanushek, E. A., and L. Woessmann. 2012. "Schooling, Educational Achievement, and the Latin American Growth Puzzle." *Journal of Development Economics* 99(2) November: 497–512.

Hanushek, E. A., and L. Zhang. 2006. "Quality-Consistent Estimates of International Returns to Skill." NBER Working Paper No. 12664. National Bureau of Economic Research, Cambridge, MA.

Harms, T., and R. M. Clifford. 1980. *Early Childhood Environment Rating Scale.* New York: Teachers College Press.

———. 1989. *Family Day Care Rating Scale.* New York: Teachers College Press.

Harms, T., R. M. Clifford, and D. Cryer. 1998. *Early Childhood Environment Rating Scale—Revised.* New York: Teachers College Press.

Harms, T., D. Cryer, and R. M. Clifford. 1990. *Infant/Toddler Environment Rating Scale.* New York: Teachers College Press.

Hart, B., and T. R. Risley. 1995. *Meaningful Differences in the Everyday Experience of Young American Children.* Baltimore, MD: Brookes Publishing Co.

Havnes, T., and M. Mogstad. 2011. "No Child Left Behind: Subsidized Child Care and Children's Long-Run Outcomes." *American Economic Journal: Economic Policy* 3(2) May: 97–129.

Heckman, J. J. 2008. "Schools, Skills, and Synapses." *Economic Inquiry* 46(3) July: 289–324.

Herrera, M. O., M. E. Mathiesen, J. M. Merino, and I. Recart. 2005. "Learning Contexts for Young Children in Chile: Process Quality Assessment in Preschool Centres." *International Journal of Early Years Education* 13(1) March: 15–30.

Hidrobo, M., J. Hoddinott, A. Peterman, A. Margolies, and V. Moreira. 2014. "Cash, Food, or Vouchers? Evidence from a Randomized Experiment in Northern Ecuador." *Journal of Development Economics* 107 (March): 144–56.

Hoddinott, J. 2010. "Nutrition and Conditional Cash Transfer Programs." In M. Adato and J. Hoddinott, eds., *Conditional Cash Transfers in Latin America.* Washington, DC: International Food Policy Research Institute (IFPRI) and Baltimore, MD: Johns Hopkins University Press.

Hoddinott, J., and L. Bassett. 2008. "Conditional Cash Transfer Programs and Nutrition in Latin America: Assessment of Impacts and Strategies for Improvement." International Food Policy Research Institute, Washington, DC. Unpublished. Available at http://papers.ssrn.com/sol3/papers.cfm?abstract_id=1305326. Accessed June 2015.

Hoddinott, J., J. R. Behrman, J. A. Maluccio, P. Melgar, A. R. Quisumbing, M. Ramírez-Zea, A. D. Stein, K. M. Yount, and R. Martorell. 2013. "Adult Consequences of Growth Failure in Early Childhood." *American Journal of Clinical Nutrition* 98(5) November: 1170–78.

Hoddinott, J., J. A. Maluccio, J. R. Behrman, R. Flores, and R. Martorell. 2008. "Effect of a Nutrition Intervention during Early Childhood on Economic Productivity in Guatemalan Adults." *Lancet* 371(9610) February: 411–16.

Hongwanishkul, D., K. R. Happaney, W. S. Lee, and P. D. Zelazo. 2005. "Assessment of Hot and Cool Executive Function in Young Children: Age-Related Changes and Individual Differences." *Developmental Neuropsychology* 28(2): 617–44.

Horton, S., and J. Hoddinott. 2014. "Benefits and Costs of the Food and Nutrition Targets for the Post-2015 Development Agenda." Food Security and Nutrition Perspective Paper. Copenhagen Consensus Center, Lowell, MA. Available at http://www.copenha genconsensus.com/sites/default/files/food_security_and_nutrition_perspective_-_horton_hoddinott_0.pdf. Accessed May 2015.

Hotz, V. J., and M. Xiao. 2011. "The Impact of Regulations on the Supply and Quality of Care in Child Care Markets." *American Economic Review* 101(5) August: 1775–805.

Howard, K. S., and J. Brooks-Gunn. 2009. "The Role of Home-Visiting Programs in Preventing Child Abuse and Neglect." *The Future of Children* 19(2) Fall: 119–46.

Howes, C., and C. E. Hamilton. 1993. "The Changing Experience of Child Care: Changes in Teachers and in Teacher-Child Relationships and Children's Social Competence with Peers." *Early Childhood Research Quarterly* 8(1) March: 15–32.

Hoxby, C. M., and A. Leigh. 2004. "Pulled Away or Pushed Out? Explaining the Decline of Teacher Aptitude in the United States." *American Economic Review* 94(2) May: 236–40.

Huebner, C. E. 2000. "Promoting Toddlers' Language Development through Community-Based Intervention." *Journal of Applied Developmental Psychology* 21(5) September–October: 513–35.

Humphries, D. L., J. R. Behrman, B. T. Crookston, K. A. Dearden, W. Schott, M. E. Penny, and the Young Lives Determinants and Consequences of Child Growth Project Team. 2014. "Households across All Income Quintiles, Especially the Poorest, Increased Animal Source Food Expenditures Substantially during Recent Peruvian Economic Growth." *PLoS One* 9(11) November: e110961. doi: 10.1371/journal.pone.0110961.

ICF International. 2012. Demographic and Health Surveys (DHS) Program STATcompiler. Rockville, MD. Available at http://www.icfi.com/insights/projects/research-and -evaluation/demographic-and-health-surveys. Accessed April 2015.

IHME (Institute for Health Metrics and Evaluation). 2014. "Baseline Data Report Salud Mesoamerica 2015." IHME, Seattle, WA.

Imdad, A., M. Y. Yakoob, and Z. A. Bhutta. 2011. "Impact of Maternal Education about Complementary Feeding and Provision of Complementary Foods on Child Growth in Developing Countries." *BMC Public Health* 11(Supplement 3) April: S25.

Isaacs, J. B. 2009. "A Comparative Perspective on Public Spending on Children." Brookings Institution, Washington, DC. Available at http://www.brookings.edu/~ /media/Research/Files/Reports/2009/11/05-spending-children-isaacs/2_comparative _perspective_isaacs.PDF. Accessed May 2015.

Johnson, M. H. 1998. "The Neural Basis of Cognitive Development." In D. Kuhn and R. S. Siegler, eds., *Handbook of Child Psychology: Volume 2: Cognition, Perception, and Language.* Fifth edition. New York: John Wiley and Sons.

Jordan, G. E., C. E. Snow, and M. V. Porche. 2000. "Project EASE: The Effect of a Family Literacy Project on Kindergarten Students' Early Literacy Skills." *Reading Research Quarterly* 35(4) October–December: 524–46.

Jurado, M. B., and M. Rosselli. 2007. "The Elusive Nature of Executive Functions: A Review of Our Current Understanding." *Neuropsychology Review* 17(3) September: 213–33.

Kagan, S. L., M. C. Araujo, A. Jaimovich, and Y. Cruz-Aguayo. Forthcoming. "Understanding Systems Theory and Thinking: Early Childhood Education in Latin America and the Caribbean." In A. Farrell, S. L. Kagan, and E. K. M. Tisdall, eds., *The SAGE Handbook of Early Childhood Research.* London: SAGE Press.

Kagan, S. L., and N. E. Cohen, eds. 1996. *Reinventing Early Care and Education: A Vision for a Quality System.* San Francisco, CA: Jossey-Bass Publishers.

Kagan, S. L., and K. Kauerz, eds. 2012. *Early Childhood Systems: Transforming Early Learning.* New York: Teachers College Press.

Kane, T. J., and D. O. Staiger. 2002a. "The Promise and Pitfalls of Using Imprecise School Accountability Measures." *Journal of Economic Perspectives* 16(4) Fall: 91–114.

———. 2002b. "Volatility in School Test Scores: Implications for Test-Based Accountability Systems." *Brookings Papers on Education Policy* 2002: 235–83.

Key, E. 1909. *The Century of the Child.* New York: G. P. Putnam's Sons.

Kisker, E. E., S. L. Hofferth, D. A. Phillips, and E. Farquhar. 1991. *A Profile of Child Care Settings: Early Education and Care in 1990.* Princeton, NJ: Mathematica Policy Research.

Kitzman, H., D. L. Olds, C. R. Henderson, Jr., C. Hanks, R. Cole, R. Tatelbaum, K. M. McConnochie, K. Sidora, D. W. Luckey, D. Shaver, K. Engelhardt, D. James, and K. Barnard. 1997. "Effect of Prenatal and Infancy Home Visitation by Nurses on Pregnancy Outcomes, Childhood Injuries, and Repeated Childbearing: A Randomized Controlled Trial." *Journal of the American Medical Association* 278(8) August: 644–52.

Kitzman, H., D. L. Olds, K. Sidora, C. R. Henderson, Jr., C. Hanks, R. Cole, D. W. Luckey, J. Bondy, K. Cole, and J. Glazner. 2000. "Enduring Effects of Nurse Home Visitation on Maternal Life Course: A Three-Year Follow-up of a Randomized Trial." *Journal of the American Medical Association* 283(15) April: 1983–89.

Kontos, S., and A. Wilcox-Herzog. 1997. "Influences on Children's Competence in Early Childhood Classrooms." *Early Childhood Research Quarterly* 12(3) January: 247–62.

Kooreman, P. 2000. "The Labeling Effect of a Child Benefit System." *American Economic Review* 90(3) June: 571–83.

Kramer, M. S. 1987. "Intrauterine Growth and Gestational Duration Determinants." *Pediatrics* 80(4) October: 502–11.

———. 2003. "The Epidemiology of Adverse Pregnancy Outcomes: An Overview." *Journal of Nutrition* 133(5 Supplement 2) May: 1592S–1596S.

Kramer, M. S., F. Aboud, E. Mironova, I. Vanilovich, R. W. Platt, L. Matush, S. Igumnov, E. Fombonne, N. Bogdanovich, T. Ducruet, J. P. Collet, B. Chalmers, E. Hodnett, S. Davidovsky, O. Skugarevsky, O. Trofimovich, L. Kozlova, S. Shapiro, and Promotion of Breastfeeding Intervention Trial (PROBIT) Study Group. 2008. "Breastfeeding and Child Cognitive Development: New Evidence from a Large Randomized Trial." *Archives of General Psychiatry* 65(5) May: 578–84.

Kramer, M. S., B. Chalmers, E. D. Hodnett, Z. Sevkovskaya, I. Dzikovich, S. Shapiro, J. P. Collet, I. Vanilovich, I. Mezen, T. Ducruet, G. Shishko, V. Zubovich, D. Mknuik, E. Gluchanina, V. Dombrovskiy, A. Ustinovitch, T. Kot, N. Bogdanovich, L. Ovchinikova, E. Helsing, and PROBIT Study Group (Promotion of Breastfeeding Intervention Trial). 2001. "Promotion of Breastfeeding Intervention Trial (PROBIT): A Randomized Trial in the Republic of Belarus." *Journal of the American Medical Association* 285(4) January: 413–20.

Kramer, M. S., T. Guo, R. W. Platt, S. Shapiro, J. P. Collet, B. Chalmers, E. Hodnett, Z. Sevkovskaya, I. Dzikovich, I. Vanilovich, and PROBIT Study Group. 2002. "Breastfeeding and Infant Growth: Biology or Bias?" *Pediatrics* 110(2) August: 343–47.

Kremer, M., C. Brannen, and R. Glennerster. 2013. "The Challenge of Education and Learning in the Developing World." *Science* 340(6130) April: 297–300.

Krueger, A. B. 1999. "Experimental Estimates of Education Production Functions." *Quarterly Journal of Economics* 114(2) May: 497–532.

Krueger, A. B., and D. M. Whitmore. 2001. "The Effect of Attending a Small Class in the Early Grades on College-Test Taking and Middle School Test Results: Evidence from Project STAR." *Economic Journal* 111(468) January: 1–28.

Kuhn, D., and R. S. Siegler, eds. 1998. *Handbook of Child Psychology: Volume 2: Cognition, Perception, and Language.* Fifth edition. New York: John Wiley and Sons.

La Paro, K. M., B. K. Hamre, J. LoCasale-Crouch, R. C. Pianta, D. Bryant, D. Early, R. Clifford, O. Barbarin, C. Howes, and M. Burchinal. 2009. "Quality in Kindergarten Classrooms: Observational Evidence for the Need to Increase Children's Learning Opportunities in Early Education Classrooms." *Early Education and Development* 20(4) August: 657–92.

La Paro, K. M., B. K. Hamre, and R. C. Pianta. 2012. *Classroom Assessment Scoring System (CLASS) Manual: Toddler.* Baltimore, MD: Brookes Publishing Co.

La Paro, K. M., R. C. Pianta, and M. Stuhlman. 2004. "The Classroom Assessment Scoring System: Findings from the Prekindergarten Year." *Elementary School Journal* 104(5) May: 409–26.

Lagarde, M., A. Haines, and N. Palmer. 2009. "The Impact of Conditional Cash Transfers on Health Outcomes and Use of Health Services in Low and Middle Income Countries." *Cochrane Database of Systematic Reviews* Issue 4. Art. No.: CD008137. doi: 10.1002/14651858.CD008137.

Lassi, Z. S., J. K. Das, G. Zahid, A. Imdad, and Z. A. Bhutta. 2013. "Impact of Education and Provision of Complementary Feeding on Growth and Morbidity in Children Less than Two Years of Age in Developing Countries: A Systematic Review." *BMC Public Health* 13 (Supplement 3): S13.

Lavy, V. 2002. "Evaluating the Effect of Teachers' Group Performance Incentives on Pupil Achievement." *Journal of Political Economy* 110(6) December: 1286–317.

———. 2009. "Performance Pay and Teachers' Effort, Productivity, and Grading Ethics." *American Economic Review* 99(5) December: 1979–2011.

Leer, J., F. López Boo, and A. Pérez Expósito. 2014. "Programas de primera infancia: calidad de programas de visitas domiciliarias para el fortalecimiento de pautas de crianza." Inter-American Development Bank, Washington, DC. Unpublished.

Levy, S., and N. Schady. 2013. "Latin America's Social Policy Challenge: Education, Social Insurance, Redistribution." *Journal of Economic Perspectives* 27(2) Spring: 193–218.

Leyva, D., C. Weiland, M. Barata, H. Yoshikawa, C. Snow, E. Treviño, and A. Rolla. 2015. "Teacher-Child Interactions in Chile and Their Associations with Prekindergarten Outcomes." *Child Development* 86(3) May: 781–99.

LoCasale-Crouch, J., T. Konold, R. Pianta, C. Howes, M. Burchinal, D. Bryant, R. Clifford, D. Early, and O. Barbarin. 2007. "Observed Classroom Quality Profiles in State-Funded

Pre-Kindergarten Programs and Associations with Teacher, Program, and Classroom Characteristics." *Early Childhood Research Quarterly* 22(1): 3–17.

Loeb, S., M. Bridges, D. Bassok, B. Fuller, and R. W. Rumberger. 2007. "How Much Is Too Much? The Influence of Preschool Centers on Children's Social and Cognitive Development." *Economics of Education Review* 26(1) February: 52–66.

Løken, K. V., M. Mogstad, and M. Wiswall. 2012. "What Linear Estimators Miss: The Effects of Family Income on Child Outcomes." *American Economic Journal: Applied Economics* 4(2) April: 1–35.

Lonigan, C. J., and G. J. Whitehurst. 1998. "Relative Efficacy of Parent and Teacher Involvement in a Shared-Reading Intervention for Preschool Children from Low-Income Backgrounds." *Early Childhood Research Quarterly* 13(2): 263–90.

López Boo, F. 2014. "Socio-Economic Status and Early Childhood Cognitive Skills: Is Latin America Different?" Working Paper No. 127. Young Lives, University of Oxford, Oxford, United Kingdom.

Love, J. M., P. Z. Schochet, and A. L. Meckstroth. 1996. "Are They in Any Real Danger? What Research Does—and Doesn't—Tell Us about Child Care Quality and Children's Well-Being." Child Care Research and Policy Paper. Mathematica Policy Research, Inc., Princeton, NJ. Available at http://www.mathematica-mpr.com/~/media/publica tions/PDFs/realdanger.pdf. Accessed June 2015.

Lowe, R. 2004. "Childhood through the Ages." In T. Maynard and N. Thomas, eds., *An Introduction to Early Childhood Studies*. London: SAGE Publications Ltd.

Lozoff, B., G. M. Brittenham, A. W. Wolf, D. K. McClish, P. M. Kuhnert, E. Jiménez, R. Jiménez, L. A. Mora, I. Gómez, and D. Krauskoph. 1987. "Iron Deficiency Anemia and Iron Therapy Effects on Infant Developmental Test Performance." *Pediatrics* 79(6) June: 981–95.

Lozoff, B., J. B. Smith, K. M. Clark, C. G. Perales, F. Rivera, and M. Castillo. 2010. "Home Intervention Improves Cognitive and Social-Emotional Scores in Iron-Deficient Anemic Infants." *Pediatrics* 126(4) October: e884–e894.

Ludwig, J., and D. A. Phillips. 2008. "Long-Term Effects of Head Start on Low-Income Children." *Annals of the New York Academy of Sciences* 1136 (June): 257–68.

Lundberg, S. J., R. A. Pollak, and T. J. Wales. 1997. "Do Husbands and Wives Pool Their Resources? Evidence from the United Kingdom Child Benefit." *Journal of Human Resources* 32(3) Summer: 463–80.

Lundeen, E. A., A. D. Stein, L. S. Adair, J. R. Behrman, S. K. Bhargava, K. A. Dearden, D. Gigante, S. A. Norris, L. M. Richter, C. H. Fall, R. Martorell, H. S. Sachdev, C. G. Victora, and COHORTS Investigators. 2014. "Height-for-Age Z Scores Increase despite Increasing Height Deficits among Children in Five Developing Countries." *American Journal of Clinical Nutrition* 100(3) September: 821–25.

Luo, Z. C., and J. Karlberg. 2000. "Critical Growth Phases for Adult Shortness." *American Journal of Epidemiology* 152(2) July: 125–31.

Maccini, S., and D. Yang. 2009. "Under the Weather: Health, Schooling, and Economic Consequences of Early-Life Rainfall." *American Economic Review* 99(3) June: 1006–26.

Macours, K., N. Schady, and R. Vakis. 2012. "Cash Transfers, Behavioral Changes, and Cognitive Development in Early Childhood: Evidence from a Randomized Experiment." *American Economic Journal: Applied Economics* 4(2) April: 247–73.

MacPhee, D. 1981. "Knowledge of Infant Development Inventory (KIDI)." Manual. University of North Carolina, Chapel Hill, NC. Unpublished.

Maluccio, J. A., and R. Flores. 2005. "Impact Evaluation of a Conditional Cash Transfer Program: The Nicaraguan *Red de Protección Social*." Research Report No. 141. International Food Policy Research Institute, Washington, DC.

Maluccio, J. A., J. Hoddinott, J. R. Behrman, R. Martorell, A. R. Quisumbing, and A. D. Stein. 2009. "The Impact of Improving Nutrition during Early Childhood on Education among Guatemalan Adults." *Economic Journal* 119(537) April: 734–63.

Mashburn, A. J., R. C. Pianta, B. K. Hamre, J. T. Downer, O. A. Barbarin, D. Bryant, M. Burchinal, D. M. Early, and C. Howes. 2008. "Measures of Classroom Quality in Prekindergarten and Children's Development of Academic, Language, and Social Skills." *Child Development* 79(3) May–June: 732–49.

Masten, A. S., and J. D. Coatsworth. 1998. "The Development of Competence in Favorable and Unfavorable Environments: Lessons from Research on Successful Children." *American Psychologist* 53(2) February: 205–20.

Mateo, M., and L. Rodríguez-Chamussy. 2015. "Who Cares about Childcare? Estimations of Childcare Use in Latin America and the Caribbean." IDB Technical Note No. 815. Inter-American Development Bank, Washington, DC.

McCartney, K., and R. Rosenthal. 2000. "Effect Size, Practical Importance, and Social Policy for Children." *Child Development* 71(1) January–February: 173–80.

Merritt, E. G., S. B. Wanless, S. E. Rimm-Kaufman, C. Cameron, and J. L. Peugh. 2012. "The Contribution of Teachers' Emotional Support to Children's Social Behaviors and Self-Regulatory Skills in First Grade." *School Psychology Review* 41(2): 141–59.

Milligan, K., and M. Stabile. 2011. "Do Child Tax Benefits Affect the Well-Being of Children? Evidence from Canadian Child Benefit Expansions." *American Economic Journal: Economic Policy* 3(3) August: 175–205.

Mizala, A., and H. Ñopo. 2012. "Salarios de los maestros en América Latina: ¿cuánto (más o menos) ganan con respecto a sus pares?" In M. Cabrol and M. Székely, eds., *Educación para la transformación*. Washington, DC: IDB.

Moffitt, T. E., L. Arseneault, D. Belsky, N. Dickson, R. J. Hancox, H. Harrington, R. Houts, R. Poulton, B. W. Roberts, S. Ross, M. R. Sears, W. M. Thomson, and A. Caspi. 2011. "A Gradient of Childhood Self-Control Predicts Health, Wealth, and Public Safety." *Proceedings of the National Academy of Sciences* 108(7) February: 2693–98.

Morris, S. S., P. Olinto, R. Flores, E. A. Nilson, and A. C. Figueiró. 2004. "Conditional Cash Transfers Are Associated with a Small Reduction in the Rate of Weight Gain of Preschool Children in Northeast Brazil." *Journal of Nutrition* 134(9) September: 2336–41.

Morrow, A. L., M. L. Guerrero, J. Shults, J. J. Calva, C. Lutter, J. Bravo, G. Ruiz-Palacios, R. C. Morrow, and F. D. Butterfoss. 1999. "Efficacy of Home-Based Peer Counselling to Promote Exclusive Breastfeeding: A Randomised Controlled Trial." *Lancet* 353(9160) April: 1226–31.

Mullis, P. E., and P. Tonella. 2008. "Regulation of Fetal Growth: Consequences and Impact of Being Born Small." *Best Practice and Research Clinical Endocrinology and Metabolism* 22(1) February: 173–90.

Muralidharan, K., and V. Sundararaman. 2011. "Teacher Performance Pay: Experimental Evidence from India." *Journal of Political Economy* 119(1) February: 39–77.

Murnane, R. J. 1975. *The Impact of School Resources on the Learning of Inner City Children.* Cambridge, MA: Ballinger Publishing Co.

Murnane, R. J., and A. J. Ganimian. 2014. "Improving Educational Outcomes in Developing Countries: Lessons from Rigorous Evaluations." NBER Working Paper No. 20284. National Bureau of Economic Research, Cambridge, MA.

National Early Literacy Panel. 2008. *Developing Early Literacy: Report of the National Early Literacy Panel.* Washington, DC: National Institute for Literacy.

National Scientific Council on the Developing Child. 2012. "The Science of Neglect: The Persistent Absence of Responsive Care Disrupts the Developing Brain." Working Paper No. 12. Center on the Developing Child, Harvard University, Cambridge, MA.

Neal, D. 2011. "The Design of Performance Pay in Education." In E. A. Hanushek, S. Machin, and L. Woessmann, eds., *Handbook of the Economics of Education.* Volume 4. Amsterdam: North-Holland.

Neidell, M., and J. Waldfogel. 2009. "Program Participation of Immigrant Children: Evidence from the Local Availability of Head Start." *Economics of Education Review* 28(6) December: 704–15.

Nelson, C. A., N. A. Fox, and C. H. Zeanah. 2014. *Romania's Abandoned Children: Deprivation, Brain Development, and the Struggle for Recovery.* Cambridge, MA: Harvard University Press.

Neuman, M. J., and A. E. Devercelli. 2013. "What Matters Most for Early Childhood Development: A Framework Paper." Systems Approach for Better Education Results (SABER) Working Paper No. 5. World Bank, Washington, DC. Available at http://wbgfiles.worldbank.org/documents/hdn/ed/saber/supporting_doc/Background/ECD/Framework_SABER-ECD.pdf. Accessed June 2015.

NICHD Early Child Care Research Network. 2002. "Child-Care Structure → Process → Outcome: Direct and Indirect Effects of Child-Care Quality on Young Children's Development." *Psychological Science* 13(3) May: 199–206.

NRP (National Reading Panel). 2000. "Teaching Children to Read: An Evidence-Based Assessment of the Scientific Research Literature on Reading and Its Implications for Reading Instruction: Reports of the Subgroups." Report. National Institute of Child Health and Human Development, National Institutes of Health, Bethesda, MD. Available at http://www.nichd.nih.gov/publications/pubs/nrp/documents/report.pdf. Accessed June 2015.

Olds, D. L., C. R. Henderson, Jr., and H. Kitzman. 1994. "Does Prenatal and Infancy Nurse Home Visitation Have Enduring Effects on Qualities of Parental Caregiving and Child Health at 25 to 50 Months of Life?" *Pediatrics* 93(1) January: 89–98.

Olds, D. L., C. R. Henderson, Jr., R. Tatelbaum, and R. Chamberlin. 1986. "Improving the Delivery of Prenatal Care and Outcomes of Pregnancy: A Randomized Trial of Nurse Home Visitation." *Pediatrics* 77(1) January: 16–28.

Olds, D. L., P. Hill, J. Robinson, N. Song, and C. Little. 2000. "Update on Home Visiting for Pregnant Women and Parents of Young Children." *Current Problems in Pediatrics* 30(4) April: 109–41.

Olds, D. L., J. R. Holmberg, N. Donelan-McCall, D. W. Luckey, M. D. Knudtson, and J. Robinson. 2014. "Effects of Home Visits by Paraprofessionals and by Nurses on Children: Follow-Up of a Randomized Trial at Ages 6 and 9 Years." *JAMA Pediatrics* 168(2) February: 114–21.

Olds, D. L., H. Kitzman, C. Hanks, R. Cole, E. Anson, K. Sidora-Arcoleo, D. W. Luckey, C. R. Henderson, Jr., J. Holmberg, R. A. Tutt, A. J. Stevenson, and J. Bondy. 2007. "Effects of Nurse Home Visiting on Maternal and Child Functioning: Age Nine Follow-Up of a Randomized Trial." *Pediatrics* 120(4) October: e832–e845.

Olds, D. L., J. Robinson, R. O'Brien, D. W. Luckey, L. M. Pettitt, C. R. Henderson, Jr., R. K. Ng, K. L. Sheff, J. Korfmacher, S. Hiatt, and A. Talmi. 2002. "Home Visiting by Paraprofessionals and by Nurses: A Randomized, Controlled Trial." *Pediatrics* 110(3) September: 486–96.

Oster, E. 2015. "Everybody Calm Down about Breastfeeding." *FiveThirtyEight.* May 20. Available at http://fivethirtyeight.com/features/everybody-calm-down-about-breast feeding/. Accessed June 2015.

Paes de Barros, R., P. Olinto, T. Lunde, and M. Carvalho. 2011. "The Impact of Access to Free Childcare on Women's Labor Market Outcomes: Evidence from a Randomized Trial in Low-Income Neighborhoods of Rio de Janeiro." World Bank, Washington, DC. Unpublished. Available at http://siteresources.worldbank.org/DEC/Resources/84 797-1104597464088/598413-1302096012728/Pedro-Olinto_access_to_free_childcare .pdf. Accessed June 2015.

Pagan, S., and M. Sénéchal. 2014. "Involving Parents in a Summer Book Reading Program to Promote Reading Comprehension, Fluency, and Vocabulary in Grade 3 and Grade 5 Children." *Canadian Journal of Education/Revue canadienne de l'éducation* 37(2) April: 1–31.

Papp, L. M. 2014. "Longitudinal Associations between Breastfeeding and Observed Mother-Child Interaction Qualities in Early Childhood." *Child: Care, Health and Development* 40(5) September: 740–46.

Paxson, C., and N. Schady. 2005. "Child Health and Economic Crisis in Peru." *World Bank Economic Review* 19(2) November: 203–23.

———. 2007. "Cognitive Development among Young Children in Ecuador: The Roles of Wealth, Health, and Parenting." *Journal of Human Resources* 42(1) Winter: 49–84.

———. 2010. "Does Money Matter? The Effects of Cash Transfers on Child Development in Rural Ecuador." *Economic Development and Cultural Change* 59(1) October: 187–229.

Penny, M. E., H. M. Creed-Kanashiro, R. C. Robert, M. R. Narro, L. E. Caulfield, and R. E. Black. 2005. "Effectiveness of an Educational Intervention Delivered through the Health Services to Improve Nutrition in Young Children: A Cluster-Randomised Controlled Trial." *Lancet* 365(9474) May–June: 1863–72.

Pérez-Escamilla, R., L. Curry, D. Minhas, L. Taylor, and E. Bradley. 2012. "Scaling Up of Breastfeeding Promotion Programs in Low- and Middle-Income Countries: The 'Breastfeeding Gear' Model." *Advances in Nutrition* 3(6) November: 790–800.

Perry, K. E., K. M. Donohue, and R. S. Weinstein. 2007. "Teaching Practices and the Promotion of Achievement and Adjustment in First Grade." *Journal of School Psychology* 45(3) June: 269–92.

Phillips, D., D. Mekos, S. Scarr, K. McCartney, and M. Abbott-Shim. 2000. "Within and beyond the Classroom Door: Assessing Quality in Child Care Centers." *Early Childhood Research Quarterly* 15(4) Winter: 475–96.

Pianta, R. C., J. Belsky, R. Houts, F. Morrison, and NICHD Early Child Care Research Network. 2007. "Opportunities to Learn in America's Elementary Classrooms." *Science* 315(5820) March: 1795–96.

Pianta, R. C., K. M. La Paro, and B. K. Hamre. 2008a. *Classroom Assessment Scoring System (CLASS) Manual: K-3.* Baltimore, MD: Brookes Publishing Co.

———. 2008b. *Classroom Assessment Scoring System (CLASS) Manual: Pre-K.* Baltimore, MD: Brookes Publishing Co.

Pianta, R. C., A. J. Mashburn, J. T. Downer, B. K. Hamre, and L. Justice. 2008. "Effects of Web-Mediated Professional Development Resources on Teacher-Child Interactions in Pre-Kindergarten Classrooms." *Early Childhood Research Quarterly* 23(4): 431–51.

Piasta, S. B., L. M. Justice, A. S. McGinty, and J. N. Kaderavek. 2012. "Increasing Young Children's Contact with Print during Shared Reading: Longitudinal Effects on Literacy Achievement." *Child Development* 83(3) May–June: 810–20.

Ponitz, C. C., S. E. Rimm-Kaufman, L. L. Brock, and L. Nathanson. 2009. "Early Adjustment, Gender Differences, and Classroom Organizational Climate in First Grade." *Elementary School Journal* 110(2) December: 142–62.

Powell, A., coord. 2014. *Global Recovery and Monetary Normalization: Escaping a Chronicle Foretold?* 2014 Latin American and Caribbean Macroeconomic Report. Washington, DC: Inter-American Development Bank.

Powell, C., and S. Grantham-McGregor. 1989. "Home Visiting of Varying Frequency and Child Development." *Pediatrics* 84(1) July: 157–64.

Powell, D. R., and K. E. Diamond. 2012. "Promoting Early Literacy and Language Development." In R. C. Pianta, ed., *Handbook of Early Childhood Education.* New York: Guilford Press.

Prentice, A. M., K. A. Ward, G. R. Goldberg, L. M. Jarjou, S. E. Moore, A. J. Fulford, and A. Prentice. 2013. "Critical Windows for Nutritional Interventions against Stunting." *American Journal of Clinical Nutrition* 97(5) May: 911–18.

Prina, S., and H. Royer. 2014. "The Importance of Parental Knowledge: Evidence from Weight Report Cards in Mexico." *Journal of Health Economics* 37 (September): 232–47.

Rasmussen, K. M. 2001. "The 'Fetal Origins' Hypothesis: Challenges and Opportunities for Maternal and Child Nutrition." *Annual Review of Nutrition* 21 (July): 73–95.

Rea, M. F. 2003. "Reflexões sobre a amamentação no Brasil: de como passamos a 10 meses de duração." *Cadernos de Saúde Pública* 19(Supplement 1): S37–S45.

Rimm-Kaufman, S. E., T. W. Curby, K. J. Grimm, L. Nathanson, and L. L. Brock. 2009. "The Contribution of Children's Self-Regulation and Classroom Quality to Children's Adaptive Behaviors in the Kindergarten Classroom." *Developmental Psychology* 45(4) July: 958–72.

Rimm-Kaufman, S. E., R. C. Pianta, and M. J. Cox. 2000. "Teachers' Judgments of Problems in the Transition to Kindergarten." *Early Childhood Research Quarterly* 15(2): 147–66.

Ritchie, S., B. Weiser, M. Kraft-Sayre, C. Howes, and B. Weiser. 2001. "Emergent Academics Snapshot Scale." Instrument. University of California at Los Angeles (UCLA), Los Angeles, CA. Unpublished.

Rivera, J. A., T. González de Cossío, L. S. Pedraza, T. C. Aburto, T. G. Sánchez, and R. Martorell. 2014. "Childhood and Adolescent Overweight and Obesity in Latin America: A Systematic Review." *Lancet Diabetes and Endocrinology* 2(4) April: 321–32.

Rivera, J. A., D. Sotres-Álvarez, J.-P. Habicht, T. Shamah, and S. Villalpando. 2004. "Impact of the Mexican Program for Education, Health, and Nutrition (PROGRESA) on Rates of Growth and Anemia in Infants and Young Children: A Randomized Effectiveness Study." *Journal of the American Medical Association* 291(21) June: 2563–70.

Rommeck, I., K. Anderson, A. Heagerty, A. Cameron, and B. McCowan. 2009. "Risk Factors and Remediation of Self-Injurious and Self-Abuse Behavior in Rhesus Macaques." *Journal of Applied Animal Welfare Science* 12(1): 61–72.

Rommeck, I., J. P. Capitanio, S. C. Strand, and B. McCowan. 2011. "Early Social Experience Affects Behavioral and Physiological Responsiveness to Stressful Conditions in Infant Rhesus Macaques (Macaca Mulatta)." *American Journal of Primatology* 73(7) July: 692–701.

Rosero, J., and H. Oosterbeek. 2011. "Trade-offs between Different Early Childhood Interventions: Evidence from Ecuador." Tinbergen Institute Discussion Paper No. 11-102/3. Faculty of Economics and Business, University of Amsterdam, and Tinbergen Institute, Amsterdam.

Rothstein, J. 2010. "Teacher Quality in Educational Production: Tracking, Decay, and Student Achievement." *Quarterly Journal of Economics* 125(1) February: 175–214.

Rouse, C. E., J. Hannaway, D. Goldhaber, and D. Figlio. 2013. "Feeling the Florida Heat? How Low-Performing Schools Respond to Voucher and Accountability Pressure." *American Economic Journal: Economic Policy* 5(2) May: 251–81.

Rubio-Codina, M., O. Attanasio, C. Meghir, N. Varela, and S. Grantham-McGregor. 2015. "The Socioeconomic Gradient of Child Development: Cross-Sectional Evidence from Children 6–42 Months in Bogota." *Journal of Human Resources* 50(2) Spring: 464–83.

Rudasill, K. M., K. C. Gallagher, and J. M. White. 2010. "Temperamental Attention and Activity, Classroom Emotional Support, and Academic Achievement in Third Grade." *Journal of School Psychology* 48(2) April: 113–34.

Ruhm, C. J. 1998. "The Economic Consequences of Parental Leave Mandates: Lessons from Europe." *Quarterly Journal of Economics* 113(1) February: 285–317.

———. 2000. "Parental Leave and Child Health." *Journal of Health Economics* 19(6) November: 931–60.

———. 2011. "Policies to Assist Parents with Young Children." *The Future of Children* 21(2) Fall: 37–68.

Rutter, M., and the English and Romanian Adoptees (ERA) Study Team. 1998. "Developmental Catch-up, and Deficit, Following Adoption after Severe Global Early Privation." *Journal of Child Psychology and Psychiatry* 39(4) May: 465–76.

Salminen, J. E. 2013. "Case Study on Teachers' Contribution to Children's Participation in Finnish Preschool Classrooms during Structured Learning Sessions." *Frontline Learning Research* 1(1): 72–80.

Samms-Vaughan, M. 2005. *The Jamaican Pre-School Child: The Status of Early Childhood Development in Jamaica.* Kingston: Planning Institute of Jamaica.

Santos, I., C. G. Victora, J. Martines, H. Gonçalves, D. P. Gigante, N. J. Valle, and G. Pelto. 2001. "Nutrition Counseling Increases Weight Gain among Brazilian Children." *Journal of Nutrition* 131(11) November: 2866–73.

Sarama, J., and D. H. Clements. 2009. *Early Childhood Mathematics Education Research: Learning Trajectories for Young Children.* New York: Routledge.

Schady, N. 2011. "Parents' Education, Mothers' Vocabulary, and Cognitive Development in Early Childhood: Longitudinal Evidence from Ecuador." *American Journal of Public Health* 101(12) December: 2299–307.

———. 2012. "El desarrollo infantil temprano en América Latina y el Caribe: acceso, resultados y evidencia longitudinal de Ecuador." In M. Cabrol and M. Székely, eds., *Educación para la transformación*. Washington, DC: IDB.

Schady, N., J. Behrman, M. C. Araujo, R. Azuero, R. Bernal, D. Bravo, F. López Boo, K. Macours, D. Marshall, C. Paxson, and R. Vakis. 2015. "Wealth Gradients in Early Childhood Cognitive Development in Five Latin American Countries." *Journal of Human Resources* 50(2) Spring: 446–63.

Schanzenbach, D. W. 2007. "What Have Researchers Learned from Project STAR?" *Brookings Papers on Education Policy* 9(2006–07) May: 205–28.

Séguin, J. R., and P. D. Zelazo. 2005. "Executive Function in Early Physical Aggression." In R. E. Tremblay, W. W. Hartup, and J. Archer, eds., *Developmental Origins of Aggression*. New York: Guilford Press.

Serdula, M. K., D. Ivery, R. J. Coates, D. S. Freedman, D. F. Williamson, and T. Byers. 1993. "Do Obese Children Become Obese Adults? A Review of the Literature." *Preventive Medicine* 22(2) March: 167–77.

Shelov, S. P., and T. R. Altmann, eds. 2009. *Caring for Your Baby and Young Child: Birth to Age Five*. Fifth edition. Elk Grove Village, IL: American Academy of Pediatrics.

Shonkoff, J. P., and D. A. Phillips, eds. 2000. *From Neurons to Neighborhoods: The Science of Early Childhood Development*. Washington, DC: National Academies Press.

Singh, G. K., and P. C. van Dyck. 2010. "Infant Mortality in the United States, 1935–2007: Over Seven Decades of Progress and Disparities." Report. Health Resources and Services Administration, Maternal and Child Health Bureau, US Department of Health and Human Services, Rockville, MD.

Snow, C. E., M. S. Burns, and P. Griffin, eds. 1998. *Preventing Reading Difficulties in Young Children*. Washington, DC: National Academies Press.

Springer, M. G., D. Ballou, L. Hamilton, V.-N. Le, J. R. Lockwood, D. F. McCaffrey, M. Pepper, and B. M. Stecher. 2010. "Teacher Pay for Performance: Experimental Evidence from the Project on Incentives in Teaching." Report. National Center on Performance Incentives, Vanderbilt University, Nashville, TN.

Stallings, J. 1977. *Learning to Look: A Handbook on Classroom Observation and Teaching Models*. Belmont, CA: Wadsworth Publishing Co.

Stallings, J. A., and G. G. Mohlman. 1988. "Classroom Observation Techniques." In J. P. Keeves, ed., *Educational Research, Methodology, and Measurement: An International Handbook*. Oxford, UK: Pergamon Press.

Stein, A. D., M. Wang, R. Martorell, S. A. Norris, L. S. Adair, I. Bas, H. S. Sachdev, S. K. Bhargava, C. H. Fall, D. P. Gigante, C. G. Victora, and Cohorts Group. 2010. "Growth Patterns in Early Childhood and Final Attained Stature: Data from Five Birth Cohorts from Low- and Middle-Income Countries." *American Journal of Human Biology* 22(3) May–June: 353–59.

Strasser, K., M. R. Lissi, and M. Silva. 2009. "Gestión del tiempo en 12 salas chilenas de kindergarten: recreo, colación y algo de instrucción." *Psykhe* 18(1): 85–96.

Straus, M. A. (with D. A. Donnelly). 1994. *Beating the Devil out of Them: Corporal Punishment in American Families*. New York: Lexington Books.

Sugarman, J. M. 1991. *Building Early Childhood Systems: A Resource Handbook*. Washington, DC: Child Welfare League of America.

Tanaka, S. 2005. "Parental Leave and Child Health across OECD Countries." *Economic Journal* 115(501) February: F7–F28.

Tavares de Araujo, I., and A. Cavalcanti de Almeida. 2014. "Government Spending on Early Childhood in Brazil: Equity and Efficiency Challenges." Unpublished.

Thaler, R. H. 1999. "Mental Accounting Matters." *Journal of Behavioral Decision Making* 12(3) September: 183–206.

Thompson, R. A., and H. A. Raikes. 2007. "The Social and Emotional Foundations of School Readiness." In D. F. Perry, R. K. Kaufmann, and J. Knitzer, eds., *Social and Emotional Health in Early Childhood: Building Bridges between Services and Systems.* Baltimore, MD: Brookes Publishing Co.

Tirole, J. 1988. *The Theory of Industrial Organization.* Cambridge, MA: MIT Press.

Tofail, F., J. D. Hamadani, A. Z. Ahmed, F. Mehrin, M. Hakim, and S. N. Huda. 2012. "The Mental Development and Behavior of Low-Birth-Weight Bangladeshi Infants from an Urban Low-Income Community." *European Journal of Clinical Nutrition* 66(2) February: 237–43.

Tylleskär, T., D. Jackson, N. Meda, I. M. Engebretsen, M. Chopra, A. H. Diallo, T. Doherty, E. C. Ekström, L. T. Fadnes, A. Goga, C. Kankasa, J. I. Klungsøyr, C. Lombard, V. Nankabirwa, J. K. Nankunda, P. Van de Perre, D. Sanders, R. Shanmugam, H. Sommerfelt, H. Wamani, J. K. Tumwine, and the PROMISE-EBF Study Group. 2011. "Exclusive Breastfeeding Promotion by Peer Counsellors in Sub-Saharan Africa (PROMISE-EBF): A Cluster-Randomised Trial." *Lancet* 378(9789) July: 420–27.

UN (United Nations). 2006. "Secretary-General's Study on Violence against Children." UN, New York. Available at http://www.unicef.org/violencestudy/. Accessed June 2015.

Undurraga, E. A., A. Zycherman, J. Yiu, J. R. Behrman, W. R. Leonard, and R. A. Godoy. 2014. "Gender Targeting of Unconditional Income Transfers and Child Nutritional Status: Experimental Evidence from the Bolivian Amazon." GCC Working Paper No. 14–03. Grand Challenges Canada, Toronto, Ontario, Canada. Available at http://repository.upenn.edu/cgi/viewcontent.cgi?article=1011&context=gcc_economic_returns. Accessed June 2015.

UNESCO (United Nations Educational, Scientific and Cultural Organization). 2015. "Data Centre." Data set. UNESCO, Paris. Available at http://www.uis.unesco.org/DataCentre/Pages/BrowseEducation.aspx. Accessed June 2015.

UNICEF (United Nations Children's Fund). 2014. "The State of the World's Children 2014 in Numbers: Every Child Counts: Revealing Disparities, Advancing Children's Rights." Report. UNICEF, New York.

US Department of Health and Human Services. 2011. "Home Visiting Evidence of Effectiveness." Available at http://homvee.acf.hhs.gov/Implementation/3/Nurse-Family-Partnership-NFP-/14/5/#ModelImplementation-AverageCostperFamily. Accessed June 2015.

Vally, Z., L. Murray, M. Tomlinson, and P. J. Cooper. 2014. "The Impact of Dialogic Book-Sharing Training on Infant Language and Attention: A Randomized Controlled Trial in a Deprived South African Community." *Journal of Child Psychology and Psychiatry.* doi: 10.1111/jcpp.12352.

Vargas-Barón, E. 2013. "Building and Strengthening National Systems for Early Childhood Development." In P. R. Britto, P. L. Engle, and C. M. Super, eds., *Handbook of Early Childhood Development Research and Its Impact on Global Policy.* New York: Oxford University Press.

Verdisco, A., S. Cueto, J. Thompson, and O. Neuschmidt. 2014. "Urgency and Possibility: Results of PRIDI: A First Initiative to Create Regionally Comparative Data on Child

Development in Four Latin American Countries." Inter-American Development Bank, Washington, DC. Unpublished.

Verdisco, A., and M. Pérez Alfaro. 2010. "Measuring Education Quality in Brazil." Briefly Noted Series No. 6. Education Division, Inter-American Development Bank, Washington, DC. Available at http://publications.iadb.org/bitstream/handle /11319/3100/Measuring%20Education%20Quality%20in%20Brazil.pdf?sequence=1. Accessed June 2015.

Victora, C. G., L. Adair, C. Fall, P. C. Hallal, R. Martorell, L. Richter, H. S. Sachdev, and the Maternal and Child Undernutrition Study Group. 2008. "Maternal and Child Undernutrition: Consequences for Adult Health and Human Capital." *Lancet* 371(9609) January: 340–57.

Vigdor, J. 2008. "Teacher Salary Bonuses in North Carolina." Urban Institute, Washington, DC. Available at http://www.urban.org/research/publication/teacher-salary-bonuses -north-carolina. Accessed June 2015.

Vollmer, S., K. Harttgen, M. A. Subramanyam, J. Finlay, S. Klasen, and S. V. Subramanian. 2014. "Association between Economic Growth and Early Childhood Undernutrition: Evidence from 121 Demographic and Health Surveys from 36 Low-Income and Middle-Income Countries." *Lancet Global Health* 2(4) April: e225–e234.

Waldfogel, J., and E. Washbrook. 2011. "Early Years Policy." *Child Development Research* 2011: 1–12. doi:10.1155/2011/343016.

Walker, S. P., S. M. Chang, M. Vera-Hernández, and S. Grantham-McGregor. 2011. "Early Childhood Stimulation Benefits Adult Competence and Reduces Violent Behavior." *Pediatrics* 127(5) May: 849–57.

Walker, S. P., T. D. Wachs, J. M. Gardner, B. Lozoff, G. A. Wasserman, E. Pollitt, J. A. Carter, and the International Child Development Steering Group. 2007. "Child Development: Risk Factors for Adverse Outcomes in Developing Countries." *Lancet* 369(9556) January: 145–57.

Ward-Batts, J. 2008. "Out of the Wallet and into the Purse: Using Micro Data to Test Income Pooling." *Journal of Human Resources* 43(2) Spring: 325–51.

Wasik, B. H., and B. A. Newman. 2009. "Teaching and Learning to Read." In O. A. Barbarin and B. H. Wasik, eds., *Handbook of Child Development and Early Education*. New York: Guilford Press.

Weaver, I. C., N. Cervoni, F. A. Champagne, A. C. D'Alessio, S. Sharma, J. R. Seckl, S. Dymov, M. Szyf, and M. J. Meaney. 2004. "Epigenetic Programming by Maternal Behavior." *Nature Neuroscience* 7(8) August: 847–54.

Welsh, M. C., S. L. Friedman, and S. J. Spieker. 2006. "Executive Functions in Developing Children: Current Conceptualizations and Questions for the Future." In K. McCartney and D. Phillips, eds., *The Blackwell Handbook of Early Childhood Development*. Oxford, United Kingdom: Blackwell Publishing.

White, T. G., and J. S. Kim. 2008. "Teacher and Parent Scaffolding of Voluntary Summer Reading." *Reading Teacher* 62(2) October: 116–25.

White, T. G., J. S. Kim, H. C. Kingston, and L. Foster. 2014. "Replicating the Effects of a Teacher-Scaffolded Voluntary Summer Reading Program: The Role of Poverty." *Reading Research Quarterly* 49(1): 5–30.

Whitehurst, G. J., F. L. Falco, C. J. Lonigan, J. E. Fischel, B. D. DeBaryshe, M. C. Valdez-Menchaca, and M. Caulfield. 1988. "Accelerating Language Development through Picture Book Reading." *Developmental Psychology* 24(4) July: 552–59.

WHO (World Health Organization). 2015. "The World Health Organization's Infant Feeding Recommendation." WHO, Geneva, Switzerland. Available at http://www.who.int/nutrition/topics/infantfeeding_recommendation/en/. Accessed June 2015.

WHO Multicentre Growth Reference Study Group. 2006. "WHO Motor Development Study: Windows of Achievement for Six Gross Motor Development Milestones." *Acta Paediatrica* 95(supplement S450) April: 86–95.

Woodward, A. L., and E. M. Markman. 1998. "Early Word Learning." In D. Kuhn and R. S. Siegler, eds., *Handbook of Child Psychology: Volume 2: Cognition, Perception, and Language*. Fifth edition. New York: John Wiley and Sons.

World Bank. 2013. "Shifting Gears to Accelerate Shared Prosperity in Latin America and the Caribbean." Latin America and the Caribbean Poverty and Labor Brief. World Bank, Washington, DC. Available at https://openknowledge.worldbank.org/handle /10986/15265. Accessed June 2015.

Wurtz, R. H. 2009. "Recounting the Impact of Hubel and Wiesel." *Journal of Physiology* 587(Pt 12) June: 2817–23.

Yoshikawa, H., L. A. Ponguta, A. M. Nieto, J. Van Ravens, X. A. Portilla, P. R. Britto, and D. Leyva. 2014. "Evaluating Mechanisms for Governance, Finance and Sustainability of Colombia's Comprehensive Early Childhood Development Policy *De Cero a Siempre*. Report. New York University, New York.

Yousafzai, A. K., M. A. Rasheed, A. Rizvi, R. Armstrong, and Z. A. Bhutta. 2014. "Effect of Integrated Responsive Stimulation and Nutrition Interventions in the Lady Health Worker Programme in Pakistan on Child Development, Growth, and Health Outcomes: A Cluster-Randomised Factorial Effectiveness Trial." *Lancet* 384(9950) October: 1282–93.

Index

CPSIA information can be obtained at www.ICGtesting.com
Printed in the USA
LVOW10s1751280116

472729LV00011B/176/P

9 781137 536488